Latin American Cooking

TIME LIFE BOOKS ®

Foods of the World

Latin American Cooking

by

Jonathan Norton Leonard

and the Editors of

TIME-LIFE BOOKS

photographed by Milton Greene

TIME-LIFE BOOKS, ALEXANDRIA, VIRGINIA

THE AUTHOR: The late Jonathan Norton Leonard *(above, left)* came to appreciate Latin American cuisines more than 30 years ago, when he lived in Venezuela, Mexico and Peru. Later he was Latin American editor of TIME before serving as science editor of the magazine for 20 years. His books include *American Cooking: New England* and *American Cooking: The Great West* in the FOODS OF THE WORLD Library and *Ancient America*, a volume in the TIME-LIFE BOOKS Great Ages of Man series.

THE CONSULTANT: Elisabeth Lambert Ortiz *(above, right)*, principal consultant for this book, is an expert on the cuisines of Mexico and other Latin American countries. Her interest in Latin American cooking was first whetted while living in Mexico with her husband, who was stationed there as an official of the United Nations Secretariat. She is the author of *The Complete Book of Mexican Cooking*. Other consultants for this book are listed on page 206.

THE CONSULTING EDITOR: The late Michael Field *(above, left)*, one of America's foremost food experts and culinary teachers, was responsible for the development and writing of recipes for this entire series. His books include *Michael Field's Cooking School, Michael Field's Culinary Classics and Improvisations* and *All Manner of Food.*

THE PHOTOGRAPHER: Milton Greene *(above, right)*, who made most of the photographs for this book, first won fame as a fashion photographer. With Joseph Eula, an artist who assisted him with lighting and composition, Mr. Greene traveled through Mexico and Central and South America on this assignment. A freelance photographer, Mr. Greene is based in New York, his native city. He is married and has two sons.

THE COVER: Brilliantly colored chili peppers in myriad shapes and sizes are the native Indian spice that lends Latin American cooking a distinctive flavor.

Contents

The Recipe Booklet that accompanies this volume has been designed for use in the kitchen. It contains all the 66 recipes at the ends of the chapters plus 42 more. It also has a wipe-clean cover and a spiral binding so that it can either stand up or lie flat when open.

The Melting Pot
South of the Border

In the nearly 500 years since the Spanish Conquest of Mexico and South America, a series of richly diverse cuisines has developed in the region. In Mexico, where there was a high Indian civilization, modern cooking is still firmly based on its Aztec-Maya foundations, while revealing clearly the impact of Spain, which introduced its own foods and cooking methods. To a lesser extent Mexico was influenced by the sophisticated dishes that were brought in from France and Austria during its brief experience as a French puppet state ruled by the ill-starred Maximilian and Carlotta. The dishes of Peru, heart of the great Inca Empire, which took in most of what is now Ecuador as well as the better part of Chile and Bolivia and a small part of Argentina, still bear the unmistakable stamp of their antique past overlaid by Spanish imports. Brazil is kaleidoscopic. There was no great Indian society here, so the indigenous peoples contributed little more than raw materials. The country's modern cooking is a mixture of Portuguese, African slave and primitive Indian influences, and it is both unique and quite good.

The cuisines of Chile, Argentina and Uruguay, with no great indigenous past to guide them, have evolved as the many European strains in the population—Spanish, English, German, Italian and others—reacted to native ingredients. Many a fine dish started as an improvisation using a local food instead of an unobtainable European one. Many home dishes suffered a sea change in the long migration. English bread sauce, surely one of the most innocent inventions of the kitchen, becomes quite complicated in Chile when as *salsa de pan* it takes the place of *béchamel* as a base for what would have been creamed dishes. Adaptations and inventions, the clash as well as the wedding of cultures, have produced a repertory as varied as the geography of the mountain-dominated continent.

Overlying all these Latin American cuisines is the influence of Spain. The pace at which Spain introduced its food to this hemisphere is remarkable in the face of the difficulties of transporting animals and seed in less than speedy ships across the Atlantic, and then up formidable mountains to cities at 8,000 to 10,000 and more feet of altitude. The beef, lamb, goat, chicken, wheat, almonds and so on that they established in the New World through this effort made possible the rounding out of the indigenous cooking.

The rapidity with which the New World accepted Old World foodstuffs was rivaled by the speed of the reverse process. The Spaniards, obsessed by gold, did not at first realize that the real treasure of the Americas was corn, potatoes, tomatoes, chilies, chocolate, tobacco, avocados, peanuts, cassava (manioc, *yuca*), beans, the squash family, vanilla, sweet potatoes, pineapples and papayas. But these foods quickly spread to other parts of the world, and today it is impossible to imagine living without them. Modern transport and food-handling methods mean, however, that *all* of the foods necessary for cooking the Latin American way are readily available in markets throughout the United States.

The editors faced a large range of choice in selecting the recipes to be included in this book. They have, in my view, succeeded in choosing dishes that are deservedly popular in their countries of origin, as well as being truly representative of the cooking of these lands. These have been exhaustively tested in the FOODS OF THE WORLD kitchen, and in the case of many older recipes that use outmoded cooking techniques, modernized to suit today's kitchens.

Comparing variant recipes to choose the most traditional, I several times found it difficult to pronounce any one version more "correct" than another, as cooks the world over tend to have their idiosyncrasies, and cooking is everywhere and always a living, growing art. The editors have solved this problem by giving variations of dishes where true variations exist.

I have spent some years discovering Mexican food and the cuisines of South America, and have found that their study demands one to be somewhat of a botanist, historian, archeologist, traveler, detective and persistent eater. I think readers will agree that Jonathan Norton Leonard, the author of the book, has admirably assumed the roles required.

Elisabeth Lambert Ortiz

I

The Indians' Gift to the World Larder

Only the plastic hat cover
worn by a young Indian
vendor in a Huancayo, Peru,
marketplace distinguishes
this scene from one that
might have been painted a
thousand years ago. The
giant squash, the potatoes,
chilies and tomatoes are all
foods that were first
cultivated by her ancestors.

South of the Rio Grande and the tip of Florida lies the colorful world of Latin America. It is a land of violent contrasts: snow-capped mountains floating like clouds over tropical rain forests; deserts threaded with green oases; cities buried in crowded jungles, like castles besieged by trees. It is a land of adventure. Its glittering capitals are as civilized as any places on earth, but nearly every country still has a wild frontier—sometimes with hostile Indians armed with bows and arrows—where every man who can afford one carries a gun.

It is also a land of adventure in food. A shy Mexican girl with glittering black hair stands by the tollgate of a modern superhighway selling brittle yellow cookies that might have been offered to an Aztec emperor. The cookies, made of cornmeal and honey, both of them pre-Columbian ingredients, are flavored with something wonderful for which the girl has no word in Spanish. They are delicious and different. Or a roast duck in Brazil turns out to be filled with a delectable stuffing made mostly of fresh-grated coconut. Or an elegant dinner party in Argentina repairs to tables in a grassy field where a dozen kinds of meat have been broiling ever since dawn on spits over smoldering logs. The meats are basted with brine while they cook, and each kind is turned and watched by an expert to see that it gets the right heat for the right length of time. This primitive cookery, a relic of Argentina's wild and violent past, produces the most delicious roast meat known to man.

Latin American cooking is not just another kind of European cooking. To be sure, there is Spanish and Portuguese influence in it, and the big ho-

tels that cater to foreigners serve standard "international" food just as they do in New York or Chicago, but under this superficial layer is food that differs sharply from anything found in Europe or the United States. It is partly African, brought by slaves from West Africa. It is partly tropical, using hot-country produce not available in Europe. Most of all it is Indian, inherited from the civilized Indians of the New World—the Aztecs, Inca and others—who were conquered by the Spaniards but whose descendants still cling tenaciously to many parts of their ancient culture, notably including their indigenous foods.

The Indian influence is naturally strongest in countries where most of the population has Indian blood. For this reason Mexican cooking is more Indian than Spanish, and in Peru, Ecuador and Bolivia, which were parts of the highly civilized Inca Empire, a large percentage of the people still eats almost unmodified Inca food. But the Indian influence shows up strongly all over South and Central America. Even in Buenos Aires, whose people are almost entirely European, characteristically Indian dishes have a traditional place in the cuisine.

Besides being distinctive, Latin American food is also extremely diverse. It could hardly be otherwise, for Latin America is enormous. Its area is nearly three times that of the United States, and the distance from the northwestern corner of Mexico to the southern tip of Argentina is nearly 7,000 miles. It has almost every climate known on earth, from very dry to very wet, from extremely hot to bitterly cold. The high mountain valleys of the Andes are cool the year around, although many of them are close to the equator. Central Chile has a climate like Southern California. Northern Brazil is almost a duplicate of West Africa, with similar jungles, savannas and dry brush country. Uruguay, Argentina and southern Brazil have some of the best temperate farmlands in the world. Northern Mexico is like the Southwestern United States.

Only a little of this great area is easy traveling country. Most of it is cut up by mountains or clogged with tangled forests that have defied exploitation to the present day. Along the west coast of South America the great range of the Andes runs like a giant picket fence, and the tortured roads that thread the passes between its tall white peaks are forced to twist and turn like tendrils of climbing vines. Only a generation ago many of these roads were mule trails, and the traveler who braved them was hardy indeed. Transportation throughout the continent was mostly by sea, which meant that each country felt closer to Europe than to its neighbors across the mountains and jungles. There was only sporadic communication among them.

Naturally, each of these countries developed its own personality and cuisine. Small sections of some nations lived apart and acquired special customs and ways of cooking. This was particularly true in Mexico, which is a tangle of mountains and intervening valleys. Even today, when roads, airplanes and modern communications have broken the isolation of its *patrias chicas* (little homelands), an expert on Mexican food could be blindfolded, taken to any part of the country and still tell where he was by the taste of its food alone.

When the Spaniards and Portuguese began exploring this part of the

New World at the end of the 15th Century, they found large areas thinly inhabited by savage Indians who lived chiefly by hunting and fishing and by gathering wild vegetable foods. Most of Brazil, Argentina and Uruguay was in this primitive "food-gathering" state, but along other coasts and on the Caribbean islands the Indians were more numerous and supported themselves by a crude sort of agriculture. The Spaniards particularly noticed a tall and beautiful plant that the people of Cuba grew in small fields and called by a name that sounded like "my-ees." It grew 10 or more feet high and bore great cylindrical ears with closely set, shiny yellow kernels. This wonderful plant was maize, or Indian corn, the staff of life of the New World. It took the place of the Old World's wheat, but it produced greater yields and it would flourish in many places where wheat would not survive.

The Spaniards soon discovered the civilized homeland of corn. Behind the hot lowlands of Mexico stood a mountain rampart, known today as the Sierra Madre Oriental, and among its peaks and ranges were fertile valleys planted with carefully tended fields and gardens and studded with attractive cities of whitewashed adobe houses. Besides corn, the Indians had many other crops, not one of which was known in Europe. All had been developed by their skillful plant breeders out of primitive wild forms. The ancestor of corn, which is now extinct, appears to have been a coarse grass that produced ears about one inch long, some of which have been found in caves once inhabited by ancient Indians. The kernels were smaller than dried peas, and each was wrapped in its individual husk. Out of this unpromising start, the Mexican Indians had conjured hundreds of improved varieties. Some were adapted to cool, high altitudes. Others grew best in tropical lowlands. Among them were white corn, yellow corn, red corn, black corn, sweet corn and popcorn. In Peru, to which corn had migrated (some scientists maintain that it originated there), the amazing plant grew in even greater variety.

Some kinds of South American corn grown today produce massive ears shaped like footballs, with flat kernels an inch long and almost as broad. The kernels of some varieties never get hard; even when wholly ripe and dry they are filled with soft, chalky material that makes them easy to grind into meal. If necessary the kernels can be chewed and eaten with no preparation. In other varieties the stalks are saturated with sweet juice, like sugar cane.

Corn by itself is not a complete and healthful diet. It has less protein than wheat and lacks certain vitamins and other desirable nutrients, but the Indians seem to have had a kind of folk wisdom that anticipated by thousands of years the modern scientific knowledge of dietary needs. Along with their corn they developed beans, the ordinary kidney beans that most of the world eats now. Beans are rich in protein, and when they were planted in the same field as corn, the bacteria on their roots collected nitrogen and helped preserve the fertility of the soil, which is quickly depleted by corn planted alone. The corn-bean combination, supplemented with other vegetables that supplied vitamins, was the solid food foundation of the Indian civilization, and millions of people in Latin America still live on it today.

Seldom seen in United States kitchens, these important ingredients of Latin American cooking are: plantains, the firm-fleshed close relative of the banana at left; *yuca*, the starchy root vegetable at center; *chayote*, the squashlike vegetable on the right, and coriander, the parsleylike, pungent herb in the foreground at right.

Continued on page 21

Latin America - A Land Divided from Itself

Stretching 7,000 miles from the Rio Grande to Tierra del Fuego are 22 Latin American countries that range in size from the vest-pocket republic, El Salvador, to the sprawling tropical giant, Brazil. The region is blessed with great natural resources—copper, tin, oil and timber—and it possesses some of the world's finest natural waterways. Yet Latin America is a victim of its own geography. As seen on the accompanying map and in the pictures on the succeeding pages, mountains, jungles and forests of great natural beauty have so divided and isolated one area from another that large regions have been barred to civilization.

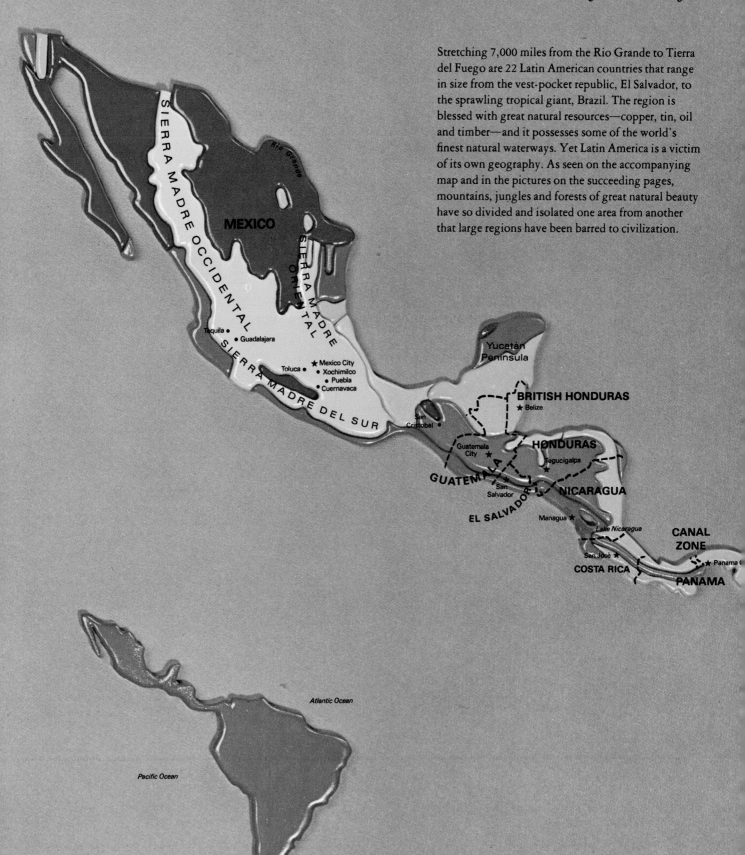

This terraced Bolivian hillside is separated from Peru by Lake Titicaca. The llamas munch on dried clumps of *ychu* grass.

A Land of Enchanting Diversity

In the heart of Brazil (*opposite*), Latin America's great river, the Amazon, winds through lush, impenetrable rain forest.

The food that a country eats depends largely upon its geography, and nowhere is geography's influence more decisive than in Latin America. Parts of this great region's west coast form the world's most absolute desert; there are places in northern Chile where no drop of rain has fallen within recorded history, and long stretches of the Peruvian coast are almost as arid. Only a few hundred miles behind these dusty shores lie vast tropical forests where rain falls almost every day. Much of Latin America is untillable or untamed, while some areas have been brought under control only by prodigious labor and ingenious farming methods such as the terracing seen above. And in striking contrast, other areas— such as the humid Pampa of Argentina and Uruguay—are naturally endowed with some of the world's richest, most productive lands.

Overleaf: The gigantic Iguassú Falls marks the Brazil-Argentina border.

15

Fat beef cattle, tended by gauchos as they graze on luxuriant grass, testify to the beneficently humid climate of the Argentine Pampa.

No rainfall has ever been recorded in much of this arid wasteland, which is part of the Atacama Desert on the northern coast of Chile.

In the high Andean valleys of South America, where corn and beans do not grow well, the Indians developed potatoes, including the standard white potato, which did not originate in Ireland, as many people assume, but in Peru or Chile. To make up for the potato's dietary deficiencies, they also grew a sturdy plant called *quinoa*, which thrives at very high altitudes and produces small seeds that are rich in protein. Another basic food was a wide assortment of squashes and pumpkins, some of which were grown not for their flesh but for their tasty, nutlike seeds. Others had sweet flesh. Still others had hard shells that could be used as containers for popular dishes.

Besides corn, beans and squash, the Indian plant breeders acquired an extraordinary range of other valuable food crops. In South America lima beans, named after Lima, the capital of Peru, may have been the first plant brought under cultivation by early Indian farmers. Limas are still important, and some varieties grow as big as pocket watches. Sweet potatoes are also of Indian origin; they probably came from some warm part of South America. Tomatoes are probably Mexican, and chili peppers, though identified with Mexico, may have come from either Mexico or Peru. The long list of Indian food crops includes peanuts, cacao (the source of chocolate), cashew nuts, vanilla, avocados, pineapples and manioc, a starchy root that yields tapioca and is important in many parts of the tropics. Besides these familiar plants, the Indians cultivated dozens of others that are known and grown only in their homelands and have only Indian names. Tobacco and rubber, while not foods, are also Indian discoveries, and so is chicle, the base for chewing gum.

The achievements of the Indians in domesticating animals did not match their contribution in plant breeding, but they did have a few tamed animals that they used for food. The Mexicans had turkeys and a kind of large duck that is probably extinct. They also ate dogs which were raised especially as food, and they kept bees for honey in hives made of hollow logs. The Peruvians did somewhat better. They kept herds of llamas and alpacas, which are improved varieties of the wild guanaco, a small relative of the camel. Llamas were used as pack animals, and alpacas were kept primarily for their fine, silky wool, but both were eaten also. But the main source of meat for the Peruvian Indians was guinea pigs, which still scurry around Indian kitchens and are fed on anything from weeds to cornhusks. In addition, the Indians made systematic use of fish and wild game. Both the Aztecs and Inca protected the deer and other edible animals that lived on the forested mountains, and collected them by regulated and organized hunting that almost amounted to genuine animal husbandry.

The Spanish conquerors of Mexico and Peru were avidly looking for gold, and they found quite a lot of it, which they sent back to Spain to be made into currency. But far more important for the world than the Indians' gold were their food crops. Like water rushing from a broken dam, they quickly spread around the earth and were passed along to inaccessible parts of Asia and Africa before white men got there. Corn had the greatest effect; it is now grown nearly everywhere and rivals rice and wheat as the world's leading food for man and beast. It is the standby of the poor

Opposite: "The Fujiyama of South America," the glacier-capped peak of an active volcano, named Osorno, looms above Petrohué River in southern Chile, near Puerto Montt.

Overleaf: The walls of the ancient Inca city of Machu Picchu, high in the Peruvian Andes, stand today amid plazas and stairways long ago carved from solid rock. To make this isolated, 6,750-foot-high stronghold self-sustaining, engineers built reservoirs and carved terraces on the mountain slopes on which small plots of corn, beans and *quinoa* were cultivated. Abandoned after the Spanish Conquest, Machu Picchu was a forgotten city for four centuries. Then in 1911 the site was rediscovered by the American archeologist, Hiram Bingham.

Continued on page 24

in many countries, and much of the world's meat, milk, butter and cheese is produced by animals fed on corn. Other Indian crops proved almost equally valuable. It is hard to imagine Italian cooking without tomatoes or Northern European cooking without white potatoes. The Indians' beans, sweet potatoes, peanuts and chocolate are used in almost every corner of the world, and their favorite spice and flavoring agent, chili peppers, warms the curries of India, the *rijsttafel* of Indonesia and the *Paprika Schnitzel* of Central Europe. There may never have been more than 12 million civilized Indians, but it can be argued that mankind owes perhaps half its present-day food supply to the achievements of Indian plant breeders.

Upon their distinctive agriculture the Indians built an equally distinctive cuisine. Its basis was corn wherever corn was obtainable, but since corn contains little gluten or other viscous protein, it could not be made into leavened bread in the European way, which depends on the ability of gluten to retain the small bubbles of gas or air that make the bread rise while it is baking. Since corn flour does not act in this way, the Mexican Indians patted corn dough into thin, unleavened cakes. When toasted briefly on a hot pottery griddle, they become tortillas, the common bread of Mexico. Properly made, tortillas hot off the griddle are truly delicious, and they combine magnificently with the lively sauces that the Indians invented to go with them. Tortillas are only the beginning of the myriad ways in which the Indians ate their precious corn. Some of these are described in the next chapter, along with dishes that they made out of their other native foodstuffs.

Even more remarkable than the formidable Indian array of edible plants is the persistence of Indian ways of cooking in the face of competition from the cooking traditions of Spain and other parts of Europe. Indian cooking has not merely survived, it has spread. With only minor modifications, its basic foods and cooking techniques are now used by many more people than ever lived in the ancient Indian empires. Both ingredients and methods have advanced into territory such as coastal Argentina, where the civilized Indians never ventured, and in combination with foods and techniques introduced from Europe they have evolved into the many Creole (that is, native-developed) cuisines that are now standard in Latin America.

The influence of the Indians' corn culture has been felt even in the United States. Hominy and succotash are typical corn-culture dishes, which the English colonists of the Eastern Seaboard learned from the relatively primitive local Indians, who in turn had acquired them from the centers of civilization in Mexico. Recently a new wave of Indian cooking has flowed into the United States. The whole country now knows chili con carne, a typical Indian-Spanish dish that originated among the Mexican-Americans of Texas. Equally familiar are Fritos, or corn chips, which are the time-honored tortillas cut into strips and fried in deep fat. In the Southwestern States many Mexican-Indian dishes—tacos, tamales, enchiladas—are firmly established, and their popularity is not limited to the Mexican-American residents; "Anglos" eat them too. The elegant Hernán Cortés, conqueror of Mexico, doubtless would be astonished if he could see Americans, whom he would consider Englishmen, enjoying in a far-off country the cooking of the Indians that he subdued.

Nowhere, of course, does the ancient Indian cooking exist without additions and modifications. The Indians were quick to adopt some of the crops and domestic animals that the Spaniards and Portuguese brought with them. They especially welcomed the Europeans' pigs, which provided the fat that their diet usually lacked. When a mixed-blood population appeared in Latin America, it selected foods, dishes and cooking methods from both sides of its ancestry.

The Negroes originally imported from Africa as slaves are another source of diversity. They brought some foodstuffs from Africa, but probably more important was their gusto. While Indians are inclined to eat sparingly even when they can afford to eat more, the Negroes of Latin America love food and eat lots of it. Perhaps because of this appreciation, Negroes are considered the best cooks of Brazil. Even in Latin American countries where Negroes are not numerous, a skilled Negro woman is likely to be bossing things in the kitchen of a restaurant or a big private house. Wherever Latin American Negroes are found, they contribute an exuberance to the food that they prepare; it tends to be highly seasoned, brightly colored and served with a flourish that adds to its attractiveness.

Since most of Latin America is tropical, its cooking makes great use of tropical products that are seldom used in the cooking of Europe or the United States. The best example is bananas, which are plentiful in all tropical regions that have sufficient rainfall, often growing in humble backyards where the trees with their broad, 10-foot leaves provide shade as well as food. They are sometimes eaten raw as in northern countries. More often they are cooked, and some of the nonsweet varieties require as much cooking as do potatoes. Coconuts both green and ripe are used in innumerable ways and so are *yuca* and other root crops that grow only in the tropics. In many countries avocados are a cheap staple food, and other tropical fruits, some of them peculiar to small regions, are an important part of the diet. Mango trees of Asian origin are often planted along the streets for shade, and their sweet, juicy fruits belong to the first person, usually a speedy small boy, who reaches them when they fall. Mango season is a time of plenty for the Latin American poor.

Most of the chapters in this book will describe regional varieties of Latin American cooking. Some countries are omitted because their styles of cooking duplicate those of other lands. Along with the discussions of the cooking of various regions, three chapters will deal with specific kinds of food —fruit, sweets, and coffee and drinks—that are highlights of the Latin American cuisine.

Not all of the food in any part of Latin America is distinctive, of course. The traveler who limits himself to the dining rooms of the major hotels can find the food as unexciting as that in the conventional restaurants of his home city, and among the working classes North American food of the hot dog and hamburger type is becoming increasingly popular. But if the visitor breaks out of this circuit and seeks good restaurants that serve *criollo* food, or if he is invited to people's homes, he will find delicious dishes that resemble nothing he has ever tried before.

In stone and clay artifacts, the pre-Inca Indians of Peru left behind them solid evidence of foods they developed and valued. Shaped like potatoes, gourds, and bean and other seed pods, the objects shown here were all found in ancient tombs.

25

II

A Cuisine from the Halls of Moctezuma

At a hacienda outside Toluca, a Mexican woman prepares tortillas in the ancient Indian way, still used in rural Mexico. She first rolls out the *masa*, or corn dough, on the stone *metate* in front of her. Then she pats each tortilla into shape by hand. The basket on the left holds cooked tortillas and *sopes*—fried tortillas filled with meat, beans and chili sauce.

When the Spaniards first reached the highlands of Mexico they found a strange and gorgeous civilization, and they soon discovered to their pleasure that among the most unusual of its glories was its food. Wonderful-smelling stews simmered in the broad marketplaces of the Aztec capital, Tenochtitlán; Indian women offered fresh-cooked corn tortillas of many shapes and sizes; piles of magnificent fruit competed in fragrance with chocolate drinks. Nothing was familiar, nothing was known in Europe, but to the weary Spaniards far from home the cooking of Tenochtitlán (now Mexico City) was a delight.

The most luxurious eating was done at the royal court, which was the scene of gastronomic magnificence rivaling the food displays of European royalty. When the Spaniards first visited Tenochtitlán, they often watched Moctezuma, the Aztec Emperor, dining in solitary splendor. His servants prepared large quantities of more than 30 different dishes and set each on a pottery brazier with live coals to keep it warm. Sometimes the Emperor would saunter among the offerings with his chefs and stewards, and they would tell him what each dish contained and recommend specialties, as modern headwaiters do. After he made his selections, he retired behind a screen embellished with golden religious figures and sat on a low upholstered stool before a table covered with white cloth. The chosen dishes on their braziers were set before him, and young women selected for their beauty brought basins of water for him to wash his hands and towels on which to dry them. Other young women brought hot tortillas in baskets, covered with white napkins, and a frothy chocolate drink, served in

27

cups of gold. For dessert they brought the varied fruits that grow in Mexico's many climates, and when Moctezuma finished eating, he took a few puffs from a gaily painted and gilded tube filled with tobacco.

The Spaniards reported that 1,000 dishes of food and 2,000 jugs of chocolate were served at Moctezuma's court. No book of recipes has survived to tell how the chefs prepared all those dishes, but the Spaniards noted that they contained meat of innumerable animals and birds, most of them wild. Bernardino de Sahagún, a Spanish friar who wrote soon after the Conquest, told about "the foods that the lords ate," and his list covers several pages. Among the items are: "Hot, white doubled tortillas; large tortillas; tortillas formed in rolls; leaf-shaped tortillas; white tamales with beans forming a sea shell on top; red tamales with beans; turkey pie cooked in a pot; roast turkey hen; roast quail; turkey with a sauce of small chilies, tomatoes and ground squash seeds; birds with toasted corn; dried duck; duck stewed in a pot; white fish with yellow chili; gray fish with red chili; frogs with green chili; newt with yellow chili; lobster with red chili, tomato and ground squash seeds; white fish with sauce of unripened plums; tamales made with honey; squash flowers; small cactus fruits with fish eggs. . . ."

The list goes on and on, mentioning hundreds of items, and finally ends with chocolate. "Then, in his house, the ruler was served his chocolate, with which he finished his meal; green, made of tender cacao; honeyed chocolate made with ground-up dried flowers and green vanilla pods; bright red chocolate; orange-colored chocolate; rose-colored chocolate; black chocolate, white chocolate. . . ."

It is safe to assume that most of the dishes that were served at Moctezuma's court were red-hot with chili. If the Spaniards did not exclaim about this startling peculiarity of Mexican food—which did not damage the Mexicans who had been eating the hotly spiced dishes all their lives—it was probably because they had been living in Cuba and other places to which the love of chili had spread along with corn.

Although the culinary secrets of the Aztec court are lost, a great deal of information has been preserved about what the ordinary Mexican Indians ate and how they prepared their food. The starting point was corn, the sacred plant of their religion. It occupied the dominant position there that was held by wheat and rye in Northern Europe before the introduction of potatoes. Corn supplied starch, the main energy source in the Indian diet, as well as protein and a little fat. Sometimes it was eaten green off the cob, either raw or boiled or roasted, or the immature kernels were cut or scraped off to be made into cakes or added to other dishes. But more generally the Mexican Indians let their corn ripen and stored the ears in ventilated corncribs like those on old-fashioned farms in the United States.

The Indians sometimes used a stone mortar and pestle to grind the hard whole kernels into meal out of which corn gruel (*atole*) was made, but this took a lot of effort. Far better was their system of heating the kernels in a mildly corrosive solution of lime until the skins came off. The skinless kernels were called *nixtamal*, an Aztec word still in use. Sometimes *nixtamal* was dried and stored, or it could be boiled in fresh, limeless water. When this was done the kernels swelled up enormously and be-

Corn, the great gift of Latin America's pre-Columbian Indians, is celebrated by this ceramic jar, fashioned by ancient Peruvian Indians. The body of the jar is composed of stylized ears of corn, while the handle is adorned with the figure of a pre-Inca deity, the corn goddess. She wears a crown made of corn ears.

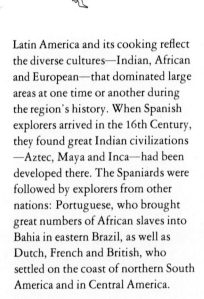

came as soft as spaghetti. The resulting dish, *pozole*, was one of the basic Indian ways to eat corn, and it was known on the farthest outskirts of the corn culture. The early New England colonists adopted it from the local Indians under the name of *samp* (a Narragansett Indian word) or "big hominy." Only a generation ago the "big hominy man" peddling his product by the quart was a familiar sight in rural New England, though few New Englanders knew they were eating Mexican *pozole*.

A more usual way of making *nixtamal* was to mash the soaked kernels into *masa*, a dough, to make tortillas. The ancient method can still be seen in some parts of Mexico. The Indian woman squats on the ground in front of a stone slab known as a *metate*. Any smooth flat rock will do, although the fancier models from the past are low, three-legged tables chipped out of porous volcanic stone. The woman puts a few handfuls of *nixtamal* on the flat surface and scrubs back and forth with a stone roller. The product, *masa*, may be white, yellow or other colors according to the color of the corn, and its appearance varies somewhat in response to the kind of mashing it receives. But if it is intended for tortillas it has to have exactly the right consistency. Modern Mexican women who make their *masa* this way never seem to have any trouble. It always comes out right.

The next step in tortilla making is wonderful to watch. The woman takes a piece of *masa* about as big as a golf ball between her wetted hands and—pat, pat, pat, pat—flattens it deftly into a round cake less than one eighth of an inch thick and six to eight inches in diameter. It looks easy but it is not, as anyone who has tried to do it will testify. The uncooked tortillas are limp and weak, but the women almost never spoil one of them and have to start over again. They must have been even more skillful in Aztec times, for the tortillas made then were a foot or more in diameter and must have been extremely difficult to handle.

Cooking tortillas is easy. They are simply tossed on a hot griddle, left there for a minute or so depending on the temperature of the griddle, and turned over once. They brown only slightly but develop a thin, tough skin on both sides. Some of them puff up momentarily like souffléed potatoes. These can be stuffed by pushing mashed beans or some other filling between the crisp skin and the body of the tortilla.

The ancient tortilla-making process is now used only on isolated farms or in remote villages, but countrywomen still make their own *nixtamal*, often out of the corn produced on their own land. Then they take it to a modern grinding machine that turns it into *masa*. Purists regret this shortcut, but what they dislike still more is the simple but ingenious machine that turns out uncooked tortillas in every city and sizable town in Mexico. It is worked by a woman who feeds *masa* between cylinders that roll it into a thin sheet and simultaneously cut tortilla-sized disks out of it. She picks up the unused parts of the sheet and stuffs them back into the machine while the disks are carried by a short conveyor belt to a second woman who piles them up and sells them to the customers. These machine-made tortillas are said to be inferior to those made by hand, but it is hard for a non-Mexican to tell the difference. All tortillas are good if hot from their first cooking and not cold or warmed over.

Another important way to utilize corn—in tamales—may be the most an-

Latin America and its cooking reflect the diverse cultures—Indian, African and European—that dominated large areas at one time or another during the region's history. When Spanish explorers arrived in the 16th Century, they found great Indian civilizations —Aztec, Maya and Inca—had been developed there. The Spaniards were followed by explorers from other nations: Portuguese, who brought great numbers of African slaves into Bahia in eastern Brazil, as well as Dutch, French and British, who settled on the coast of northern South America and in Central America.

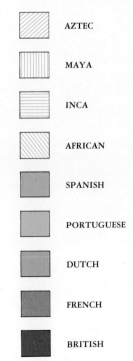

AZTEC

MAYA

INCA

AFRICAN

SPANISH

PORTUGUESE

DUTCH

FRENCH

BRITISH

cient of all. In very early times tamales were made without the pots needed for boiling *pozole* and even without the pottery griddle needed for
toasting tortillas. They were made by wrapping corn dough in the tough,
pliant husks so conveniently provided by the corn ear. In this method,
which is still sometimes used, the package is buried in the hot ashes of a
campfire; the husk protects the meal from the heat long enough for it to
cook properly. Tamales made in this ancient way, with no cooking utensils at all, have a fine primitive quality about them. Some of the cooked
corn is crusty or slightly browned and a powdering of ashes adds to the
primitive effect.

Long before the Spaniards arrived in Mexico, however, the Indians had
acquired pottery and had developed new methods of cooking tamales.
They generally steamed them in an underground pit or in a covered pot
in which some sort of trivet held the tamales above an inch or so of
water. Corncobs sometimes were used in place of a trivet on the bottom
of the pot. Some of the Indian tamales may have been flavored merely
with the bland taste of the cornhusk, but most of them were hotly
spiced, probably with chili, as modern tamales tend to be. The American
who buys tamales in a Mexican market or humble restaurant had better
taste one with caution, but if the chili is not too much for him, he will
have the pleasure of eating an unusual and delicious food that does not differ appreciably from the tamales the Indians cooked long ago.

The prize-package act of unwrapping the steaming cornhusk adds to
the pleasure, and the excitement is greatest when the tamales are of different kinds. Then eating them becomes a treasure hunt. The little packets of corn may have nothing but streaks of chili in their centers, but
they may also have meat, turkey, fish, chopped olives or anything the makers happened to have around. There are also sweet tamales, which the Aztecs made with honey since they had no sugar. Tamales are a world of
food, and a varied kettleful of them, easy to heat on a small fire, is a sure
center of excitement for a picnic or cookout.

Some of the foods that the Indians cooked in a wrapping of cornhusks
contained no corn, for many other things can be prepared in this primitive but effective way. Many modern Mexican markets, such as the famous market in Toluca, feature an item that looks like a kind of large
tamale but contains hundreds of inch-long fish instead of corn. This is
baked in ashes or on hot stones until the outer layers of cornhusk are slightly charred. The mass of tiny fish is then well cooked and flavored.

Although corn was the Indians' staple, beans were important, too, for
they supplied protein. In Aztec times there were probably even more
kinds of beans than corn. They came in many sizes from very small to
very large. They were white, black, yellow, red, brown, pink and speckled
in various colors, and the Indian plant breeders had adapted them to all
the climates of Mexico. They were boiled in stews and soups or mashed
and mixed with chili or other flavorings. To judge by modern Mexican habits it is safe to say that even the poorest Aztecs usually had a dab of
beans to eat with their tortillas or to boil with their *pozole*.

Squash was another food available to the poorest Indians, and squashes
and pumpkins were grown in great variety, as they still are. Some sci-

30   *Continued on page 34*

Corn, the Key Crop

Since pre-Conquest days corn has been the mainstay of the Latin American diet. In many places where traditional methods persist the ears of dried corn are still brought to markets, like the one at San Cristóbal de las Casas, Mexico, in loosely woven wicker hampers (*above*). There the corn is shelled by women workers. Most of it is then sold to commercial shops to be made into *masa*, the meal used for tortillas and tamales, but it can also be bought in bulk by housewives (*left*) who prefer to make their own *masa* at home by soaking the corn in limewater and then grinding it on a stone called a *metate*.

Completely Mechanized Tortillas

The Mexican woman at the right would have spent
many hours in the old days—her rural relatives still do
—laboriously preparing her own tortilla dough and
molding tortillas by hand. Now, thanks to the machine
age, she can walk into a *tortillería* like this one in a
Mexico City suburb and buy her daily supply for a
few pesos. Here machine-made dough is shaped into
tortillas by mechanical cutters. A conveyor belt *(above)*
passes the tortillas over a flame that bakes them to
just the right consistency. The customer can buy them
uncooked or get them while they are hot, and take
them home to be combined with other ingredients.

entists who have studied the history of agriculture in Mexico believe that pumpkins or squashes were the first crop to be cultivated by the Indians, but the most ancient types were not like the modern vegetables. The earliest examples had no edible flesh at all but were grown for their large seeds, which were rich, oily and nutritious and could be stored in baskets for a time of need. *Pepitas* (squash seeds) are still grown in Mexico in considerable quantities. They are roasted and eaten like peanuts or shelled and ground to a greenish meal that makes delicious sauces. Dishes made of tortillas garnished with squash seed sauce are still popular, and some of them follow recipes that are probably 4,000 or 5,000 years old.

The ancient Mexicans had many other cultivated plants that have not spread appreciably beyond Mexico. Most interesting and important is the *maguey*, a large and beautiful "century plant" that thrives on Mexico's arid uplands. Its thick, stiff leaves, rimmed and pointed with strong, sharp thorns, get to be 10 feet long and form a wonderfully graceful cluster that grows gradually larger for 10 to 15 years. All this time the enormous plant is storing up food in its leaves and starchy root. At last it has enough reserves to make a grand effort and produce flowers. If nothing interferes, it will send up a flower stalk sometimes 40 feet tall, displaying high in the air thousands of gleaming white flowers. In spite of their name, most century plants flower once every 10 to 15 years.

The Mexican country people watch the *maguey* closely, and when the flower bud—as big as a cabbage—begins to appear in the center of the cluster of spiny leaves, it is cut out in a way that forms a basinlike cavity. The poor *maguey* does not realize that it has been deflowered, and it keeps filling the cavity with sweet sap provided by the starchy reserve. This sap is collected regularly in large gourds and fermented to yield *pulque,* a mildly alcoholic beverage that is drunk while it is still fermenting and milky with living yeast.

Few non-Mexicans like *pulque;* it has a sour, rotten-apple smell that comes from the carbon dioxide that the still-active yeast is giving off, and its taste is no better. But Mexicans love it and drink enormous quantities of it. Its modest content of alcohol and its price may be its main attractions, but the living yeast cells suspended in the cloudy liquid are a rich source of vitamins and an invaluable supplement to the basic diet of corn, beans and chili.

The *maguey* plant has other uses besides providing *pulque.* Its leaves contain a coarse, strong fiber that is made into mats, sacks and rope, and its massive root can be dug up and eaten as a starchy vegetable. When the plant is dying, as it does after flowering or attempting to flower, it yields another kind of food. Its fleshy leaves become infested with great burrowing grubs, *gusanos de maguey,* which were an Indian delicacy in pre-Conquest times and are still a celebrated food. Modern Mexican gourmets try to persuade their foreign friends to try *gusanos,* usually without success.

Other Indian specialties are less bizarre than *gusanos.* The prickly-pear cactus that grows in many dry parts of Mexico is an excessively spiny desert plant that looks about as edible as a barbed-wire fence, but the ancient Indian plant breeders were not discouraged by its hostile appearance. They gradually improved the prickly pear until it became a tall, stately, cultivated variety that has few thorns and bears delicious fruit, called *tunas,* that are three inches long and an inch in diameter. The thick young leaves of the prickly pear are edible, too. They have only rudimentary thorns and can be cooked as an excellent green vegetable.

Mexico was not the only Indian country whose agriculture contributed to the cuisine of modern Latin America. Peru was just as important, and the Inca Empire of which it was the center was at least as advanced as the Aztec Empire of Mexico. When the Spanish conquerors under Francisco Pizarro invaded Peru in 1531, they found the country had just been torn by a war between two claimants to the Inca throne. The victor, the Inca Atahuallpa, was campaigning 600 miles from Cuzco, the Empire's capital, but nevertheless, he lived in magnificent state, surrounded by wives, concubines, courtiers, soldiers, entertainers and servants of all kinds.

Like Moctezuma, Atahuallpa had food prepared in great variety and served by beautiful girls whose only duty was to attend him. If he so much as touched a dish, the uneaten part of the food was thrown away, and the container itself was destroyed so that no lesser person could ever eat from it. Atahuallpa was captured by the Spaniards and held prisoner for several months. He continued to live in his accustomed luxury under their eyes, but none of the captors recorded what foods were served to him. The Spaniards themselves seem to have lived mostly on meat, recklessly slaughtering the herds of llamas that grazed on the nearby mountains. So even less is known about Peruvian royal food than about its Mexican equivalent. It was probably elaborate and ostentatious, consuming great amounts of materials and labor to glorify the ruling Inca, who was considered a living god. When residing at Cuzco, for instance, the Inca had fish from the Pacific brought to his table by relays of trained runners who covered 300 miles of high, rugged mountains in less than two days. The fish must have arrived in very good condition since most of the time they would have been refrigerated by the mountain cold.

Though the Inca luxury cuisine can only be vaguely guessed at, the food eaten by the common people today has changed little from that of their ancestors. This continuity is the result of the extraordinarily difficult topography of Peru. The Andes are almost incredibly lofty and rugged; passes higher than the peaks of any mountain in the United States or Europe are commonplace, and often a traveler is confronted by a steepsided valley two miles deep. In many inaccessible crannies the Indians live much as they did before the Spanish conquest. They speak their ancient language, Quechua, grow their ancient crops and prepare their food in ancient ways. Modern Peruvian scholars who study their customs get a pretty good idea of what their ancestors ate in Inca times.

One thing is obvious immediately: The Peruvian Indians rivaled the Mexicans in their genius for plant breeding. They may have got their original corn from Mexico, but they soon improved it and found new ways to utilize it. The dry, mature kernels of many varieties of Peruvian corn are soft enough to chew and so can be eaten without any preparation at all. They are usually roasted, however, in a special pottery vessel with a narrow opening and a handle so that the containers can be held over a fire and shaken like a corn popper. The grains do not pop but turn a rich

Overleaf: Mexico's versatile tortilla and its principal uses are displayed against a detail from a famous Diego Rivera mural, the market in Tenochtitlán, the ancient Aztec capital. Tortillas may be eaten plain or combined with various ingredients, such as those shown on the left, to make soft or unfried tacos. They may also be cooked with a variety of ingredients to make the popular dishes shown on the right. Listed below are sauces and condiments and tortilla-based dishes (*pages 36 and 37*).

INGREDIENTS SERVED WITH TORTILLAS:
  1 *Guacamole* (crushed avocado)
  2 Chopped raw onion
  3 *Chiles chipotles* (whole fiery chilies)
  4 *Salsa cruda* (uncooked tomato sauce)
  5 *Salsa verde* (uncooked green tomato sauce)
  6 *Chiles serranos* (whole hot chilies)
  7 Coarsely grated Parmesan cheese
  8 Shredded lettuce
  9 *Salsa de chile rojo* (cooked red chili sauce)
  10 Grated breast of chicken

TORTILLA-BASED DISHES:
  11 *Enchiladas rojas*
  12 *Enchiladas verdes*
  13 *Tacos*
  14 *Tostadas*
  15 *Quesadillas*

Continued on page 38

Chilies come in a variety of shapes, sizes, colors and flavors, and experienced cooks can usually tell whether a particular chili is hot, pungent or sweet by its shape and color. The seven different types shown above are among the most widely used in Latin America:

1 Cayenne: grows in most parts of world; always hot
2 *Mirasol colorado:* mild; widely used in Peru
3 A smaller Cayenne: as hot as larger ones of this species
4 Small variety of Cayenne: hot; common in U.S. markets
5 *Pequín* (or *tepín*): tiny red chili; hot; generally used dried
6 Japanese *hontaka:* hot; usually used dried; widely available
7 *Ancho:* mild; very pungent; most used of dried red Mexican chilies
8 *Güero* (California green pepper): mild; used fresh
9 *Mulato:* very pungent; large; dark in color; always used dried

brown and have a fine toasted flavor. This toasted corn, *cancha,* was the field ration of the Inca soldiers, and it is still carried by Peruvian Indians on journeys or at work in places far from their homes. It was sometimes ground up and combined with dried vegetables and *ají,* the Peruvian chili, to make a soup mix to which meat, fish or other available ingredients could be added. This very practical instant food, which sounds more characteristic of the age of supermarkets than of the Inca Empire, is still in use in the Andes. It produces in a few minutes a satisfying one-dish meal.

Peru does not have pronounced seasons, so corn matures over much of the year, and most of the time it can be harvested and eaten when not quite ripe. The ears are cut in sections and boiled; fishing them out of a stew and eating them with the fingers is a messy but rewarding process. The Indians also cut the soft kernels off the cobs and boil them, making a dish like the Mexican *pozole* but better in taste. They sometimes mash or grind the kernels into a dough for corncakes and tamales, often called *humitas* in the Andes. All these preparations of immature corn are popular and excellent, with a somewhat nutty flavor. They can be made out of sweet corn, but the usual raw material is more like the field corn that is fed to hogs and chickens in the United States.

A great deal of Peruvian corn was, and still is, ground in a simple and ingenious mill that is peculiar to the Andes. It is a heavy piece of stone with one side cut in a curve so the stone can be rocked back and forth on a flat stone surface. Little strength is needed; a small child can put a few handfuls of corn kernels under the stone and keep it rocking like a cradle until the corn is reduced to meal. Other grains can be ground in the same effortless way. The meal, which is often flavored with *ají* and other spices, is made into tortillas or *humitas* or into corn mush or soup.

High in the Andean valleys, where corn does not grow well because of the cold, the potato reigned supreme in Inca days as it does today. An Indian market in the mountains shows a bewildering assortment of potatoes. The skins of some of them are red or black; their shapes vary from almost spherical to long and thin. A much-prized kind of "white" potato has bright-yellow flesh and a distinctive flavor. Some varieties are favored because of their solidity: They contain much more dry matter and less water than ordinary potatoes.

The Indians eat their potatoes baked, boiled, mashed and in soups and stews, just as other people do, but they also do many other things with them. Perhaps the most interesting uses start with a freeze-drying process that turns them into a material, *chuño,* that will keep practically forever. After the potato harvest, the Indians carry a large part of their crop to ravines at an altitude of more than 13,000 feet and expose the potatoes to the bitter cold air that cascades down the mountainsides almost every night. The potatoes freeze, thaw when the sun hits them, and then freeze again at night. Their moisture departs into the thin, dry air, which is always too cold to permit decay. Finally they turn into a dry material almost as hard as wood and light as cork.

There are many kinds of *chuño.* Sometimes the potatoes are cooked and cut up before freeze-drying, and sometimes they are crushed during the drying process. The most attractive *chuño* is made of small, very solid potatoes grown at high altitude. They keep their shape during freeze-drying and do not shrink much. When sold in the mountain markets they look like grayish pebbles about two inches long, but a short period of soaking and boiling turns them back into potatoes that have a mild but distinctive and very pleasant flavor. Other root crops are also freeze-dried, and so are meat, fish, frogs' legs and almost everything else that the Indians want to preserve. The dry foods are often finely ground and made into cakes or added to soups or stews.

Some of these stews have names in the Indian language, Quechua, but others are nameless combinations of whatever ingredients happen to be on hand. Many of the stewlike dishes or thick soups for sale in the Indian markets are spiced with *ají*, which is almost as prevalent in Indian Peru as chili is in Mexico, and are apt to be too spicy for North American tastes. If this difficulty is overcome, and a short training period can overcome it, the mysterious *picantes* of the markets prove to be delicious. Yet even for a Spanish-speaking person it is hard to find out what they contain. The women with shining pigtails who ladle these delicacies out of great earthenware pots will identify some of the ingredients in Spanish—tomatoes, corn, potatoes and various kinds of beans and meat. But other ingredients, including many powerful spices, have names only in Quechua. The women smile and shrug their shoulders. "What does it matter?" they ask. "Doesn't it taste good?" Generally it does.

The cooking of the ancient Indians lacked, of course, many ingredients that the modern world considers essential. Except among the ruling classes, meat was usually scarce. The turkeys of the Mexican Indians were not raised in sufficient numbers to be a staple food. The Peruvian Indians were somewhat better off for meat: They had their llamas and alpacas, which they usually killed for food only after they had grown old and tough. Guinea pigs, though small—it takes a whole one to satisfy a hungry man—were fairly plentiful. When broiled or stewed they are rather like small rabbits, but with lighter-colored meat.

The pre-Conquest Indians lacked milk, butter and cheese. They had no chickens, and eggs from turkeys, ducks and wild birds must have been scarce luxuries. Since they lacked grease or cooking oil they did no frying. Their foods were usually boiled or steamed, or toasted on a dry griddle. They broiled meat and fish by holding it on a stick near a wood or charcoal fire, but they had no real ovens. Their only way to bake food was the ancient method of digging a hole in the ground and filling it with wood fuel and some good-sized stones. When the wood in such an oven has burned away, the stones are hot enough to bake or steam any food that is put into the hole and properly covered.

It takes a great deal of work, time and fuel to cook this way, but for festive occasions its appeal is unfailing. It is the origin of the New England clambake, which the early settlers copied from the New England Indians. In Mexico the same method is called *barbacoa*, a name that may be the source of the English word barbecue; in Chile it is *curanto* and in Peru it is *pachamanca*. No matter by what name it is called, the ancient Indian cooking hole is still a center of cheerful gaiety and produces excellent baked or steamed food with a special nostalgic flavor.

Mexico's Venerable Brew

The wizened old Mexican above is savoring a bowlful of *pulque*, the taste of which was described by someone sampling it for the first time as "sour milk mixed with a bit of gunpowder and Limburger cheese." Nevertheless this inexpensive, nutritious beverage has been consumed in great quantities by Mexican country people and city workers since pre-Conquest days. Slightly stronger than beer—it is about 6 per cent alcohol—*pulque* is made from sap in the heart of the spiky mature *maguey* plants *(right)*. The sap, *aguamiel* (literally, "honey water"), is collected by sucking it into *acocotes*, long, slender gourds narrowly opened at both ends *(near right)*. Emptied into casks *(far right)* or jugs, the sap is transported to vats, where it ferments for several days. The resulting *pulque* is best when drunk fresh at the ranch where it is made, but it is sold by the barrel to *pulquerías* and restaurants where it is served plain or flavored with various fruit juices.

40

To make 12

2¼ cups instant *masa harina* (corn
   flour)
1 teaspoon salt
1⅓ cups cold water

Tortillas

In a mixing bowl, combine the *masa harina* and salt, and gradually pour
in 1 cup of water, stirring constantly. Knead the mixture with your
hands, adding more water, a tablespoon at a time, until the dough becomes firm and no longer sticks to the fingers. If you have a tortilla
press, break off small pieces of dough and shape them into balls the size
of a walnut. Place one ball at a time between two 8-inch squares of wax
paper, and press them into 5- to 6-inch circles. Or divide the dough into
3 or 4 batches and, with a rolling pin, roll each batch between long strips
of wax paper until the dough is about ¹⁄₁₆ inch thick. With a plate or
pot lid as a pattern, and a knife or pastry wheel, cut the dough into 5-
inch rounds. Stack the rounds between pieces of wax paper.

  Preheat the oven to 250°. Cook the tortillas one at a time. Heat an ungreased *comal*, a cast-iron griddle or a 7- to 8-inch cast-iron skillet over moderate heat. Unwrap the tortilla and cook it for 2 minutes on each side,
turning it once with a spatula when the bottom becomes a delicate
brown. Adjust the heat if it browns too fast. As you proceed, wrap the tortillas, 4 or 5 at a time, in foil, and keep them warm in the oven.

  Tortillas may be cooked ahead and kept warm in the oven for 2 or 3
hours: Stack 10 together and wrap each batch with paper toweling, then
with a damp cloth and finally in foil. To rewarm tortillas, brush both
sides with water, and heat, one at a time, in a skillet for a few seconds.

  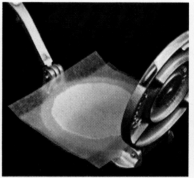 

Tortillas are such a staple in
Mexico that cooks use special
presses to flatten them speedily
and special pans called *comales* to
bake them. Tortilla making,
shown above from left to right, is
simple. A ball of dough is placed
on the press between two pieces
of wax paper and flattened by
closing the press. After the paper
is peeled off, the tortilla is baked
on a *comal (right)*. The press and
comal shown are available in the
U.S., but the dough can be
flattened with a rolling pin and
the tortillas baked in a skillet.

Enchiladas Rojas
FRIED SAUSAGE-FILLED TORTILLAS WITH RED CHILI SAUCE

NOTE: Before using hot chilies, read the instructions on page 51.

Under cold running water, pull the stems off the chilies. Cut or tear the chilies into halves, and brush out the seeds. With a small, sharp knife, cut away any large ribs; then tear them into small pieces. In a small bowl, soak the chilies in 1 cup of boiling water for 30 minutes.

Pour the chilies and their soaking water into the jar of an electric blender and blend at high speed for about 15 seconds. Add the tomatoes, ½ cup of the onions, the garlic, *epazote,* sugar, salt and black pepper, and blend for 30 seconds, or until the mixture is reduced to a smooth purée. (To make the sauce by hand, purée the chilies, tomatoes, onions, garlic and *epazote*—a cup or so at a time—in a food mill set over a large mixing bowl. Discard any pulp remaining in the mill. Stir in the sugar, salt and black pepper.)

In an 8- to 10-inch skillet, melt 1 tablespoon of the lard over moderate heat until a haze forms above it. Pour in the chili and vegetable purée and, stirring frequently, cook it for 5 minutes. Remove the pan from the heat. In a small bowl, beat the eggs with a fork until they are well combined, then stir in the cream. Slowly pour the egg-cream mixture into the sauce in the skillet, stirring constantly to prevent the eggs from curdling. Cover the skillet and set it aside.

In another 8- to 10-inch skillet, melt 1 tablespoon more of the lard over moderate heat and add the chopped sausages. Fry for about 5 minutes, stirring constantly, until the sausages have rendered most of their fat and are lightly browned. With a slotted spoon, remove the sausages from the skillet and drain them on paper toweling. Discard the fat from the skillet. Place the sausages in a small bowl and stir in 3 tablespoons of the chili sauce and ⅓ cup of the grated cheese.

Preheat the oven to 350°. In the heavy skillet, melt the remaining 3 tablespoons of lard over moderate heat until a light haze forms above it. Fry and fill the tortillas, one at a time, in the following fashion: Dip a tortilla in the tomato sauce, drop it into the hot lard, and fry it for a minute or so on each side, or until it becomes limp but not brown. Transfer the tortilla from the pan to a plate and place about ¼ cup of the sausage mixture in the center. Fold one side of the tortilla over the filling, then roll the tortilla completely into a thick cylinder. Place it seam side down in a shallow 8-by-12-inch baking dish. Fry and fill the remaining tortillas similarly, replenishing the lard in the frying pan when necessary. When the tortillas are all arranged in one layer in the baking dish, pour the remaining tomato sauce over them, and sprinkle the top with the ½ cup of the chopped onions and the remaining cheese. Bake in the middle of the oven for about 15 minutes, or until the cheese has melted and the enchiladas are lightly browned on top.

To serve, gently transfer the enchiladas with a spatula to heated individual plates and spoon some of the sauce over them.

NOTE: 3 cups of leftover lean roast pork or cooked chicken, finely shredded, may be substituted for the sausage. In that case, do not brown the pork or chicken, but simply combine it with the tomato sauce and the grated Parmesan cheese.

To serve 6

THE SAUCE
6 dried *ancho* chilies
1 cup boiling water
5 fresh tomatoes, peeled, seeded and coarsely chopped *(see salsa cruda, page 44)*, or substitute 1⅔ cups chopped, drained, canned Italian plum tomatoes.
½ cup coarsely chopped onions
¼ teaspoon finely chopped garlic
½ teaspoon crumbled dried *epazote,* if available
Pinch of sugar
1 teaspoon salt
¼ teaspoon freshly ground black pepper
5 tablespoons lard
2 eggs
1 cup heavy cream

6 Spanish *chorizo* sausages, skinned and coarsely chopped, or substitute ¾ pound smoked, spiced pork sausage, skinned and chopped
⅔ cup freshly grated Parmesan cheese
12 tortillas *(opposite)*
½ cup coarsely chopped onions

To make about 2 cups

4 medium tomatoes (about 1 pound)
⅓ cup finely chopped onions
1 tablespoon coarsely chopped fresh
   coriander (*cilantro*)
1 teaspoon drained, rinsed, and finely
   chopped canned *serrano* chili
½ teaspoon salt
⅛ teaspoon freshly ground pepper
Pinch of sugar

To serve 6

2 whole chicken breasts, each about
   ¾ pound
1 cup chicken stock, fresh or canned
6 ounces cream cheese
2 cups heavy cream
¾ cup finely chopped onions
6 fresh *poblano* chilies, about 5 inches
   long, or substitute 6 fresh green
   peppers, about 3½ inches in
   diameter
A 10-ounce can Mexican green
   tomatoes, drained
2 canned *serrano* chilies, drained,
   rinsed in cold water and finely
   chopped
5 teaspoons coarsely chopped fresh
   coriander (*cilantro*)
1 egg
1½ teaspoons salt
¼ teaspoon freshly ground black
   pepper
3 tablespoons lard
12 tortillas (*page 42*) or 12 ready-
   made tortillas
⅓ cup freshly grated Parmesan cheese

Salsa Cruda
UNCOOKED SPICED TOMATO SAUCE

Drop the tomatoes into a pan of boiling water and remove them after 15 seconds. Run them under cold water, and with a small, sharp knife, peel them. Cut the stem out of each tomato, then slice the tomatoes in half crosswise. Squeeze the halves gently to remove the seeds and juices, and chop the tomatoes fine. In a large mixing bowl, combine the tomatoes, onions, coriander, chili, salt, pepper and sugar, and with a large spoon mix them together gently but thoroughly. Taste for seasoning. If the sauce is not to be served immediately, cover the bowl with plastic wrap and refrigerate. It will keep for at least 2 days. *Salsa cruda* is traditionally served with cooked meats, poultry, fish, tacos and *tostadas*.

Enchiladas Verdes
FRIED CHICKEN-FILLED TORTILLAS WITH GREEN TOMATO SAUCE

Place the chicken breasts in a heavy 2- to 3-quart saucepan, pour in the stock and bring it to a boil over high heat. Then reduce the heat to its lowest point, cover the pan, and simmer the breasts for about 20 minutes, or until they are tender but not falling apart. Transfer the breasts to a plate and reserve the stock. When the chicken is cool enough to handle, remove the skin, cut the meat away from the bones and shred it into small pieces. In a large mixing bowl, beat the cream cheese with a wooden spoon until it is smooth, then beat into it ½ cup of cream, 3 tablespoons at a time. Stir in the onions, add the shredded chicken, mix thoroughly, and put the mixture aside while you make the sauce.

Roast the *poblano* chilies or green peppers by impaling them, one at a time, on the tines of a long-handled fork and turning them over a gas flame until the skin blisters and darkens on all sides. Or place the chilies on a baking sheet or broiler pan, and broil them about 3 inches from the heat for about 5 minutes or so, turning them so that they color on all sides. Be careful not to let them burn. Wrap the chilies in a damp, clean towel and let them rest in the towel for a few minutes. Gently rub them with the towel until the skins slip off. Cut out their stems and thick white membranes, and discard the seeds. Chop the chilies coarsely and place them in the jar of an electric blender. Add the tomatoes, *serrano* chilies, coriander and ¼ cup of the reserved chicken stock. Blend at high speed until the mixture is reduced to a smooth purée. Pour in the remaining 1½ cups of cream, the egg, salt and pepper, and blend for 10 seconds longer. Scrape the purée into a large bowl. (To make the sauce by hand, purée the chilies, tomatoes, *serrano* chilies and coriander in a food mill set over a bowl. Discard any pulp remaining in the mill. Stir in the ¼ cup of stock, 1½ cups of cream, the egg, salt and pepper, and mix together thoroughly.)

Preheat the oven to 350°. In a heavy 8- to 10-inch skillet, melt the lard over moderate heat until a light haze forms above it. Fry and fill the tortillas, one at a time, in the following traditional fashion: Dip a tortilla in the chili-tomato sauce, drop it into the skillet and fry it for a minute or so on each side, or until limp. Transfer the tortilla from the pan to a plate and place ¼ cup of the chicken filling in its center. Fold one side of the tortilla over the filling, then roll the tortilla up completely into a thick cylinder. Place it, seam side down, in a shallow 8-by-12-inch baking dish. Fry and fill the remaining tortillas in a similar fashion, replenishing the lard in the frying pan when necessary. When the tortillas are all arranged in one layer in the baking dish, pour the remaining chili-tomato sauce over them and sprinkle the top evenly with grated cheese. Bake on the middle shelf of the oven for about 15 minutes, or until the cheese melts and the enchiladas brown lightly on top. Serve at once.

NOTE: You may substitute 2 cups of leftover lean roast pork, finely shredded, for the chicken.

Tostadas Estilo Guadalajara
FRIED TORTILLAS WITH BEANS AND PIG'S FEET

Combine the tomatoes, 1 cup of finely chopped onions, oregano, garlic, vinegar, sugar and salt for the sauce in a bowl and, with a large spoon, mix them together thoroughly. Set the sauce aside.

For the topping, prepare the *frijoles refritos* according to the recipe on page 72; cover them and keep them warm over the lowest possible heat. In a large bowl, beat the oil, vinegar and salt together until they are thoroughly combined. Drop in the lettuce and toss lightly with a spoon until the lettuce is coated evenly with the dressing.

In a heavy 8- to 10-inch skillet, melt 2 tablespoons of the lard over moderate heat until a light haze forms above it. One at a time, fry the tortillas for 1 minute on each side, or until they are light gold. Drain on a double thickness of paper towels. As you proceed, replenish the lard in the pan, 1 tablespoon at a time, when necessary.

Assemble the *tostadas* in the following fashion: Place 2 tortillas side by side on each serving plate. Spread about ⅓ cup of the refried beans on the surface of each tortilla, scatter ¼ cup of lettuce on the beans, then top with layers of pig's feet, coarsely chopped onions and finally the sauce. Sprinkle each *tostada* with 2 teaspoons of grated cheese and garnish with a few strips of *jalapeño* chili.

Guacamole
AVOCADO SAUCE WITH TOMATO AND CORIANDER

Cut the avocados in half. With the tip of a small knife, loosen the seeds and lift them out. Remove any brown tissuelike fibers clinging to the flesh. Strip off the skin with your fingers starting at the narrow or stem end (the dark-skinned variety does not peel as easily; use a knife to pull the skin away, if necessary). Chop the avocados coarsely; then, in a large mixing bowl, mash with a fork to a smooth purée. Add the chopped onion, chili, tomato, coriander, salt and a few grindings of black pepper, and mix them together gently but thoroughly. Taste for seasoning. To prevent the *guacamole* from darkening as it stands, cover it with plastic wrap or aluminum foil and refrigerate until ready to use. Stir before serving, and serve either at room temperature or chilled as a dip with fried tortillas *(page 42)*, as a sauce for tacos or *tostadas*, or as a salad heaped on chilled lettuce.

To serve 6

THE SAUCE
6 medium tomatoes, peeled, seeded and finely chopped *(see salsa cruda, opposite)*
1 cup finely chopped onions
2 teaspoons dried oregano
½ teaspoon finely chopped garlic
½ cup red wine vinegar
1 teaspoon sugar
1 teaspoon salt

4 cups *frijoles refritos (page 72)*
5 tablespoons olive oil or vegetable oil
2 tablespoons red wine vinegar
¼ teaspoon salt
3 cups finely shredded iceberg lettuce
⅓ cup lard
12 tortillas *(page 42)* or ready-made tortillas
2 or 3 pickled pig's feet, boned and coarsely chopped
1 cup coarsely chopped onions
Freshly grated Parmesan cheese
4 canned *jalapeño* chilies, rinsed in cold water and cut lengthwise into ⅛-inch strips

To make about 2 cups

2 large ripe avocados
1 tablespoon finely chopped onion
1 tablespoon rinsed and finely chopped canned *serrano* chili
1 medium tomato, peeled, seeded and coarsely chopped *(see salsa cruda, opposite)*
1 tablespoon finely chopped fresh coriander *(cilantro)*
½ teaspoon salt
⅛ teaspoon freshly ground black pepper

To make about 2 cups

5 dried *ancho* chilies
1 cup boiling water
1 dried *pequín* chili, crumbled
3 medium tomatoes peeled, seeded and coarsely chopped *(see salsa cruda, page 44)*, or substitute 1 cup drained, canned Italian plum tomatoes
½ cup coarsely chopped onions
¼ teaspoon finely chopped garlic
¼ cup olive oil or vegetable oil
1 tablespoon finely chopped fresh parsley
½ teaspoon sugar
½ teaspoon salt
⅛ teaspoon freshly ground black pepper
1 tablespoon red wine vinegar

To make 24 tamales

24 dried cornhusks, or substitute 24 sheets of baking parchment paper, 4 by 9 inches
⅓ cup lard
2 cups instant *masa harina* (corn flour)
2 teaspoons double-acting baking powder
1½ teaspoons salt
1½ cups lukewarm beef or chicken stock, fresh or canned

THE FILLING

1½ cups *mole poblano* made with turkey, chicken or pork *(page 73)*, cut in ¼-inch dice and moistened with its sauce; or 1½ cups *pollo en adobo (Recipe Booklet)*, cut in ¼-inch dice and moistened with its sauce; or 1½ cups *picadillo (Recipe Booklet)*

Salsa de Chile Rojo
RED CHILI SAUCE

NOTE: Before using hot chilies, read the instructions on page 51.

Under cold running water, pull the stems off the *ancho* chilies, tear them in half and brush out their seeds. With a small, sharp knife, cut away any large ribs. Tear the chilies into small pieces and place them in a bowl. Pour 1 cup of boiling water over them and let them soak for 30 minutes. Then combine the *ancho* chilies, ¼ cup of their soaking water, the *pequín* chili, tomatoes, onions and garlic in the jar of a blender. Blend at high speed for 1 minute, or until the mixture is reduced to a smooth purée. (To make the sauce by hand, purée the chilies, tomatoes, onions and garlic in a food mill set over a bowl. Discard any pulp left in the mill. Stir ¼ cup of chili soaking water into the purée and mix well.) In an 8- to 10-inch skillet, heat the oil over moderate heat. Add the purée and cook, uncovered, stirring occasionally, for 5 minutes. Stir in the parsley, sugar, salt and pepper, remove the skillet from the heat, and add the vinegar. *Salsa de chile rojo* is traditionally served with cooked meats and tortilla dishes. It keeps, covered and refrigerated, for 3 to 4 days.

Tamales
STEAMED MEAT-FILLED CORNHUSKS

In a large bowl or pot, cover the cornhusks (if you are using them) with hot water and let them soak for 30 minutes. Then drain and pat the husks dry with paper towels.

Meanwhile, cream the lard with an electric beater at medium speed for 10 minutes, or beat and mash it against the sides of a bowl with a spoon for about 20 minutes, or until light and fluffy. In another bowl, mix the *masa harina,* baking powder and salt together, then beat it about ¼ cup at a time into the creamed lard, continuing to beat until the ingredients are thoroughly combined. Slowly pour in the lukewarm stock, stirring constantly; beat for 4 or 5 minutes until a soft, moist dough is formed.

Assemble the tamales one at a time in the following fashion: Place about a tablespoon of dough in the center of a cornhusk or sheet of paper and, with a knife or metal spatula, spread it into a rectangle about 3 inches by nearly 4 inches to reach almost to the long sides of the husk or paper. Drop a heaping tablespoon of filling in the center of the dough. Then fold one side of the wrapper a little more than halfway across the filling and bring the opposite side over the first fold. Turn the ends up to cover the seam, overlapping them across the top. Lay the tamales, seam side down, in a large colander in as many layers as necessary.

Place the colander in a deep pot about 1 inch larger in diameter than the colander, and pour enough water into the pot to come to an inch below the bottom of the colander. Bring the water to a vigorous boil over high heat, cover the pot securely and reduce the heat to low. Steam the tamales for an hour, keeping the water at a slow boil and replenishing it with boiling water as it evaporates. When the tamales are done, remove them from the colander with tongs, arrange them on a heated platter and serve at once. The tamales may be cooked ahead if you like and reheated by steaming them again for half an hour.

Dried cornhusks are the traditional wrapper for the Mexican tamale—shown freshly cooked, in a basket, and newly opened, on a plate.

1 To make a tamale, smooth out a tablespoon of dough almost to the sides of a presoaked cornhusk.

2 Drop a heaping tablespoonful of the ground meat filling onto the center of the dough.

3 Fold one of the long sides of the cornhusk over, bringing it a little more than halfway across the filling.

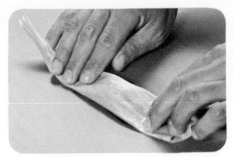

4 Fold the opposite side over the first fold, covering it by about an inch to enclose the filling in its wrapper.

5 Bring the ends up over the seam, overlapping them. Stack the tamales in a colander (*right*), for steaming.

III

Mexico: A Blend of Indian and Spanish

At a restaurant near Mexico City, a waiter displays a variety of regional Mexican dishes. Starting at his right hand and moving clockwise are: grilled shrimp from Campeche (shown with tortillas), squash-flower soup from the Federal District (Mexico City), red snapper Veracruz style, lobster tails from Isla Mujeres, chicken tacos (especially popular in the Federal District), chicken *pibil* from Yucatán, and enchiladas in a Pueblan sauce. In the center is the nationally favored dish, *guacamole*, along with *chiles en nogada* from Puebla.

When the Spaniards and Portuguese settled among the Indians of Latin America in the 16th Century, they brought with them the foods and cooking of the Mediterranean world: their edible plants, domestic animals—especially hogs—along with onions, garlic, cinnamon, rice and many other things. The reception of these imports varied a good deal. Some conservative Indian communities accepted only a few; others were more open-minded or were compelled as slave laborers to grow European crops for their conquerors and prepare European dishes for them.

In most areas a gradual mixing and blending took place, with differences in each locality. Spanish foods were cooked by Indian methods, producing such hybrids as tortillas made of wheat instead of corn. Indian foods were cooked by Spanish methods (meats were often fried rather than being roasted or stewed). Rice, introduced from the Old World, was enlivened with New World tomatoes and chili and became the familiar Spanish rice that is eaten under various names in most of Latin America. European onions and garlic must have filled an aching need. They made an immediate hit and are now grown in every tucked-away valley. Their flavor is strong in dishes that in other respects are Indian.

Out of this culinary interbreeding came the regional or Creole cuisines of Latin America. Probably the most varied and remarkable of them is the Mexican, which managed to preserve the best of pre-Conquest Indian cooking while freely adopting and modifying many good things from Spain. At its best Mexican cooking is very, very good, and the Mexicans are enormously proud of it. Their scholarly gourmets dig into old records

49

to find the first mention of a famous dish, and gastronomic nationalists campaign against the snobbism and commercial propaganda that they blame for the inroads of French and international cooking among the upper classes and the growing popularity of American hot dogs and hamburgers among the common people.

The Creole cooking so honored by the gourmets evolved in a variety of fascinating ways. The story is told of a banquet that Hernán Cortés, the commander of the Spanish conquistadors, gave for his Indian allies at Coyoacán, which is now a suburb of Mexico City. A feature was roast pork from Spanish swine, but far more important than the meat itself was the lard that dripped from it. The Spaniards showed the Indians how it could be used to cook many foods in a new and handy way, by frying. The pre-Conquest Indians had used no cooking fats or oils, but they cooked tortillas on pottery griddles called *comales;* these were easily modified into frying pans, some of which were made with depressions to hold fat. As pigs multiplied and rapidly spread over Mexico, the Indians learned to elaborate many of their ancient foods by frying them in lard.

It would be an exaggeration to say that modern Mexican cooking is Aztec cooking plus pigs, but the statement is not far out of line. The food of the Aztecs was boiled, broiled, steamed or eaten raw. Their fancy dishes were elaborate stews containing many ingredients cooked in a thick sauce. Modern Mexican cooking retains all these methods but adds frying, both in deep fat and on a lightly greased griddle. Perhaps half of all Mexican food is fried in some way before it is served. Tortillas may be fried, and vegetables and meats are fried before or after boiling; even cooked beans are fried. Good Mexican food is seldom greasy, but most of it could not be produced without frying, which was the great contribution of the Spaniards' swine.

Mexican cooking starts, now as in Aztec days, with tortillas, the "bread of Mexico," and only those who have tasted them hot off the griddle know how good tortillas can be. They are not at all hard to make *(page 42)*, and are fine with butter or eaten plain along with other foods. Tortillas are eaten by the humbler Mexicans with just a little chili, beans or sauce. Mexicans use them also as plates, forks and spoons. They dip their tortillas into stews and use torn-off pieces of them to scoop up sauces. They can even, with skill, eat soup with them. Almost any kind of food that is not too liquid can be dumped on a tortilla and rolled up in it. This combination is a taco, the Mexican equivalent of a sandwich. It may be taken directly from the griddle, in which case it will be soft, or it may be stuffed, rolled and fried. Whether soft or fried, tacos may contain nothing more than chopped chili, or they may be bursting with meat and rich sauce. If so, they should be eaten with caution to keep the contents from squirting out the far end. A good precaution is to bend the taco a little, holding the far end closed and slightly raised. Also important is to bite with the teeth only, keeping the lips from having any squeezing effect. With a little practice this is easy, and it makes one's taco eating much more free and seemly.

A more elegant adaptation of the tortilla is the enchilada *(page 43)*. This is a tortilla that has been dipped in a thin sauce, usually green or red tomato, and fried rapidly. It is then rolled up like a taco, but unlike the improvised taco, the enchilada may have an elaborate filling of pork or shredded chicken breast, as well perhaps as onion, cheese, coriander and tomato. The remaining sauce is poured over the enchilada before serving, and the top may be decorated with cheese and chopped onion. Thrifty Mexican housewives customarily use leftover tortillas to make, among other things, not only enchiladas but also *chilaquiles* (tortillas that have been shredded, fried and layered in a casserole with chili sauce).

The ways to use tortillas are almost endless. Tortillas two to five inches in diameter that have been fried crisp and sprinkled with chopped onion, chili, grated cheese or bits of meat are called *tostadas (page 45)*. The smaller *tostadas* are fine as canapés. Like little edible plates, these fried tortillas, which are flat, round versions of the corn chips so widely sold in the United States, can support almost anything that is not too juicy, and they taste better than conventional cocktail crackers.

Another excellent variation is the *quesadilla*, which is a freshly made tortilla filled with meat and sauce, beans, cheese or vegetables, and folded like a turnover. The dough is sometimes flavored with grated cheese, bone marrow or ground chili. The edges of the tortilla are crimped to make them stick together, and the whole thing is fried crisp in fat. *Quesadillas* are excellent and easy, and anyone who happens to have raw tortilla dough can experiment with them. When made very small they are delicious two-bite canapés.

Besides giving variety to the tortilla base of the Mexican diet, lard—that great gift of the Spaniards—also revolutionized the cooking of beans. In Aztec days beans were grown and eaten as much as now, but although they came in many sizes and colors, there were few ways to cook them. They were generally simmered in an earthenware pot and flavored with chili and herbs. Beans are still cooked in much this same way and served *de olla* (out of the pot), but equally popular are fried beans *(page 72)*. They are first boiled until soft, then mashed and fried slowly in lard until the paste is stiff and dry enough to hold its shape. It is usually sprinkled with grated cheese, and may be decorated with bits of fried tortilla stuck into its sides and top. Fried beans, which are illogically called *frijoles refritos* (refried), are served in nearly every home and restaurant in Mexico. Americans are apt to find them rather dry, but a little water added after frying solves this problem.

Anyone who eats beans or almost any other Mexican food must face the chili problem. Most Mexicans are crazy about chili, that vegetable dynamite, which they inherited from their ancestors and which comes in at least 140 varieties. Almost every part of Mexico has its own special chilies, of which the local citizenry is assertively proud. Grocery stores and markets are piled high with the fiery stuff. Country people grow chilies in their backyards and munch the hottest of them raw as if they were strawberries. Most of the wonderful-looking stews and sauces sold in Mexican markets are spiced with chili that is too hot for Americans to touch with the tips of their tongues, and some recipes call for doses of it that will knock the average American off his chair.

"How can the Mexicans eat that stuff?" ask once-bitten foreigners.

How to Handle Hot Chilies

Hot chilies are cousins to the familiar green bell peppers, but they require special handling. The volatile oils in their flesh and seeds can make your skin tingle and your eyes burn. Wearing rubber gloves is a wise precaution, especially when you are handling fresh hot chilies. Be careful not to touch your face or eyes while working with them.

To prepare chilies, first rinse them clean in cold water. (Hot water may make fumes rise from dried chilies, and even the fumes might irritate your nose and eyes.) Working under cold running water, pull out the stem of each chili and break or cut the chilies in half. Brush out the seeds with your fingers. In most cases the ribs inside are tiny, and can be left intact, but if they seem fleshy, cut them out with a small, sharp knife. Dried chilies should be torn into small pieces, covered with boiling water and soaked for at least 30 minutes before they are used. Fresh chilies may be used at once, or soaked in cold, salted water for an hour to remove some of the hotness.

Canned chilies always should be rinsed in cold water to remove the brine in which they were preserved. For finer-textured sauces, they sometimes are stemmed and seeded as well.

After handling hot chilies of any kind it is essential always to wash your hands thoroughly with soap and warm water.

Continued on page 56

Mexico's abundance of fresh foods is reflected by mounds of fruits and vegetables at Guadalajara's bustling market, Mercado Libertad.

Popular Foods
from Mexican Markets

ABOVE: CHÍCHAROS (PEAS). BELOW: GREEN TOMATOES.

BELOW: CACTUS LEAVES AND GREEN BEANS.

ABOVE: PLUM TOMATOES (TOP); CHILIES. BELOW: FRIJOLES COLORADOS (BEANS).

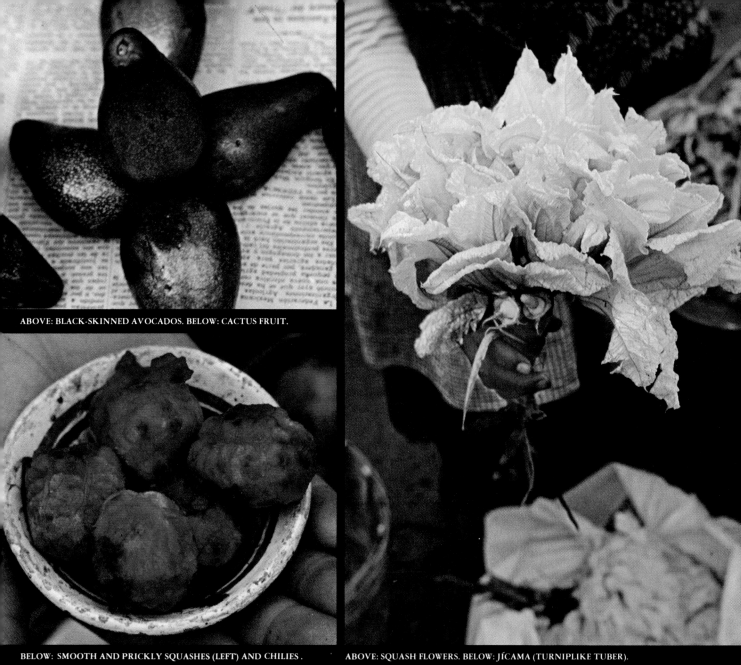

ABOVE: BLACK-SKINNED AVOCADOS. BELOW: CACTUS FRUIT.

BELOW: SMOOTH AND PRICKLY SQUASHES (LEFT) AND CHILIES .

ABOVE: SQUASH FLOWERS. BELOW: JÍCAMA (TURNIPLIKE TUBER).

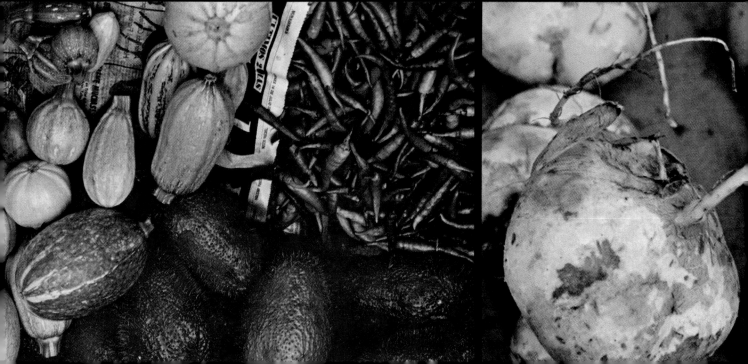

The answer is not simple, and race and nationality have nothing to do with it. Some Mexicans do not like chili; they testify that it burns their mouths and has all the other distressing effects on them that it has on Americans. Young Indian boys who have spoken forbidden words have their mouths washed out with chili as a punishment, a fact seeming to prove that even Indians are not born with immunity to burn. On the other hand some Americans who have lived in Mexico for a long time become so accustomed to chili that they hardly enjoy eating without it. Apparently, the human system can become desensitized to the irritating chemical, capsaicin, that is so abundant in chili. And even when chili seems hot at first, the burning sensation gradually disappears, leaving only a pleasant warmth and agreeable flavor.

Heavy chili eating does not seem to do any damage; Mexicans do not suffer from ailments that can be blamed on it. Indeed, their gourmets consider it a private national asset that other people cannot properly enjoy. Chili, they say, is the wine of the Mexican poor, which ennobles their otherwise monotonous diet of corn and beans. Some recipes call for several kinds of chili, and gourmets claim they can tell at a taste whether any has been omitted or substituted.

In spite of this chili mystique, Americans who visit Mexico need not worry about having their tongues burned. Restaurants patronized by foreigners are careful to serve denatured "native" dishes that contain little or no chili. They sometimes make two versions of each dish, the mild one for foreigners. In the larger Mexican cities many private homes are as free of chili as if they were located in Philadelphia. An appreciable part of the Mexican upper class copies American or European customs and even feels that there is something low-class about chili.

Although jarring accidents do happen now and then when unwary tourists gulp numbing mouthfuls, it would be a shame if chili eating should die out. Once a modest immunity has been acquired, which is not difficult, the hot Indian stews and sauces become wonderfully interesting. Within this book the amounts of chili called for in the recipes have been adjusted to suit American tastes. By experimenting with these recipes the housewife can vary the "hotness" of these dishes to suit her own particular preference and that of her guests.

Chili is actually a boon reserved for educated tastes. Traditional Mexican dishes are still delicious and unusual even when they contain little or none of it. Many of them consist of a sauce, usually a very thick one, that is poured over solid food or contains solid material, such as beans, pieces of tortilla or shredded meat mixed with chili. Plain roast meat or chicken is rare in traditional Mexican cooking, partly because in the old days meat and chicken were so tough that they had to be boiled for hours before human teeth could cope with them. Their quality has since improved, but Mexican cooking still features stews and sauces. Mexican cookbooks give their main attention to them, and at least one is devoted solely to sauces. Many of the mysterious concoctions that perfume Indian markets with their enticing smells are sauces pure and simple. The purchaser gets a small amount in an earthenware bowl and eats it with hot tortillas cooked in a nearby stall.

If local variations are included, the full Mexican cuisine has hundreds of sauces. Some are simple, merely chilies—or chilies, onions and tomatoes —chopped fine, mixed with water or vinegar and served either raw or boiled to enliven tortillas, tamales or any other dish that needs enhancement. Mexicans generally believe that nothing should be eaten without some sort of sauce.

More complicated sauces are generally called *moles*, which comes from an Aztec word, *molli*, meaning a sauce flavored with chili. Some of these are very complicated indeed. The most famous of them, *mole poblano*, is the essence of Mexico's national holiday dish, *mole poblano de guajolote* (turkey in Pueblan sauce). The dish is not only complicated but has a special legend about its origin. The story goes that in the 16th Century the nuns of the convent of Santa Rosa in the city of Puebla heard that the archbishop was coming to visit them. They went into a panic because the convent had nothing suitable to offer such a distinguished visitor, but after a while they rallied, prayed and—with heavenly guidance—began to grind and chop everything edible that they had in the kitchen. Into the mix went (among other things) many kinds of chili, almonds, tomatoes, onions, garlic, bread, tortillas, bananas, sesame seeds, sugar, raisins, lard, toasted avocado leaves and innumerable herbs and spices. All were finely ground and cooked for hours. The final touch was a small quantity of chocolate, which gave the *mole* its subtle flavor. While the sauce was simmering in a great pot the nuns killed their one and only turkey (which was intended for the local bishop), cut it up and cooked the meat. When the archbishop arrived, they served the turkey with the miraculous *mole* poured over it. The noble guest was, of course, delighted. The angels who guided the hands of the nuns had created the most delicious dish that he had ever tasted.

This appealing story probably contains a considerable amount of truth. The convents of post-Conquest Mexico were famous as strongholds of good eating, and they may have improved the dish. But *mole poblano* is not likely to have originated as an invention of Spanish nuns. It contains only a few Spanish ingredients; it is typically Aztec. When the first Spaniards entered Tenochtitlán and wandered around the great central market of the Aztec capital, they probably could have found a thick brown sauce very much like that *mole* simmering in the pots of the Indian food sellers.

A modern version of *mole poblano (page 73)* varies a good deal according to the recipe used. When the most complicated formula is followed, the tedious job of chopping, grinding, frying, simmering and blending the ingredients takes three days. Most recipes are much simpler, and since the sauce is the thing, it can be poured over chicken or pork as well as turkey. When properly prepared it is extraordinary, like nothing else. The chocolate, the most unusual ingredient in this famous dish, cannot be tasted but adds a necessary something. If it is omitted, the *mole* loses much of its character.

Moles can now be bought in a package. But a generation ago traditional Mexican kitchens were small factories where numerous servants were needed to prepare a *mole* and other time-consuming dishes. For grinding and blending the ingredients they used a technique that was descended from

Overleaf: For breakfast or for brunch, *huevos rancheros* (country-style eggs) is a Mexican favorite, served with avocado slices and a hot sauce of tomatoes and chilies, as well as tortillas, kidney beans and chili peppers. To complement this hearty meal, Mexicans prefer a steaming cup of chocolate, a drink that was enjoyed by pre-Columbian Indians of Moctezuma's time.

Continued on page 60

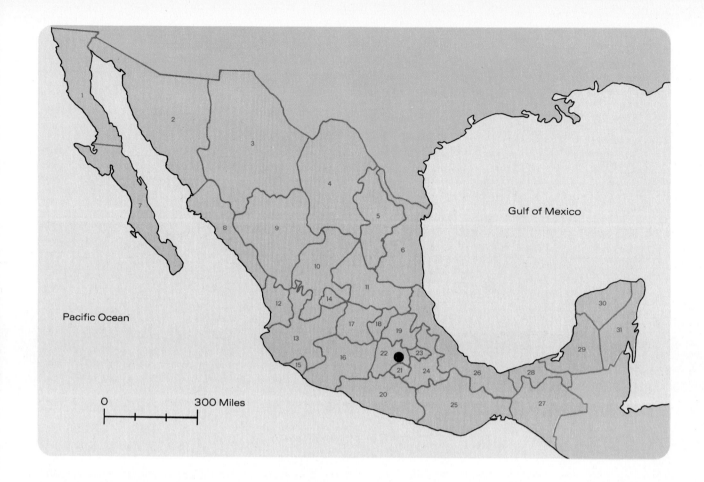

Mexico's Makeup

Mexico includes the Federal District (Mexico City) plus 29 states and two territories. In each of these areas, customs and cooking have retained a distinctive flavor through the years.

FEDERAL DISTRICT (Mexico City) ●

STATES

Aguascalientes (14)	Nayarit (12)
Baja California (1)	Nuevo León (5)
Campeche (29)	Oaxaca (25)
Chiapas (27)	Puebla (24)
Chihuahua (3)	Querétaro (18)
Coahuila (4)	San Luis Potosí (11)
Colima (15)	Sinaloa (8)
Durango (9)	Sonora (2)
Guanajuato (17)	Tabasco (28)
Guerrero (20)	Tamaulipas (6)
Hidalgo (19)	Tlaxcala (23)
Jalisco (13)	Veracruz (26)
México (22)	Yucatán (30)
Michoacán (16)	Zacatecas (10)
Morelos (21)	

TERRITORIES

Baja California Sur (7)
Quintana Roo (31)

Aztec times, employing a stone pestle and a *molcajete*, a three-legged mortar usually made of pocked volcanic stone. The work was slow, but servants were cheap and plentiful, and the results were worth the investment in time and manpower.

Molcajetes are still the mainstay of humbler Mexican kitchens, and are still on sale in stores and marketplaces. Hundreds of thousands of them must have been carried home by American tourists. Small ones make excellent ashtrays, especially for pipe smokers who want something solid against which to knock their pipes. But in up-to-date kitchens *molcajetes* are obsolete. Servants are not as plentiful or humble in modern, prosperous Mexico as they used to be. Today the Mexican servant disdains the slow and laborious *molcajete* and demands an electric blender. Indeed, the kitchens of large houses need two or more blenders to reduce chilies, nuts, tomatoes, squash seeds and what-have-you to *mole* smoothness.

Mexican cooking is still laborious, even with blenders. In most kitchens numerous chilies and tomatoes must be heated over a flame or glowing charcoal to make the skins come off; tortillas must be toasted; earthenware pots and casseroles must be watched for long hours of simmering. But American convenience foods are beginning to penetrate Mexico. In prosperous residential districts of the larger cities, modern supermarkets are replacing the little specialty shops and open-air marketplaces that traditionally distributed Mexico's produce. The supermarkets look much like their American prototypes, and they offer the same bewildering variety of canned and packaged food, most of it produced in Mexico. Along with the items familiar to Americans are others peculiar to the country, such as many kinds of dried or powdered chili, enclosed in plastic envelopes. Packaged dried meat and dried shrimp are also popular items, and the shelves offer more kinds of beans and corn than would be found in American supermarkets. The ultimate in Mexican convenience foods is ready-made *mole poblano* in paste or powdered form. Gourmets denounce all brands of it, but something must be said for a short-cut that saves so much labor.

In spite of convenience foods and laborsaving devices, many Mexicans still insist on eating in an elaborate style. Families who can afford to do so eat four meals per day, all of which are served in the dining room with much changing (and washing) of dishes. Breakfast is substantial, with fruit, tortillas, bread or sweet rolls, coffee or chocolate with milk, and eggs or meat, or sometimes both. The big meal is dinner, *comida*, in the middle of the day, usually starting between 1 and 2 p.m. Around 6 p.m. comes *merienda*, a sort of tea-less high tea, when the father of the family, exhausted by the daily grind, restores himself with coffee or chocolate, sweet rolls, cookies or cake, and *atole*, a rich corn broth usually fortified with sugar, milk, eggs or fruit. Supper *(cena)* comes late, 8 to 10 p.m. It is often skipped, and is usually light if eaten at home. On formal occasions or at restaurants it can be heavy indeed.

But the midday meal is the traditional feast. When served *comme il faut* in a wealthy house, *comida* has at least six courses, with a change of plates for each course and a stream of hot tortillas circulating continuously in their napkin-lined baskets. First comes soup, and Mexican soups are apt to be nourishing beyond the call of duty, swarming with dumplinglike tortilla balls, vegetables, noodles or pieces of meat and chicken. The next course is also called soup, although it has nothing to do with soup. This *sopa seca* (dry soup) is actually a highly seasoned, starchy dish of rice, noodles, macaroni or cut-up tortillas that is cooked in an elaborate sauce. Then comes a course of chicken or fish, or perhaps wild game, followed by a salad. The main course is beef, pork, lamb or *cabrito* (young goat), roasted, boiled or fried, and several vegetables, and this is followed by "refried" beans smothered with grated cheese. Finally comes dessert, usually a pudding, custard or cooked fruit dish, and then—after coffee and fresh fruit in season—the family retires for a well-earned siesta.

Except when entertaining formally, most modern Mexican families do not serve these blockbuster midday dinners. Some of them have even taken to American habits, eating their main meal in the evening and skipping the afternoon *merienda*. Hunger pangs caused by such deprivation are stilled by the extraordinary amount of between-meals eating that goes on in Mexico. In most residential districts hardly a block lacks a booth or sidewalk peddler selling some sort of handy food. Some sell tacos, tamales, sandwiches, sweets, peeled fruit or fruit juices. More elaborate establishments have rotating grills that broil chickens, pork or great masses of sliced bacon whose outer layers curl and whose grease drips into a pan. At every hour of the day these vendors have customers, and office workers who cannot get to them keep stocks of nourishment hidden away in their desks. By American standards Mexico is poor, but most of its people, in the cities at least, seem to have enough money to nibble whenever the spirit moves them.

Continued on page 64

In the convents of colonial Puebla such celebrated Mexican delights as *mole poblano de guajolote (page 73)* and *chiles en nogada (page 74)* were perfected. These kitchens set a standard of beauty and convenience as well as culinary innovation. As seen in this replica displayed at the San Antonio, Texas, Hemisfair, *poblano* kitchens were equipped with open-counter stoves *(center)* and graced by tasteful and attractively arranged pottery, tiles and utensils. Light meals were served at a table conveniently placed near the cooking area.

63

Nearly all food in Mexico, from the street-corner snack to the eight-course dinner served in a lordly mansion, tastes different from its counterpart in the United States, if a counterpart exists. Often the difference is chili, which shows up in unexpected places, such as scrambled eggs, or in a sauce for another favorite, *huevos rancheros (page 70)*. Even a bright green garnish that looks like chopped parsley turns out to have a wholly novel flavor, perhaps of fresh coriander. Sometimes half a dozen unfamiliar herbs and spices contribute to the effect of a Mexican soup or stew. Other differences of taste come from Mexican ways of cooking. Even in modern kitchens many utensils are apt to be made of earthenware, and the slow, burnless simmering permitted by this material affects the flavor. The popular Mexican habit of frying skinned tomatoes slowly in lard until they turn into a thick paste yields a sauce that tastes unlike tomatoes treated in any other way.

Another big difference in Mexican food is that it varies widely from region to region. In the United States, a traveler can drive from New York City to Los Angeles and eat almost identical meals at roadside restaurants along the way. Mexico is not that homogenized. It is not really a single country; it is many small countries tied together in a loose package. In pre-Spanish days it was inhabited by Indians speaking at least 14 distinct families of languages and varying in culture from fierce savagery to rather surprising sophistication. Many of them were independent of the Aztecs, and even those who were subject to these Indians stubbornly clung to their own peculiar customs.

This situation continued after the Conquest. There was little travel or commerce across Mexico's rugged mountains, so the Indian communities kept their identities and passed them along to the populations of mixed Spanish and Indian ancestry that developed locally. The effect can be seen to this day. The country people in adjacent valleys wear different hats, live in different kinds of houses, and cook different food. A pleasant recreation of Mexican gourmets is to travel around their country sampling the local cuisines. Often they find in remote places distinctive traditional dishes that are unknown in Mexico City.

Northern Mexico, especially the big states that border on the United States, was thinly inhabited in pre-Conquest times by warlike, primitive Indians, mostly nomadic hunters whom the civilized Aztecs called Chichimecs (Sons of the Dog). When the Spaniards arrived with their hardy long-horned cattle, a wave of pioneers—Spaniards, mestizos and Indians—moved north to graze their animals on the rich grasslands of the Chichimecs. They also took varieties of wheat that thrived on less rainfall than corn required. The north is still cattle country with wheat grown in favorable places, and beef and wheat are more prominent in its cuisine than they are in other parts of Mexico.

One beef dish from the north—chili con carne—is not considered Mexican in Mexico proper. It was developed in Texas, the Mexicans say, and therefore is American. Supposedly it was invented in Texas when that state was part of Mexico's wild frontier. Few Mexican cookbooks describe it, but they give many recipes for beans cooked with meat, onion, tomato, chili and spices. Originally the beef in chili con carne was cut into

small pieces instead of being ground into hamburger. It is much better when the meat is prepared that way.

Since northern Mexico is arid cattle country where moisture evaporates quickly in the hot, dry air, it is only natural that dried beef, called *cecina*, should be one of the traditional staples. This interesting material is not the thin-sliced, unnaturally pink, almost flavorless stuff that is sold in the United States under the name of chipped beef. It is robust, even overwhelming, and the way it is made in northern Mexico should tell why. The first step is to buy a large solid chunk of beef and form it into a single long sheet by making alternate knife cuts from opposite sides that do not reach quite all the way through. Opened up in accordion folds, this ribbon of meat is sprinkled with salt on both sides and folded up again for two hours to absorb the salt. It is then unfolded and exposed to the sun until it is fairly dry but not stiff. It is rubbed with lemon juice and pepper and stretched out in the cool shade for two days to ripen. After this it is pounded with a mallet (or a stone) to tenderize it. Finally it is folded up for future use. During these vicissitudes it acquires a powerful fla-

Chiles en nogada, stuffed peppers topped with red pomegranate seeds, green coriander leaves and white sauce *(page 74),* is a festive salute to the colors of the Mexican flag. Legendarily, the dish originated in Puebla about 1822 to honor the country's newly won independence.

65

vor like those marvelous ripened steaks that are served by expensive restaurants but cannot be bought in supermarkets. It can be boiled in stews, soaked and fried, or chopped and made into fillings for tacos, enchiladas and tamales. Everywhere it goes, *cecina* makes itself known in no uncertain manner, like high-powered cheese. American chipped beef could well use a touch of its character.

The Mexican north is also a land of cheese. It is not very fancy cheese and is used mostly in cooking, for which it does very well. A fine dish from Chihuahua, the big state opposite west Texas, is made of beans cooked barely soft, fried in lard and heated carefully with cheese until the cheese melts. In Sonora, another northern state, they make a rich potato soup (first frying the potatoes with onions, tomatoes and chili) that is covered with a substantial layer of melted cheese.

In other parts of Mexico beef and cheese are not as important. The place of beef is taken by pork, goat, turkey or chicken. Goat, if it is young, is excellent eating, and only an unreasonable prejudice keeps it from being enjoyed in the United States. Some Americans think that young goats are "too cute to eat," but they are no more endearing than the calves and lambs that are eaten without compunction.

In the small central state of Aguascalientes, *cabrito* is rubbed with a sauce of garlic, chili and spices in vinegar and left overnight to marinate. The next day, while it is slowly roasting it is basted with the same sauce, which dries to a savory crust on the meat. An even more festive dish in the north is a whole *cabrito* elaborately stuffed with a mixture of tomatoes, ground pork, ham cubes, raisins, almonds, pine nuts, hard-boiled eggs and many spices. Few who taste this gorgeous roast worry much about the cuteness of the sacrificed *cabrito*.

In the tropical parts of Mexico, which lie mostly along the coasts, hot-country fruits and vegetables play a prominent part in the cuisine. The banana, which grows nearly everywhere, is used both as a fruit and a vegetable. The sweet varieties are generally eaten ripe and fresh or made into desserts, though they are also fried. The nonsweet kinds, plantains, which are more important, are always cooked. A typical dish of the Gulf Coast is boiled, mashed plantains fried in oil with onions and tomatoes. It is usually served hot with shrimp and chili sauce and has only a very faint banana flavor.

The favorite fruit-vegetable of Mexico is the avocado, which is grown in many varieties in warm regions. It may be a Mexican native, but most authorities think it was domesticated in Peru or some other part of South America several thousand years ago. Some avocados have black skins and are no bigger than plums, while others are green and grow to the size of cantaloupes. Flavors vary from poor to wonderful. American-grown avocados are but pale (and expensive) shadows of the best specimens that are grown in the tropics.

Mexicans eat avocados in salads with salad dressing just as Americans do, but that is only the beginning. They are also eaten with salt or lime juice, to enhance their bland flavor. Pieces of avocado show up in almost any dish, including soups and stews. An excellent soup is made almost entirely of mashed avocados *(page 85),* and sometimes a few avocado slices

Opposite: Mexico's national dish, *mole poblano,* is an adaptation of an old Indian recipe calling for turkey and a chili sauce made with chocolate. The sauce also includes cinnamon, cloves, raisins, almonds and sesame seeds. Since it requires elaborate preparation, and because turkey is a holiday bird in Mexico as well as the United States, *mole poblano* is reserved for special occasions.

are spread on the top, where they almost melt if the soup is hot enough. The most famous avocado dish is *guacamole (page 45)*, which is mashed avocado mixed with tomato, chopped onion, fresh coriander and chili. The proportions of this dish vary all over the lot, and the chili may be omitted. Salt and pepper are generally included and often olive oil. *Guacamole* is commonly served with tortilla dishes, refried beans or anything that can benefit from its green, soft smoothness and contrasting flavor, or it is served as a separate dish. It can be eaten with a fork or spoon or used as a dip, but Mexicans like to make tacos of it by rolling it in tortillas. They take the tacos on picnics, and since this paste turns brown on exposure to air, Mexicans cover its surface with avocado seeds in order to avoid the discoloration.

The cuisine of southern Mexico is exotically different from that of other regions. The State of Oaxaca, for example, is a southern center of Indian tradition whose cooking features red, yellow, green and black *moles*. Famous Oaxaca dishes are made of the flowers and young shoots of squash vines and of "sea chestnuts," a kind of crustacean with a shiny dark-brown shell. One of the oddest is made of *chalupines,* crickets that are gathered in the cornfields. In Oaxaca and other warm parts of Mexico tamales are wrapped in banana leaves instead of cornhusks. The stiff center rib of the banana leaf is removed and the remainder of the great leathery leaf is put in water and brought to a boil. It is then soft and pliable and can be torn into squares and wrapped around a tamale as handily as if it were a sheet of parchment paper. The result is unusually attractive, and the pleasure of unfolding a green Oaxaca tamale increases the enjoyment of eating the food inside.

Perhaps the most distinctive of all the local cuisines of Mexico is that of Yucatán, a state so hemmed in by jungles and swamps that, until a modern highway was finally built, it could not be reached from the rest of the country except by air or sea. Yucatán is the land of the Maya, whose civilization reached amazing heights and went into decline long before the arrival of the conquering Spaniards. Many Yucatecs are descendants of these Maya; their profiles look like the bas-reliefs carved on the ancient ruined temples of the area. These people still speak the Maya language, and some of the names of their favorite local dishes baffle tongues that are accustomed to English. A perch broiled with a spicy sauce, for example, is called *mero en tikin-xik.*

Shrimp are plentiful in Yucatán, and a pleasant local way to serve them as a cold appetizer is to arrange four very large ones in a soup plate and cover them with vinegar, olive oil, finely chopped onions and chili, tomatoes cut in half-inch cubes and chopped fresh coriander. The dish is partly a salad and partly a shrimp cocktail—a far better way to present shrimp than sticking them in tomato ketchup.

A well-known Yucatec specialty is *papatzul,* which means "food of the lords." It is tortillas rolled into tacos stuffed with shredded pork or hardboiled eggs and served with a sauce made principally of ground, toasted squash seeds and another sauce made with tomatoes. The tacos are then decorated with a clear green oil that is pressed from the squash seeds during their grinding.

Another agreeable specialty of Yucatán is *panuchos*. These are small tortillas stuffed with mashed beans or chopped meat, and covered with a special spicy sauce. The stuffing operation is a delicate one. It is quite a trick to lift the thin skin that forms when a tortilla is cooked, and the women who do it are not eager, perhaps not able, to tell how they accomplish this feat.

Many meat or fowl dishes in Yucatán are called *pibil* to tell that they are steamed in a pit, a *pib* in Maya. In some cases the cooking is actually done in this laborious way, but much more often *pollo pibil* (steamed chicken, Yucatán style) is steamed for hours in a covered pot, which gives much the same effect *(page 72)*. The chickens are cut up and the pieces marinated for 24 hours in a sauce that contains *achiote* (annatto), the red-orange spice and coloring agent that is so dear to the Yucatecs. Then they are folded like tamales in banana leaves and steamed until tender. Opening one of these packages is a delight. The banana leaf is pulled apart with two forks and a wonderfully fragrant steam arises. The chicken *pibil* inside has a pungent flavor and a bright red color that no one would expect.

For the adventurous traveler, Mexico offers many such tempting foods, yet American tourists who hear about the strange and delicious dishes of the many local cuisines usually make no attempt to taste them. The expensive tourist hotels, which look so sanitary and seem so American, serve mostly international food with perhaps a few standard Mexican dishes that are carefully watered down to suit the palates of the most timid guests. Tourists may be tempted to eat in purely Mexican restaurants, many of which look marvelous, but they have heard dire tales about compatriots who have died after drinking unbottled water, or even after a single bite of a septic taco.

The rebuttal to such doleful stories is that modern medicine has worked an enormous change in what a tourist should or should not eat. Mexican standards of sanitation are certainly well below those of most parts of the United States, but immunization wards off the worst disease, typhoid, which is carried by food and water, and other food and drink diseases are not the terrors that they were before antibiotics were developed. Still other exotic terrors—such as malaria, yellow fever and typhus—have nothing to do with either food or water.

Many Americans who visit Mexico suffer from diarrhea, sometimes called *turista* or "Moctezuma's revenge." It generally goes away by itself, but there is no reason to let it spoil the trip for even a little time. A few doses of paregoric usually restore the intestinal tract to tranquility. In most cases the upset was not caused by dangerous disease germs but merely by exhaustion or change of routine or climate. It is interesting to know that Mexicans and other Latin Americans frequently suffer from the same affliction while visiting New York.

The best policy for exploring strange Mexican foods off the sheltered tourist tracks is simply to use elementary caution and a reasonable amount of common sense. Then stop worrying. Both Mexico and the other parts of Latin America have an endless variety of unusual but wonderful dishes waiting for you to taste them.

To serve 6

THE SAUCE

3 tablespoons vegetable oil

1 cup finely chopped onions

½ teaspoon finely chopped garlic

5 medium tomatoes, peeled, seeded
and finely chopped (see *salsa cruda,
page 44*), or substitute 2⅔ cups
chopped, drained, canned Italian
plum tomatoes

3 canned *serrano* chilies, drained,
rinsed in cold water and finely
chopped

½ teaspoon sugar

1 teaspoon salt

Freshly ground black pepper

2 tablespoons finely chopped fresh
coriander (*cilantro*)

⅓ cup vegetable oil

12 fresh tortillas (*page 42*) or ready-
made tortillas

6 tablespoons butter

12 eggs

1 large ripe avocado, peeled, pitted
and sliced thin (see *guacamole,
page 45*)

To serve 8

3 cups chicken stock, fresh or canned

3 pounds lean boneless pork loin,
cut into 1½-inch cubes

1 bay leaf

¼ teaspoon dried thyme

¼ teaspoon dried oregano

⅛ teaspoon ground cloves

THE SAUCE

6 dried *mulato* chilies, 4 dried *ancho*
chilies and 2 dried *pasilla* chilies;
or substitute 12 dried *ancho* chilies

1 cup boiling chicken stock, fresh or
canned

1 cup shelled walnuts

A 10-ounce can Mexican green
tomatoes, drained

½ cup coarsely chopped onions

¼ teaspoon finely chopped garlic

2 tablespoons coarsely chopped fresh
coriander (*cilantro*)

1 teaspoon salt

2 tablespoons lard

Huevos Rancheros
RANCH-STYLE EGGS

In a heavy 2- to 3-quart saucepan, heat 3 tablespoons of vegetable oil over moderate heat until a light haze forms above it. Add the onions and garlic, and cook, stirring frequently, for 4 or 5 minutes, or until the onions are soft and transparent but not brown. Stir in the tomatoes, chilies, sugar, salt and a few grindings of black pepper. When the mixture comes to a boil, reduce the heat and simmer uncovered, stirring occasionally, for 15 minutes, or until most of the tomato juices have evaporated and the sauce is a thick purée. Then add the coriander, turn off the heat, and cover the pan to keep the sauce warm.

In one or two *comales* or heavy 8-inch skillets, fry the tortillas in the following fashion: Heat 2 tablespoons of the oil in a skillet over high heat until a light haze forms above it. One at a time, fry the tortillas for 1 or 2 minutes on each side, or until they are slightly golden, replenishing the oil 1 or 2 teaspoons at a time when necessary. As you proceed, transfer the finished tortillas to a double thickness of paper towels to drain.

Place 2 tortillas side by side on each of 6 individual heated plates. Over moderate heat, melt 3 tablespoons of the butter in a heavy 10- to 12-inch skillet. When the foam subsides fry the eggs, 6 at a time (using the remaining butter for the second batch), until the whites are set and the yolks still soft. Separate them with a spatula and carefully place an egg on each tortilla. Spoon a 1-inch ring of the hot sauce around each egg, garnish with the slices of avocado, and serve at once. Present the extra sauce in a small serving bowl.

Mancha Manteles de Cerdo
PORK TABLECLOTH STAINER

NOTE: Before using hot chilies, read the instructions on page 51.

In a heavy 5-quart flameproof casserole, bring the 3 cups of chicken stock to a boil over high heat. Add the pork, bay leaf, thyme, oregano and ground cloves, and reduce the heat to low. Cover the casserole, and simmer for 30 minutes, or until the pork shows only the slightest resistance when pierced with the tip of a sharp knife.

Under cold running water, pull the stems off the chilies, break them in half and brush out their seeds. With your fingers or a small, sharp knife, remove any large ribs. Tear the chilies into small pieces and place them in a small bowl. Pour 1 cup of boiling chicken stock over them and let them soak for 30 minutes. Then place the walnuts in the jar of an electric blender and blend them at high speed until they are completely pulverized. Sieve and return them to the blender with the green tomatoes, onion, garlic, coriander, salt, chilies and chili soaking liquid, and blend at high speed until the mixture is reduced to a smooth purée. (To make the sauce by hand, put the tomatoes, onion, garlic, chilies and coriander through a food mill set over a bowl and discard any pulp remaining in the mill. With a pestle, pound the walnuts in a mortar until they are pul-

The villains that give the stew *mancha manteles* (tablecloth stainer) its name and deep red color are the three chilies at lower right.

verized; then stir them into the purée. Stir in the soaking liquid from the chilies and add the salt.) In a heavy 10-inch skillet, melt 2 tablespoons of lard over moderate heat, pour in the purée and cook it, uncovered, stirring constantly, for 5 minutes. Cover the skillet to keep the sauce warm and set it aside off the heat.

When the pork is done, drain its cooking juices into a small mixing bowl and skim off as much fat from the surface as possible. Add the juices to the walnut-tomato sauce and mix together thoroughly.

Arrange the pear wedges, banana slices, apple wedges, pineapple cubes and zucchini slices in layers on top of the pork, in the casserole. Pour the sauce over them, distributing it as evenly as possible, and cover the casserole. Over low heat, cook undisturbed for 40 minutes. Then sprinkle the green peas over the fruit and zucchini, and cook, covered, for about 5 minutes longer, or until the peas are tender. Serve at once, directly from the casserole.

1 pound firm, ripe pears, peeled, cored and cut lengthwise into 8 wedges

⅔ pound bananas, peeled and sliced ¼ inch thick (about 1 cup of slices)

3 firm, ripe apples (about 1¼ pounds), peeled, cored and cut lengthwise into 8 wedges

1 cup fresh pineapple, cut into ½-inch cubes

1 pound unpeeled zucchini, sliced ¼ inch thick (about 3 cups of slices)

1 cup cooked fresh green peas, or 1 cup thoroughly defrosted frozen peas

To serve 4 to 6

2 cups dried pink beans or dried red
  kidney beans
6 cups cold water
1 cup coarsely chopped onions
2 medium tomatoes, peeled, seeded
  and coarsely chopped *(see salsa
  cruda, page 44)*, or substitute ⅔
  cup chopped, drained, canned
  Italian plum tomatoes
½ teaspoon finely chopped garlic
1 teaspoon crumbled and seeded dried
  pequín chili
¼ teaspoon crumbled *epazote*, if
  available
¼ teaspoon freshly ground black
  pepper
½ cup lard
1 teaspoon salt

Frijoles Refritos
REFRIED BEANS

NOTE: Before using hot chilies, read the instructions on page 51.

Place the beans in a colander or sieve and run cold water over them until the draining water runs clear. Pick out and discard any black or shriveled beans. In a 3-quart heavy pot, combine the water, ½ cup of the onions, ¼ cup of the tomatoes, ¼ teaspoon of the garlic, the chili, *epazote* (if used) and pepper, and drop in the beans. Bring the water to a boil over high heat, then half-cover the pan and reduce the heat to low. Simmer the beans for about 15 minutes and stir in 1 tablespoon of the lard. Simmer, half covered, for 1½ hours, add the teaspoon of salt, and over the lowest possible heat, simmer for another 30 minutes, or until the beans are very tender and have absorbed all their cooking liquid. During the last half hour of cooking, stir the beans gently now and then to prevent their sticking to the bottom of the pan. Remove the pan from the heat, and cover it to keep the beans warm.

In a heavy 12-inch skillet, melt 2 more tablespoons of the lard over high heat until a light haze forms above it. Add the remaining chopped onions and garlic, turn the heat down to moderate, and fry for about 5 minutes, or until the onions are translucent but not brown. Stir in the remaining tomatoes and simmer for 2 or 3 minutes. Fry the cooked beans in the following fashion: Add 3 tablespoons of the beans to the pan of simmering sauce, mash them with a fork, then stir in 1 tablespoon of the remaining lard. Continue adding and mashing the beans in similar amounts, following each addition with another tablespoon of lard until all the lard has been used. Then gradually add the remaining beans, mashing them as you proceed. Cook over low heat for 10 minutes, stirring frequently, until the beans are fairly dry. Serve at once.

Frijoles refritos are a traditional accompaniment to tortilla dishes.

To serve 4

⅔ cup fresh orange juice
⅓ cup fresh lemon juice
1 tablespoon annatto *(achiote)* seeds,
  ground in a blender or pulverized
  with a mortar and pestle
1 teaspoon finely chopped garlic
½ teaspoon dried oregano
½ teaspoon ground cumin seeds
¼ teaspoon ground cloves
¼ teaspoon ground cinnamon
2 teaspoons salt
¼ teaspoon freshly ground black
  pepper
A 3½- to 4-pound chicken, cut into
  6 or 8 pieces
12 hot tortillas *(page 42)*, or 12 heated
  ready-made tortillas

Pollo Pibil
CHICKEN STEAMED WITH FRUIT JUICE

In a small bowl, combine the orange and lemon juice, ground annatto seeds, garlic, oregano, cumin, clove, cinnamon, salt and pepper. Place the chicken in a shallow baking dish just large enough to hold the pieces snugly in one layer and pour the seasoned fruit juice over it. Cover the dish with plastic wrap and marinate the chicken for 6 hours at room temperature, or 12 hours or overnight in the refrigerator, turning the pieces over in the marinade from time to time.

Line a large colander with 2 crossed, overlapping sheets of aluminum foil and arrange the chicken on it. Pour in the marinade, then bring the ends of the foil up over the chicken and twist them together to seal in the chicken and its marinade securely.

Place the colander in a deep pot, about 1 inch larger in diameter than the colander, and pour enough water into the pot to come to within an inch of the bottom of the colander. Bring the water to a vigorous boil over high heat, cover the pot securely and reduce the heat to low. Steam for 1¾ hours, or until the chicken is tender, checking the pot from time to time and adding more boiling water if necessary.

To serve, remove the package of chicken from the colander, open it, and transfer the chicken and all of its sauce to a heated bowl or platter. Accompany it with tortillas, served in a basket, in place of bread.

NOTE: In Yucatán, the chicken is wrapped in banana leaves and steamed in a special pit called a *pib*.

Mole Poblano de Guajolote
TURKEY IN CHOCOLATE AND CHILI SAUCE

NOTE: Before using hot chilies, read the instructions on page 51.

Place the turkey in a 4- to 5-quart heavy flameproof casserole. Add the salt and enough cold water to cover the turkey completely. Bring to a boil over high heat. Then reduce the heat to low, cover the casserole and simmer for 1 hour; the turkey will be almost cooked through. Set the casserole aside off the heat.

Meanwhile, prepare the *mole* (sauce) in the following fashion: Under cold running water, pull the stems off the chilies, break or cut the chilies in half, and brush out their seeds. Cut away and discard any thick ribs and tear the chilies into small pieces. In a large bowl, pour 2 cups of boiling chicken stock over the chilies and soak them for about 30 minutes.

Blend the almonds in the jar of an electric blender until they are completely pulverized. Force the nuts through a sieve and return them to the blender with the chilies, their soaking liquid, the onions, tomatoes, raisins, 2 tablespoons of sesame seeds, tortilla, garlic, cinnamon, cloves, coriander, anise seeds, salt and pepper, and blend at high speed until the mixture is reduced to a smooth purée. (To make the sauce by hand, put the chilies, onions, tomatoes, raisins, tortilla and garlic through a food mill set over a large bowl and discard any pulp remaining in the mill. With a pestle, pound the almonds, sesame seeds and anise seeds in a mortar until they are pulverized, force them through a sieve, then stir the mixture into the chili purée. Stir in the chilies' soaking liquid and add the cinnamon, cloves, coriander, salt and pepper.)

In a heavy 10-inch skillet, melt 2 tablespoons of the lard over moderate heat. Pour in the *mole* and simmer it, stirring constantly, for about 5 minutes. Add the cold stock and the chocolate. Cook, uncovered, over low heat, stirring frequently, until the chocolate has melted. Cover the skillet and set it aside off the heat.

Remove the turkey from the casserole and lay the pieces on a double thickness of paper towels to drain. Then pat them thoroughly dry with extra towels. In a heavy 12-inch skillet, melt the remaining 4 tablespoons of lard over moderate heat until a light haze forms above it. Add the pieces of turkey and brown them well on all sides, turning them frequently in the hot lard. Drain off the fat from the skillet, and then pour the *mole* sauce over the turkey, turning the pieces about in the sauce to coat them evenly. Cover the skillet and simmer over low heat for about 30 minutes, basting the turkey now and then with the sauce.

To serve, arrange the pieces of turkey on a heated platter and pour the sauce over them. Sprinkle the top with 2 tablespoons of sesame seeds.

NOTE: In Mexico, chicken and pork are often prepared and served in the same sauce.

To serve 8

An 8- to 9-pound turkey, disjointed and cut into 8 serving pieces
1 teaspoon salt
4 dried *pasilla* chilies, 4 dried *mulato* chilies and 6 dried *ancho* chilies; or substitute 14 dried *ancho* chilies
2 cups boiling chicken stock, fresh or canned
¾ cup blanched almonds
1 cup coarsely chopped onions
3 medium tomatoes, peeled, seeded and coarsely chopped (*see salsa cruda, page 44*), or 1 cup drained, canned Italian plum tomatoes
½ cup lightly packed seedless raisins
2 tablespoons sesame seeds
1 tortilla, broken in small pieces
1 teaspoon finely chopped garlic
½ teaspoon ground cinnamon
½ teaspoon ground cloves
½ teaspoon ground coriander seeds
½ teaspoon anise seeds
1 teaspoon salt
¼ teaspoon freshly ground black pepper
6 tablespoons lard
2 cups cold chicken stock, fresh or canned
1½ squares unsweetened chocolate

2 tablespoons sesame seeds

To serve 6

6 fresh *poblano* chilies, or substitute
   6 fresh green peppers, each about
   4 inches in diameter

THE FILLING

2 tablespoons lard
2 pounds ground beef, preferably
   chuck
1 cup coarsely chopped onions
½ teaspoon finely chopped garlic
5 medium tomatoes, peeled, seeded,
   and coarsely chopped (*see salsa
   cruda, page 44*), or substitute 1⅔
   cups chopped, drained, canned
   Italian plum tomatoes
¾ cup seedless raisins
¼ cup distilled white vinegar
1½ teaspoons sugar
2 teaspoons cinnamon
½ teaspoon ground cloves
2 teaspoons salt
½ cup slivered blanched almonds

THE TOPPING

2 cups heavy cream
½ cup shelled walnuts, ground in a
   blender or pulverized with a mortar
   and pestle
½ cup blanched almonds, ground
   in a blender or pulverized with a
   mortar and pestle
2 tablespoons finely chopped fresh
   parsley
½ teaspoon ground cinnamon
Pinch of salt
2 tablespoons fresh pomegranate
   seeds, or 12 pimiento strips, 2
   inches long and ⅛ inch wide

To serve 4 to 6

4 fresh *poblano* chilies, or substitute
   4 green peppers, each 4 inches in
   diameter
4 cups chicken stock, fresh or canned
1 cup coarsely chopped fresh parsley
½ cup coarsely chopped onions
¼ teaspoon finely chopped garlic
1 teaspoon salt
⅛ teaspoon freshly ground black
   pepper
¼ cup olive oil
2 cups raw long-grain rice

Chiles en Nogada

FILLED ROASTED GREEN CHILIES WITH WHIPPED CREAM AND NUT SAUCE

NOTE: Before using hot chilies, read the instructions on page 51.

Roast the chilies by impaling them, one at a time, on the tines of a long-handled fork, and turning them over a gas flame until the skin blisters and darkens. Or place the chilies on a baking sheet and broil them 3 inches from the heat for about 5 minutes, turning them so that they color on all sides. As the chilies are roasted, wrap them in a damp towel and let them rest for a few minutes. Rub them with the towel until the skins slip off. Cut out the stems and white membranes, discard the seeds.

In a heavy 10- to 12-inch skillet, melt the lard over high heat. Add the beef and brown it lightly, stirring constantly with a fork to break up any lumps. Reduce the heat to moderate, add the onions and garlic, and cook 5 minutes. Stir in the tomatoes, raisins, vinegar, sugar, 2 teaspoons of cinnamon, cloves and 2 teaspoons of salt; then reduce the heat and simmer, uncovered, for 15 minutes. Add the slivered almonds.

Whip the cream with a whisk or a rotary or electric beater until it forms soft peaks. Fold in the ground nuts, parsley, ½ teaspoon of cinnamon and pinch of salt. (If you like, you may beat in a little sugar.)

To assemble, fill the roasted chilies with the warm beef mixture, packing it down and mounding it slightly on top. Spoon the whipped cream over the top of each pepper. Scatter a teaspoon of pomegranate seeds on the cream or arrange 2 strips of pimiento over it. Serve at once.

Arroz Verde

GREEN RICE

NOTE: Before using hot chilies, read the instructions on page 51.

Roast the chilies over a gas flame or under a broiler as described above and wrap them in a damp towel. After they have rested for a few minutes, gently rub off their skins with the towel. Cut out the stems and thick white membranes and discard the seeds. Chop the chilies into chunks. Combine 1 cup of the chunks and ½ cup of stock in the jar of a blender and blend at high speed for 15 seconds. Then gradually add the remaining chilies and the parsley, onions, garlic, salt and pepper, blending until the mixture is reduced to a smooth purée. (To make the sauce by hand, purée the chilies, parsley, onions and garlic, a cup or so at a time, in a food mill set over a bowl. Discard any pulp left in the mill. Stir in ½ cup of stock and the salt and pepper.)

Pour the oil into a 2- to 3-quart casserole and set it over moderate heat. When the oil is hot but not smoking, add the rice and stir constantly for 2 to 3 minutes until the grains are coated with oil. Do not let them brown. Now add the puréed chili mixture and simmer, stirring occasionally, for 5 minutes. Meanwhile, bring the remaining 3½ cups of stock to a boil in a small saucepan and pour it over the rice. Return to a boil, cover the casserole and reduce the heat to its lowest point. Simmer undisturbed for 18 to 20 minutes, or until the rice is tender and has absorbed all the liquid. Before serving, fluff the rice with a fork. If the rice must wait, remove the cover and drape the pan loosely with a towel. Place in a preheated 250° oven to keep warm.

Smothered in an olive and pimiento sauce, a red snapper baked Yucatecan style rests on a bed of shredded lettuce and radishes.

Pescado Yucateco
BAKED FISH WITH OLIVE AND PIMIENTO SAUCE

Preheat the oven to 400°. In a heavy 8- to 10-inch skillet, heat the olive oil until a light haze forms above it. Add the onions and cook over moderate heat, stirring frequently, for 5 minutes, or until the onions are soft and transparent but not brown. Stir in the olives, fresh red pepper or pimiento, fresh coriander and ground annatto seeds, and cook, stirring occasionally, for 3 minutes longer. Then add the orange juice, lemon juice, salt and a few grindings of black pepper.

With a tablespoon of soft butter, grease the bottom and sides of a shallow heatproof casserole large enough to hold the fish comfortably. Place the fish in the casserole and pour the sauce over it. Bake, uncovered, in the middle of the oven for 30 minutes, basting the fish with its sauce every 10 minutes. The fish is done if its flesh feels firm when pressed with a finger. Be careful not to overcook.

Serve the baked fish directly from the casserole, sprinkled with the chopped egg, or—with one or two spatulas—transfer the fish carefully to a large heated platter, pour the sauce over and around it and garnish with the chopped egg or with the shredded lettuce and radishes.

To serve 8

3 tablespoons olive oil
½ cup coarsely chopped onions
⅔ cup pimiento-stuffed olives, quartered lengthwise
½ cup coarsely chopped sweet fresh red pepper or canned pimiento
2 tablespoons coarsely chopped fresh coriander (*cilantro*)
1 teaspoon annatto (*achiote*) seeds, pulverized with a mortar and pestle
½ cup fresh orange juice
¼ cup fresh lemon juice
½ teaspoon salt
Freshly ground black pepper
1 tablespoon soft butter
A 4- to 5-pound red snapper, cleaned but with head and tail on, or any firm white whole fish
2 finely chopped hard-cooked eggs, or 2 cups shredded lettuce combined with 3 or 4 sliced radishes

75

IV

A Matchless Bounty of Tropical Fruits

Piled high like a bountiful offering to the ancient Texcocoan Indian Rain God, Tlaloc, a lavish array of Latin American fruits combines a variety of familiar and unusual species. Among the bananas, melons, pineapples, citrus fruits, coconuts and sugar cane (considered part fruit, part candy) are such exotic tropical fruits as: green *sapote (1)*, mango *(2)*, papaya *(3), granadilla (4), chirimoya (5)* and *mamey (6)*.

Every Latin American cuisine, and notably that of Mexico, features a year-round abundance of wonderful fruit. In the markets of most countries appears an endless parade of fruits big and small, of every color and almost every shape. Some of them, such as pineapples and bananas, are familiar exports to other continents. Some are so delicate that they cannot be transported more than a few miles, and these are often the most delicious. Still others are grown in only a few localities or are the products of wild jungle trees. The supply of the rarer fruits is often sporadic; a truck will show up in a town, loaded with knobby things that look like green hand grenades. For a few days the market will be flooded with them; then none of that particular kind of fruit can be bought for weeks.

In the United States and Europe tropical fruit is sometimes a luxury, but in many parts of Latin America it is an indispensable part of the diet, even for the poorest people. Peasant huts are apt to be surrounded by banana plants and papaya trees, both of which start bearing when they are about a year old and produce enormous amounts of fruit. What is not eaten at home is peddled in the town at prices almost everyone can afford.

Bananas in the tropics are not the standardized fruit that North Americans know so well. Latin American markets commonly display a dozen kinds, and many more can be found with a little searching. Some of them, called "fingers," are slender, only three inches long and very sweet. Others are fat and stubby or long and curved. Many kinds have red skins or even red flesh, and their flavors vary from sweetly insipid to powerfully aromatic. They may be offered while they are still green, to be cooked or ripened at home. Plantains, which are members of the banana family, sometimes grow more than a foot long. They are almost always marketed green and must be cooked before eating. The flesh is firm and only slightly sweet; some varieties are not sweet at all.

Americans could have a lot of fun experimenting with plantains and green bananas, which can be found in any city where Latin Americans have settled. Both of these fruits are not only good but cheap, and can be boiled, fried or baked. Slices dipped in batter or rolled in egg and bread crumbs and fried in deep fat make marvelous crisp fritters to serve with meat dishes. These fruits can also be fried in butter and baked with a covering of cheese. Any number of puddings and desserts are based on bananas. Most recipes for cooking them are vague as to cooking time because of the wide variation in the sweetness and firmness of the flesh. A ripe, soft, sugary banana comes apart if fried very long, while a firm, green, starchy one browns like a fried potato.

The other universal and extremely cheap fruit of the tropics is the papaya, which occurs in countless varieties. It grows on a small, odd-looking tree that generally has an unbranched trunk and a single tuft of large star-shaped leaves. Under the leaves grow the papayas, looking, someone has said, "like Hubbard squashes hung on a baby palm tree." A single tree may have 50 of them in all stages of growth, and they may become 20 inches long, weighing over 20 pounds apiece.

Like cantaloupes, papayas are formed with thin green or yellow skin and bright orange-yellow flesh that may be two inches thick. Their flavor varies: Ripe papayas are always sweet, but certain varieties are sickly sweet while others have a slight but saving acidity. The musky fragrance is unappealing to some people on first trial, but addiction comes quickly and easily. Papayas are the common breakfast fruit in most of Latin America and an after-dinner fruit as well. They are almost always in season, and one large papaya is enough for a dozen servings. Latin Americans eat them with a spoon or knife and fork, either plain or with salt, pepper or lime juice, and they can be made into pies, puddings and candies. But the best varieites do not ship well, so they seldom reach North American markets in good condition. The small, tough papayas developed for long-distance shipping give no idea of how good a good papaya can be.

Many Latin Americans believe papayas have medicinal powers and will cure almost anything. This is not true, but the papaya plant does have some remarkable properties. When cut, the bark and leaves exude a milky juice containing an enzyme called papain that digests animal tissues. Pre-Columbian Indians were aware of its power; they wrapped bruised papaya leaves around tough meat to make it tender. Nowadays the juice is tapped from the unripe fruit and used in the familiar meat tenderizers.

Another native of Latin America is the avocado. It grows on a fine, shiny-leafed tree and is considered a fruit, but for eating purposes it is more like a vegetable. Its bland flesh has no appreciable sugar or acid. Instead, it contains fat—as much as 18 per cent—and important amounts of starch and protein and is much more nourishing than other fruits.

In many parts of Latin America avocados are cheap enough to be used in everyday meals. They are often eaten raw, either on the half shell or in

A patient mule is loaded with plantains on the outskirts of Salvador, capital of the Brazilian state of Bahia. This ubiquitous Latin American fruit, a member of the same family as the banana, is widely used for dishes ranging from soups to desserts.

decorative salads. Mashed avocado mixed with gelatin, grated onion, lemon juice and seasoning makes a delicious mousse when chilled. Avocados are also cooked. A tempting Brazilian dish is baked avocado stuffed with shrimp purée and covered with grated cheese. The soft flesh cannot be fried, but the common custom of slicing dead-ripe avocado into hot soups and stews just before serving is a kind of cooking. The buttery flesh partly disintegrates and blends delightfully with the liquid.

Pineapples, another important tropical fruit, were cultivated by pre-Columbian Indians in the Caribbean region, and sometimes the thorny, sharp-pointed plants were massed around their villages like barbed-wire entanglements to ward off intruders. Since they ship fairly well, are attractive when canned and are easy to raise on large plantations, they have been for many years an important article of commerce. But none of the forms in which pineapples reach their markets in temperate countries gives a true idea of what they are like in their native tropics. Canned pineapple tastes canned, and even frozen pineapple is not like the real thing. As for the fresh pineapples that are sold in the United States, they are mostly inferior varieties that will stand shipping, and they are picked green and sour, and ripen after a fashion during the voyage to market.

A prime pineapple ripened on the plant is in a wholly different class. In Mexico pineapples as big as footballs sell for 40 or 50 cents, and they are so fragrant that one of them perfumes an entire room. A good Mexican pineapple is so sweet that no one would think of adding sugar to it.

During the pineapple season, everyone eats this marvelous fruit. Fresh pineapple juice is also widely consumed. In addition the fruit is made into candies and desserts, often combined with rice. It is used to stuff chickens and ducks and is served in all sorts of salads. An impressive cold appetizer can be made by cutting off the top of a large, ripe pineapple and scooping out the flesh and core without damaging the skin. The cavity is packed with pieces of lobster and shrimp mixed with mayonnaise, chopped apple and pineapple. The leafy top is then replaced, and the stuffed pineapple is brought to the table as a decorative serving dish.

Oranges and other citrus fruits in Latin America are often better flavored than their Florida counterparts because they are allowed to ripen naturally on the trees instead of being picked when the market calls and colored artificially. Tropical oranges are not ordinarily dyed with the deep chemical color that American consumers expect. When fully ripe their skins are no more than yellowish orange, and often they are green—even though the juice may be fully sweet. This is presumably one of the reasons why breakfast oranges in elegant tropical hotels are often brought to the table peeled: The shock of seeing orange halves with their natural grass-green skins might be too much for North American guests.

Citrus fruits almost end the list of tropical fruits successfully marketed in temperate parts of the United States, but Latin America grows many other fruits—and they range in quality from terrible to delightful. Even in the jungle there are many kinds of them; the tall trees in rain forests produce edible fruits and then monkeys and other arboreal animals propagate the trees by scattering the seeds well away from the parent tree where they have a bet-

ter chance of growing. In some places it is possible to look up at the forest canopy and see fruits as big as melons hanging under the stiff green leaves, and often the ground for many yards around the base of a tree will be littered with the debris of the fruit feast far above.

People who live in the jungle sometimes know the location of fruit or nut-bearing trees, but they also search for them by sound. A man riding along a trail will stop his horse and listen carefully. If he hears in the distance an unusual amount of bird or monkey noise concentrated at a particular spot, he may ride off the trail and find a bounteous tree dropping great quantities of fruit on the ground.

Not all jungle fruits are attractive to civilized humans, but a good proportion are, and a few kinds were cultivated selectively by Indian orchardists

A fruit stand in Huancayo, Peru, provides a colorful display of native fruits. Among them are: yellowish, plumlike *nísperos,* at lower left; dark, knobby *guanábanas* and dark, mottled *chirimoyas,* the pulpy fruits in the foreground; pearlike *peros* in the box with red lining; potato-shaped *tumbos* in the box with blue lining; and thirst-quenching *granadillas,* clustered on the vine at upper left.

81

and brought to heights of perfection centuries ago. The botanical origin of some of these fruits is obscure. The Indians kept no genetic records, and nothing like the cultivated types is known in the wild.

One of the best of these improved native fruits is the guava, whose small, bushy trees with cinnamon-brown bark grow wild along the roadsides of many Latin American countries. Some kinds of guava get to be four inches long, but most guavas are yellow fruits about the size of plums, with a layer of flesh, usually reddish, surrounding a central cavity full of pulp and small, hard seeds. The fruits can be eaten as they come from the tree, but the seeds are rather unpleasant to eat, almost like sand in texture, so the flesh is generally stewed separately. An even commoner use for guavas is to make them into firm, dark-red paste. In some countries this delicious fruit is the standard dessert and is often eaten with a slice of crumbly white goat cheese. It is also sold on the streets to be eaten as a quick snack like a candy bar.

Almost anywhere in the Andean or Caribbean countries the traveler may see a peasant woman trudging along the road with a heavy basket of fruit on her back. When she sets down her basket, it may prove to contain nothing but green bananas or perhaps a quantity of small, hard things like crab apples. It may also be a cornucopia of strange and delicious fruits. If the traveler is thirsty and does not trust the local water, he should look for sweet cucumbers. These are plump, about six inches long, with pointed ends and a roughly triangular cross section. The skin is green blotched with purple, and the flesh is faintly sweet, crisp like the cucumber familiar to North Americans but much juicier. A few cucumbers are as good for quenching thirst as a glass of cold water and much better than the bottled soft drinks that Latin Americans so admire.

Out of the woman's basket may come another pleasant thirst quencher, the *granadilla*, or passion fruit. The name has nothing to do with passion in its common meaning, and the fruit is not an aphrodisiac as is sometimes claimed. The name comes from the flowers whose complicated parts were held by imaginative Spanish missionaries to represent the Crucifixion, or Passion, of Christ. There are many kinds of *granadilla*, some of which are cooked green as a vegetable. The best of them is a deep-reddish fruit slightly bigger than a hen's egg. The skin is thin and brittle, and the fruit can easily be broken in two, revealing an interior packed with small seeds, each one encased in a delicate envelope full of juice that has a mild and pungent flavor and is about as acid as a ripe strawberry. The little bags of juice can be "drunk" almost like water out of a cup. People who worry about tropical germs can break a virgin *granadilla* and be sure that they are getting an absolutely safe drink.

Another native Latin American fruit that seldom if ever reaches the United States is the cashew apple, which is not only a fruit but a nut. That is, its seed is a nut, the familiar cashew, which hangs like a comma from the end of a soft, peachlike fruit that may be white, yellow or reddish in color. Since the seed is carried outside, the whole fruit is pulp and juice. Some varieties are sweet and deliciously flavored. Others are as puckery as green persimmons. In any case the eater of a cashew apple had better watch his step; the nut that hangs from the fruit is encased in a shell whose acrid juice is dangerously irritating. The nut must be roasted before it is edible, and the fumes given off during this process are dangerous too.

Tropical fruits are commonly members of large botanical families, just as apples are closely related to pears and quinces. One of the most popular fruits in Mexico and the Caribbean countries is a *sapote*, or marmalade plum, mistakenly called a *mamey* in Spanish. The "mamey" has a hard, rough skin like cinnamon-brown sandpaper, and inside is a single large seed surrounded by a firm, sweet flesh that looks like the reddest kind of canned salmon. It is enormously popular with sweet-toothed Latin Americans, but foreigners find it a bit insipid because it has no trace of acidity to temper the cloying taste. A squeeze of lime juice does it a world of good, and its marmalade, made with lime or lemon, is delicious.

Closely related to this fruit are many other kinds of *sapote* and *sapote* cousins. The *sapodilla*, one of the best, is borne by a tree that yields chicle, the base for chewing gum. The fruit is about as big as a small apple. It must be eaten when dead-ripe and squashy-soft. In this condition it has an extremely attractive flavor though a bit lacking in acidity for many tastes. Other *sapote* relatives are white, yellow, black—almost any color— and most of them closely resemble the wild forms. The queen of the whole tribe is the *lucuma*, a high-bred product of ancient Peruvian arboriculture that is the pride of modern Peru and Chile. It is about the size of a small orange and has a yellow-green shiny skin that crinkles a little when it is fully ripe. The flesh has a distinctive and delightful flavor and is so soft and mealy that it can be eaten with a spoon.

Another great group of native Latin American fruits, *Annona*, might be called the royal family. Its queen is the *chirimoya*, another triumph of Peruvian Indian plant breeders. Many Americans must have been disappointed by *chirimoyas* brought to the United States or even by those bought in the tropics that were not in prime condition. But no one was ever disappointed by a perfectly ripened *chirimoya*. The solid, heavy fruit is heart-shaped and about five inches long, with soft, greenish-brown or greenish-yellow skin covered with shallow indentations like finger marks. The flesh is pure white and contains shiny black seeds that are separated from the flesh as easily as are watermelon seeds. A good *chirimoya* is intensely sweet but contains plenty of acid to prevent its sweetness from cloying. Because of its delightful flavor it has been called "strawberry in heaven."

Other members of the *Annona* family are the sweetsop of the West Indies, which is like a *chirimoya* but not quite as good, and the custard apple, which is generally rated another step down. Rated much higher is the *guanábana*, or soursop, whose green, warty fruit gets as big as a football. The white pulp inside is rather too acid to eat by itself, but it makes marvelous drinks and excellent sherbet or ice cream when frozen.

The list of tropical fruits could be extended indefinitely, but many of them must be tasted near their point of origin to be believed. None of them except bananas reaches North American customers in top condition. But the commercial arboriculture of Latin America is improving rapidly and so are methods of shipping delicate fruits. Perhaps the time is not far off when perfect *lucumas* and *chirimoyas* will be as common as bananas in the United States.

Looking like a family of hedgehogs clambering over each other, a pile of *jáca* (jackfruit) awaits buyers at the busy marketplace in Salvador, Brazil. In the background lie bright green avocados. *Jáca*, which grows on trees in Brazil, has a texture resembling that of the pomegranate. The rind and center of the fruit are discarded and only the sweet seedy pulp is eaten, raw, boiled or fried.

To make about 1½ cups of sauce

1 small ripe tomato
1 large ripe avocado
¼ cup olive oil
1 tablespoon red wine vinegar
½ teaspoon chili paste *(page 105)* or
    very finely chopped, seeded, fresh
    hot chili
1 teaspoon salt
½ teaspoon freshly ground black
    pepper
2 tablespoons finely diced green
    pepper
1 cold hard-cooked egg, finely
    chopped
1 tablespoon finely chopped fresh
    parsley
1 teaspoon finely chopped fresh
    coriander *(cilantro)*

Salsa Guasacaca
SPICY AVOCADO SAUCE

NOTE: Before using hot chilies, read the instructions on page 51.

Cut out the stem of the tomato, then slice the tomato in half crosswise. Squeeze each half gently to extract the seeds and juices, discard them, and chop the tomato into ¼-inch dice. Cut the avocado in half. With the tip of a small knife, loosen the seed and lift it out. Remove any brown tissuelike fibers clinging to the flesh. Strip off the skin with your fingers, starting at the narrow stem end (the dark-skinned variety does not peel easily; use a small, sharp knife to pull the skin away, if necessary). Chop the avocado into small dice.

In a large mixing bowl combine the oil, vinegar, chili paste (or fresh chili), salt and black pepper, and, with a large wooden spoon, mix well. Add the diced tomato, avocado, green pepper, chopped egg, parsley and coriander, and mix together gently but thoroughly. Taste for seasoning.

Salsa guasacaca is traditionally served with grilled meats.

Creme de Abacate
CREAM OF AVOCADO DESSERT

With the back of a spoon, force the diced avocado through a sieve set over a bowl. Stir in the lime juice and sugar. Serve from chilled parfait glasses or dessert dishes, and garnish each serving with a lime wedge.

Sopa de Aguacate
AVOCADO CREAM SOUP

Purée the diced avocados in 3 batches, combining ⅓ of the dice and ½ cup of cream at a time in the jar of a blender and blending at high speed for 30 seconds. (To make the purée by hand, force the diced avocados—with the back of a large spoon—through a sieve set over a bowl. Beat the cream into the purée, a few tablespoons at a time.) In a 3-quart enameled or stainless-steel saucepan, bring the stock to a boil over high heat, reduce the heat to low, and when the stock is simmering, stir in the avocado purée. Add the sherry, salt and pepper, and taste for seasoning. To serve the soup hot, pour it into a tureen and strew the top with tortilla quarters or avocado slices. Or refrigerate and serve it cold.

To serve 4

2 large, ripe, chilled avocados, peeled, halved, seeded and diced (*see salsa guasacaca, opposite*)
¼ cup fresh lime juice
6 tablespoons confectioners' sugar
½ lime, cut into 4 thin wedges

To serve 8

3 large ripe avocados, peeled, halved, seeded and diced (*see salsa guasacaca, opposite*)
1½ cups heavy cream
6 cups chicken stock, fresh or canned
¼ cup pale dry sherry (optional)
1 teaspoon salt
½ teaspoon ground white pepper
3 tortillas (*page 42*), quartered and fried until crisp, or 1 ripe avocado, peeled and thinly sliced

Technically, the highly nutritious avocado is a fruit, but in Latin America it is the main ingredient for a wide variety of delights. Here, on a base of avocados, are three dishes that are made with the popular food (*recipes, opposite and above*). At the far left is a piquant Venezuelan relish, *salsa guasacaca*, in the center is *sopa de aguacate*, a delicate soup from Mexico, and on the right is *creme de abacate*, a Brazilian dessert.

V

Peru:
Heir to the Inca

Since ancient Inca days, the indigenous Peruvian potato —called *papa*—has been the staple diet in the high sierra of the Andes. Today potatoes are the basis for dishes like *papas a la huancaina* (top; recipe, page 102), which includes boiled potatoes, made rich and zesty by a cheese and chili sauce, and the cartwheel- shaped *causa a la limeña* (page 104), a combination of mashed potatoes, shrimp, ripe olives, cheese, *yuca*, corn and hard-boiled eggs.

Between the desert on the West Coast of South America and the Amazon rain forest rears the great range of the Andes whose peaks climb
above 20,000 feet and glitter forever with ice and snow. This stupendous
mountain chain, longest and second highest in the world, dominates the
continent's entire West Coast. In its valleys and on its fringes lived all of
South America's civilized Indians. The rest of the continent, including
the fertile, temperate Pampa of Argentina, remained savage or almost uninhabited until the coming of the Europeans in the 16th Century.

The Andes are the controlling fact of South America and the home of
the customs and traditions that produced its most extraordinary and distinctive foods. In their central section arose the strange Inca Empire,
which included at its maximum Peru, Ecuador, the better part of Chile
and Bolivia, and the mountainous northwestern corner of Argentina. This
great domain was ruled by a single family whose head, the Inca, was a living god and a despot with unlimited power. But along with this absolutism,
the empire had many of the characteristics of a modern welfare state.
Each citizen was assigned sufficient land to grow his family's food and
was also required to cultivate the lands of the state and to support the official religion. Part of the crop from these common lands went to feed
the Inca court, the priests, the bureaucrats who ran the empire and spe-
cialized workers such as the engineers who built bridges and maintained
the excellent roads and irrigation systems. The old people, the sick and
the orphaned children enjoyed their due shares of the crop without working for it. The surplus was stored in warehouses as insurance against crop

failures. The empire knew no money or written language, but it was almost uncannily orderly and well governed. As the wondering Spaniards, fresh from the turmoil and misery of 16th Century Europe noted: "No one went hungry in that land."

The order and abundance of the Inca Empire did not survive the Spanish Conquest; plenty of people go hungry in the Andes now. But the descendants of the Indians who were the Inca's subjects still inhabit their mountain valleys and are probably more numerous than ever before. They have clung with amazing tenacity to their ancient customs and have created a native cuisine that, like Mexico's, contains both Indian and Spanish elements but is more than a simple mixture of the two. In the opinion of many connoisseurs and of this author, an American who married a Peruvian and has traveled through this area many times, the Creole cooking of Peru is the best in Latin America. Ecuadorian cooking is similar and is also excellent.

Except for their common background of Indian civilization, Peru and Ecuador differ from Mexico in nearly every respect, and the main reason is their eccentric climate. On most of the seacoast, a narrow zone under the towering wall of the Andes, the land is a treeless, bushless, grassless desert. In a few places the bare reddish hills behind the beach are thinly sprinkled with spiny brown objects known as *achutalla* that look like the dead tops of pineapples. They are living plants and are actually related to pineapples, but they have no roots; they can be kicked around as freely as empty beer cans. The almost totally dry soil has no interest for them; they get the moisture that keeps them barely alive out of the dank fog that sometimes blows off the sea. A droplet of water that falls on one of their stiff leaves is instantly absorbed.

Except for such curious fog plants, which grow with extreme slowness, nothing could live on the rainless coast if it were not for the 50-odd rivers that trickle down from the Andes. None is large, and many flow intermittently and are hardly ever bigger than brooks, but each supports a green oasis, watered by irrigation ditches, where practically everything thrives with lavish abandon. Frost is unknown and so is extreme heat. Inside the magic perimeters of the irrigation ditches flowers bloom and crops increase all the year round. When enough water is available, a second crop is planted as soon as the first is harvested. Every inch of soil is lovingly cultivated. From the air it looks like snippets of bright-green cloth pinned on a brownish land as barren as an asphalt road.

In pre-Spanish times these irrigated valleys supported dense populations of Indians whose isolation gave rise to varying local customs, although all were ruled by the Inca in the high Andes. They lived well on corn, beans, root crops and fruit from their tiny but highly productive farms and on fish from the teeming waters off the coast. Trains of pack llamas brought these coastal people highland products such as freeze-dried potatoes and alpaca wool. They made magnificent pottery and wove beautiful textiles. Their nobles lived in brightly painted palaces and worshiped in temples roofed with gold.

With the completion of the Spanish conquest the brilliant coastal Peruvian civilizations vanished almost as suddenly as if they were made of smoke. Nearly all their people died of European diseases or of hunger when war and disorder destroyed their irrigation systems. For years the valleys were almost uninhabited, and the desert crept close to the riverbanks. Then, slowly, life revived. Spanish colonists established great estates, haciendas, and recruited Indians from the Andes to work the fields and mend the ancient irrigation ditches. A mixed population appeared, part Spanish, part Indian. The fields sprouted crops again, and fruit trees grew where the desert sand had blown.

The revived oases supported a rich, aristocratic life. The Indian and mestizo laborers might be sorely oppressed, but the great landowners in their fortress-mansions enjoyed all the lavish fruits of their favored lands. Gradually a Creole cuisine evolved, differing considerably from valley to valley. At first it was Spanish in spirit, though making the most of local materials, but Indian ideas and foods came down from the Andes and were gradually blended into a growing galaxy of truly Peruvian dishes.

Meanwhile in the high Andes a different kind of mingling was taking place. The tougher highland Indians diminished in numbers after the Conquest, but never to the point of near extinction, as on the coast. Spaniards established haciendas among them and made them work as serfs in the fields or as slaves in the mines but were never able to dominate them completely. Many of the mountain valleys are inaccessible, and in them the Indians continued to speak their own language, Quechua, and they kept their local government, a kind of village communalism. They made their clothes out of home-woven cloth as they always had, and they still do. They cooked in much the same way. Only when a Spanish food or cooking technique really fitted their way of life did they adopt it.

The mingling of Indians and Spaniards in the valleys and the high Andes gave Peru two Creole cuisines, coastal and mountain. Today the coastal cooking is more appealing because the coast is rich and fertile, while the sierra, as Peruvians call their mountains, is comparatively poor. The same distinction prevails in Ecuador and Bolivia, which were outlying parts of the Inca Empire, although the coast of Ecuador is not desert and Bolivia owns no coastal oases. There is also a third kind of cooking, that of the primitive jungle country to the east of the Andes, but most of its specialties, which include stewed monkey and alligator steaks, have limited appeal to nonjungle people.

The staple food of the high sierra, especially the cold plateau of Bolivia, is potatoes, some of which thrive in spite of nightly frost. The poorest Indians eat them simply boiled or perhaps with a little hot *ají* (Andean chili; pronounced "ah-HEE") or some local herbs, but those who are somewhat better off have ways of embellishing them that could well be copied by American cooks in search of attractive economy dishes.

The commonest embellishment is a thick sauce made of cheese, milk or water, *ají* and various local spices. It is stirred with lard in a frying pan over a low fire until it is smoothly blended, then poured over boiled potatoes. The cheapest kinds, those that cost just a few cents a serving in Indian marketplaces, have plenty of *ají* and not much cheese, but these sauces of poverty make an interesting dish out of boiled potatoes.

When economy is not the controlling factor, the cheese-and-potato dish becomes the elaborate *papas a la huancaina* (potatoes of Huancayo, a mountain city), whose rich sauce has lots of cheese, cream, chili and olive oil *(page 102)*. The best potatoes for this luxury food are those with yellow flesh, which grow only in Peru. After they are covered with the sauce, the dish is decorated with hard-boiled eggs, black olives, sliced onions, sliced *aji* and anything else that comes to mind. Yet even when served in sophisticated Lima with elaborate additions, this is still basically the earthy, satisfying dish that the mountain Indians invented when their Spanish conquerors taught them to make cheese.

Another good dish of Indian origin, *causa a la limeña (page 104)*, is essentially stiff mashed potatoes mixed with salt and pepper, lemon juice, olive oil, chopped onions and *aji*. In festive dress it is molded into a form or individual servings and gaily decorated with cheese, hard-boiled eggs, sweet potatoes, *yuca*, black olives, prawns and corn.

An excellent Indian food that is seldom appreciated outside the Andean countries is guinea pig, called *cuy*. The image of children's pets makes North Americans balk at eating these animals, but actually they are clean vegetarian rodents like small, short-eared, tailless rabbits, and there is no nutritional reason why they should not be eaten. In both mountain and coastal Peru they are commonly raised for food. They are fine when simply broiled over coals and brushed with oil and garlic, but for a party dish the Peruvians make them into an elaborate stew. The *cuyes* (a Quechua word pronounced "kwee-ess") are skinned and rubbed with salt, then cut in quarters and fried to a golden brown. Onions, garlic and *aji* are fried separately in a pot until the onions are golden too. Boiled cut-up potatoes are added with a little water and cooked until they begin to disintegrate. Then the *cuyes* are put into the pot and stirred for a few minutes. The result is a hearty Andean version of the German *Hasenpfeffer* (rabbit stew) that is hard to beat. If the guests are hungry men, one *cuy* should be provided for each of them.

Most Andean dishes contain *aji*, which is botanically related to Mexican chili but has different flavors. There are many kinds; one that is popular with mountain people, especially in southern Peru, is flaming red with thick flesh—and as hot as its appearance. It is generally sliced and served in careful isolation in a separate saucer. The safest way to use it is to pick up a slice on a fork and gently touch its cut surface to meat or other food. This gingerly kiss of fire is enough for most tastes; only hardened connoisseurs ever eat the explosive flesh itself.

The commonest Peruvian *aji*, called *mirasol* (looking at the sun), is much milder. It is orange-yellow and tapers to a sharp point. Most of its hotness is in its seeds and their supporting "veins." Its thin flesh is only slightly hot and has a characteristic and attractive flavor. This mild-tempered vegetable is what most Peruvians mean by *aji*. They use it in all sorts of ways: dried and powdered as a spice; combined in soups, stews and sauces; or chopped or thinly sliced as a bright-colored garnish. A little saucer of cooked and mashed *mirasol* is often provided to eat with meat, and a touch of it does the finest steak a favor.

The great Andean party specialty is the *pachamanca*, which means earth oven in Quechua and is the local variant of the American clambake and the Mexican *barbacoa*. This feat of ancient cookery is not lightly undertaken; it requires both time and skill as well as considerable money for its ingredients, but almost any joyous occasion warrants a *pachamanca*: a wedding, a political victory, the end of a school term when the teachers and pupils of a district are briefly freed from teaching and learning.

The first step in preparing a *pachamanca* is to dig a circular hole three or four feet wide and about as deep and to line its bottom and sides with good-sized stones. The hole is filled with dry wood and straw; more stones are placed on top and the fuel is ignited. The fire should be kept going for two hours or more, or until the stones are nearly red-hot. Then any unburned wood and loose stones are cleared away and the pit is lined with moist green leaves or aromatic herbage. On this steaming, sweet-smelling mattress is placed a whole young pig or goat, sometimes both, surrounded by guinea pigs, chickens and as many other kinds of meat as the host can afford. Deep casseroles of pig's feet in broth and of rice, *ají* and water are nestled among the chunks of meat, and on top go tamales, ears of green corn, potatoes both sweet and white, and other kinds of vegetables. The whole is covered with more greenery. Hot stones are set on top and the pit is sealed thickly with earth so that most of the heat is trapped. The final touch is to decorate the mound with flowers, and to stick green branches in the earth around it.

Preparations for this gaudy feast begin at dawn. Around midday the guests begin to gather; they admire the flower-decked heap of warm earth and sniff the savory steam that seeps out of it. They play guitars and sing, or if they are mountain Indians, an orchestra, sometimes of curious homemade instruments, plays the strange, haunting indigenous music of the Andes, which sounds like no other music on earth. They dance in couples or groups: odd, fast, shuffling steps or vigorous adaptations of Spanish dances. They also drink, and many a guest at a *pachamanca* drinks so much that he does not eat at all.

At last comes the moment when the *pachamanca* is opened. The earth is carefully pulled away, the cap of green stuff removed, and out of the pit with a burst of steam come all the delicacies, to be dunked in bowls of hot sauces and eaten with rejoicing and with more rounds of drinks. If the job has been done by an expert, all the different foods are properly cooked and are subtly flavored by the aromatic herbs lining the pit, just as the food of a New England clambake is flavored by seaweed. If the ceremony is performed at an elegant hacienda, or estate, near Lima, there are modern accessories such as wine, sweetmeats, plates, knives and forks, but essentially the *pachamanca* descends from very ancient times when cutlery was made of stone and the crudest pottery had not yet been invented.

The cuisine of coastal Peru and of Ecuador, which is a continuation of Peru, overlaps Andean highland cooking, sharing many of its dishes, but it is richer and more elaborate because many more ingredients are commonly available on the coast. It is the product of great houses with cavernous kitchens and troops of patient servants. Until recently the preferred cooking fuel, as in all Spanish-influenced countries, was charcoal burned in ranges with many small, elevated hearths. The smokeless fires burned under iron grills. For long, slow simmering only a few coals glowed

Taking a break between customers, a shoeshine boy in Lima enjoys an *anticucho*. These grilled, skewered strips of marinated beef hearts are served as hors d'oeuvres by the wealthy, but the 30 cents apiece they cost make them a rare treat for a shoeshine boy who earns under two dollars a day.

dimly in the center of each fire, but when high heat was needed, a servant would crouch in front of the hearth and force air through a hole in the side with a palm-leaf fan. In Lima and other modern cities much cooking is now done with gas or electricity, but the old charcoal ranges are still numerous, and traditionalists claim that proper Creole cooking cannot be done without them.

One typical product of charcoal cookery, the delight of rich and poor, is *anticuchos*, the popular Peruvian equivalent of the hot dog but much better eating. *Anticuchos* are pieces of beef heart, somewhat less than one inch across, from which all tough tissue has been removed. The pieces are marinated overnight in spiced vinegar and then impaled by sixes on thin skewers of sharpened cane *(page 104)*. While grilling over the coals, they are brushed with a hot sauce of oil, *ají* and spices applied, traditionally, with a feather or a strip of cornhusk. The sauce cooks into them, and more can be added after they are done.

Anticuchos are really delicious. They are served as hors d'oeuvre before a formal meal but are also sold on the streets and in parks, especially during fiestas. People of all ages are addicted to them, and children come back from celebrations boasting of how many they have eaten. *Anticuchos* of a sort can be made of other things, such as seafood, beef, liver or kidney, or of many meats in alternation on the skewer. But these are corruptions. True *anticuchos* are made only of beef heart, whose odd, crisp texture has much to do with their effect. Beef heart has the further advantage of being very cheap; a cookout of *anticuchos* is more trouble than one of hot dogs, but it is immeasurably superior.

In the more prosperous households in Peru, as in Mexico, the main meal usually comes in the middle of the day. In Lima most stores and offices close at noon and stay closed until 3 o'clock. There is much to say for this custom in hot countries where midday is a good time to take things easy, but although Lima is near the equator and almost at sea level, it is never very hot. It is cooled by the ice-cold Peru Current, which runs northward along the coast. Even so, at the stroke of noon everybody downtown makes a dash for home. The narrow streets are jammed to a standstill, and traffic moves so slowly that only the fortunate few get home in time for a leisurely meal and the traditional nap before they start the struggle back to the city again. Lima has grown far too big for this daily double battle. Unlike Mexico City, it has no subway. One is planned, but pessimists predict that before it arrives to ease double commuting, the long, stately midday meal will have been eroded, and businessmen will have contracted the ugly North American habit of lunching downtown, far from their familes.

In spite of the difficulties, the ceremonious midday meal is still the thing in Peru. It begins with an appetizer, which is commonly cold but is otherwise hard to classify. Peruvian meals are lavish; few men and hardly any women can eat everything that is set before them, but the courses are not as sharply defined as in Mexico.

Dishes of Indian origin based on potatoes, such as *causa a la limeña*, are often served as appetizers. So are *anticuchos* garnished brightly with paper-thin sliced onions, radishes and *ají*. Another popular appetizer is fried fish slices bedded in lettuce, covered with a sauce of onions and *ají*. They are cooked in oil and vinegar and decorated with olives and hard-boiled eggs. Peruvian tamales are also in the appetizer class. Although tamales are sometimes called *humitas*, the two dishes differ somewhat. Both use corn, but *humitas* traditionally are made with fresh corn dough wrapped in cornhusks, while tamales use soaked, dried corn ground into a paste and wrapped in banana leaves. The Peruvian tamales are more elaborate than Mexican ones; they may contain almost anything—pork, chicken, meat, sausage, eggs, raisins, olives, cooked peanuts—and they are often slightly sweet, which sounds all wrong but is not wrong at all.

The most famous appetizer is *ceviche,* the raw fish dish that was invented in Peru but is now made in most countries of Latin America, some of which claim to have invented it themselves. Many visitors who are horrified by the idea of raw fish have eaten *ceviche* with delight, and with no suspicion that it was not cooked. The trick is to cut the fish in half-inch cubes, cover it with salted lime and lemon juice, then flavor it with pepper, garlic, thinly sliced onions and *ají,* and let it marinate for three to five hours *(page 103)*. After one hour the fish is opaquely white; after three hours the pieces have shrunk and their texture is like that of cooked fish. They are served with lettuce and colorful garnishings of sweet potatoes and *choclos* (fresh corn on the cob).

Continued on page 96

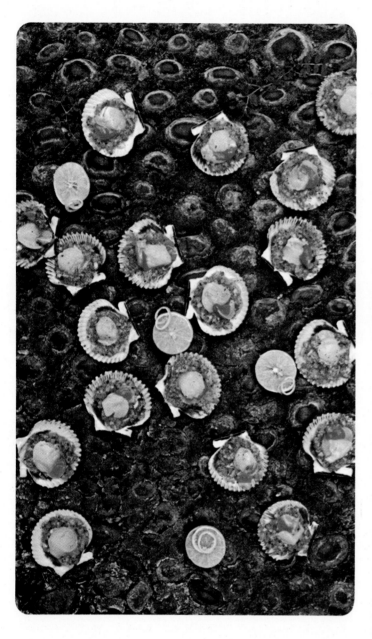

Catch from a Cold Current

A superb variety and abundance of seafood abound
in the icy, mineral-rich Peru Current, which washes
the hot, barren coast of Peru. Some species of marine
life that feed on the current's rich plankton are unique
to Peru. These include the *conchita (above)*, a pink-
and-white scallop, and the *corvina (right)*, a relative
of the sea bass. The *corvina* is surrounded by two
kinds of *ají*, plus the onions and lemons with which
it is marinated to make *ceviche (page 103)*.

When properly made from the right kind of fish *ceviche* is magnificent. For people who are still leery of its rawness, it can be said that the lime and lemon juice have much the same effect on the fish that boiling has. The citric acid in the juice precipitates albumen in the fish, turning it firm and white.

The question as to what kind of fish to use has no answer that satisfies everyone. Peruvians prefer *corvina*, a large fish rather like a striped bass that is common off their coast, but *ceviche* is made successfully in other Latin American countries that have no *corvinas*. Perhaps the best advice for American housewives is to try several kinds of locally available white-fleshed fish that are dependably fresh, firm and free of hard-to-find bones, and test them to see which one makes the best transplanted *ceviche*. Success will be worth the effort.

Shellfish, especially scallops, are also made into *ceviche,* but Peruvians often eat their scallops raw on the half-shell with various sauces and are rather surprised to hear that North Americans do not, even though the latter have no objections to raw clams or oysters. Peruvian scallops are a little bigger than the bay scallops of the East Coast of the United States but smaller than sea scallops, and they come to the market in their shells. When they are opened, the large white chunk of meat, the swimming muscle, is extracted along with a small pink part that lies next to it.

Many Peruvian appetizers and main courses feature shrimp. The Peruvian shrimp is one of the best of shellfish. Although it is called *camarón*, the regular Spanish word for shrimp, it is more like a crayfish, or perhaps should be considered a small, fresh-water lobster. *Camarones* live in the rivers and irrigation canals and grow about six inches long with claws like a lobster's. Peruvian country people of all classes keep an eye on every trickle of water to see if it has nurtured a population of these easily captured delicacies. The edible part is the meaty tail, which tastes more like a small lobster tail than like shrimp, and when a *camarón* is boiled, its shell turns red. Peruvians peel most of the shrimp they serve, but in certain dishes they leave a few of them whole so their shells will add brilliant bits of color. For Peruvian recipes calling for shrimp, the shrimp of the United States do very well, except that they are not as decorative.

After the appetizer, the next course in a full-dress Peruvian meal is soup. A typical recipe for meat broth calls for two kinds of meat, eight kinds of vegetables, pepper, salt, husked wheat, rice and chick-peas. All this is boiled for two hours; then it is strained and only the liquid part is served. The rest is eaten by the servants or their relatives.

Other kinds of soup come to the table intact. Some of them, called *chupe,* are made of shellfish, vegetables and milk, which is added at the last minute *(Recipe Booklet)*. They are somewhat like New England fish or clam chowder but were probably invented at a much earlier date. Peruvians are seldom economical unless they are forced to be so, but one of their tricks that should appeal to economy-minded New Englanders is to break raw eggs into the *chupe* just before adding the milk. If the *chupe* is stirred slightly and gently at this point the eggs poach in large pieces, and the yolks do not break. They add body and interest to the dish and permit a saving in expensive ingredients such as shrimp or lobster.

Some of the heartier Peruvian soups are served in two installments.

After the cooking is finished, the liquid is carefully ladled out of the pot and put in another container to keep it hot. Then the solid parts of the soup are arranged on plates, making sure that each plate has a share of each ingredient. The plates go to the table first along with a special sauce that is often as complicated as the soup. Then the liquid part of the soup is served in cups or soup plates. This custom has definite advantages. Besides giving all the guests or customers an even break, it helps them cope with large pieces of meat or chicken, a trick that is hard to accomplish with grace when the pieces are immersed in liquid.

In old-fashioned Peruvian households one course of a proper dinner was always a standard meat-and-vegetable stew that was brought to the table in bowls and quickly taken away. It was seldom touched by members of the family or their guests; it was really meant for the servants and perhaps was originally intended to show that they were properly fed. This custom has now all but disappeared, but not long ago a Peruvian family living in New York and well adjusted to American ways entertained an elderly countryman who dropped in unexpectedly and was invited to dinner. He enjoyed the first course, soup, but when the main course, an American beef stew, appeared, he ignored it, expecting it to be taken away just as it would have been in his own house in Lima. The host told him tactfully that he had better eat it. Not much more was coming.

The more elaborate Peruvian meals include so many substantial preliminaries that the main meat dish does not dominate the meal to the extent that it does an American dinner. Peru does have roasts, however, and they can be very elaborate. The meat, whether a large or smaller cut, is usually coated before roasting with lard mixed with salt, garlic, pepper and herbs. Some of the mixture stays in place, making a fine brown crust and flavoring the outer parts of the meat. The rest, mixed with the juice and drippings, may be served as a sauce.

Much more common are meat dishes in which the meat or fowl is cut in smallish pieces or finely shredded, a custom inherited from an age when most of the meat in the markets came from old, mountain-climbing animals and was tough. In some cases the meat is merely coated with a delectable sauce; in others it is mixed with a large amount of rice or cooked vegetables, which are pleasantly flavored by its juices.

Many inexpensive but excellent Peruvian dishes are made of a small amount of meat fried with onions, garlic, *ají* and other flavorings, and then boiled with water and cornmeal. The result is a thick, nourishing corn mush with enough meat in it to make it interesting. In some Latin American countries this dish is called *tamal en cazuela* (casserole tamale). If left overnight the mush solidifies and does not liquefy on reheating. In this condition it is called *dormido* (slept) and is delicious. *Tamal en cazuela* is an excellent way to use up mixed accumulations of leftover meat, which the Latin Americans call *ropa vieja* (old clothes).

Peruvian cooking also features dishes with many ingredients that require more work than most American cooks are willing to expend. A traditional one called *carapulchra* (beautiful face) might be called a pork dish, but it also contains fine-cut chicken, yellow potatoes, freeze-dried potatoes, onions, garlic, peanuts, olives and hard-boiled eggs, as well as

Overleaf: Coriander leaves and beer give *arroz con pato* (rice with duck) a distinctive flavor. Before the duck is cooked with the beer, it must be marinated, then browned in olive oil (*page 102*). *Arroz con pato*, like many other Latin American dishes based on rice, shows a Spanish influence.

Continued on page 100

many spices. It is cooked slowly for hours, with different items added at the proper stages. The dried potatoes are slightly browned in the oven, pounded to bits and mixed with lard before they are added to the pot. The yellow potatoes are boiled separately and added toward the end. The eggs and olives are thinly sliced and used with *ají* as garnishing. Properly made *carapulchra* is appetizing and interesting, although a lot of work.

In spite of the popularity of *ají,* most Peruvian cooking is not too hot for tender American tongues. The traveler in Peru does not generally need to taste with caution as he should in Mexico; only certain local cuisines are fiery hot. One of them centers in Arequipa, a charming city in southern Peru whose houses are largely built of white volcanic stone that looks like the purest marble. Arequipa is a delightful place, but its cooking has a reputation for incandescence. The word *arequipeño* after the name of a dish in a Lima restaurant is a hint to Peruvians and Americans alike that the first mouthful should not be a big one.

Most other Peruvian cities of any size have their specialties. Usually the differences are not as sharp as in Mexico, but the cuisine of Piura in the extreme north is distinctive and much like the cooking of coastal Ecuador. Like the Ecuadorians, the people of Piura make great use of bananas and plantains, and they are partial to peanuts as a cooked food.

Peanuts originated in South America, probably somewhere in the Inca Empire, and they are found perfectly preserved in pre-Inca tombs more than a thousand years old. Peanut butter was an ancient Indian invention that did not require much inventing. Roasted peanuts ground in a mortar turn into peanut butter with no additions or urging. There is no record that the Incas made anything equivalent to the peanut butter sandwiches that are the staff of life of North American school children, but they probably made sauces out of ground peanuts, as modern Peruvians do. Peanuts can be ground for the occasion or peanut butter can be stirred into water and added to the mix.

Boiled whole peanuts, which are called for in many Peruvian recipes, do not soften and turn into mush like beans, to which they are related botanically. They swell up a little and become somewhat mealy, but they hold their shape after as much as three hours of boiling. They do not contribute much to the flavor of the dish in which they are cooked. Generally they are not boiled very long and remain crisp like the almonds that the Chinese put in so many dishes.

Ecuador and the northernmost parts of Peru are strongholds of banana cookery, which takes many interesting forms. One of them, banana chips, is the equivalent of our potato chips and is made the same way, by frying slices in deep fat. Firm green bananas or plantains are used, and the slices are cut on a slant so the chips are oval. They do not curl up like potato chips, and they usually have only a faint trace of sweetness. They are stronger than potato chips and make fine implements for dipping up stiff mixes at cocktail parties.

In Ecuador, a large producer of bananas, a staple food is banana flour, which is made into all sorts of breads and pastries. Bananas are also puréed, often nowadays in an electric blender, and used to make bread with ordinary wheat flour, or the same purée is baked with beaten eggs as a

delicious soufflé. Banana desserts are innumerable. The commonest and simplest one, which is made in some form all over Latin America, is merely ripe—but not soft—bananas cut across and lengthwise and fried slowly in butter. When the banana slices begin to brown, sugar is added and the frying is continued carefully until the pieces are brown on both sides. Then a little brandy is poured over them, and they are dusted with confectioners' sugar. Just before they are served, a little more brandy is delicately dribbled on each piece. This recipe makes an excellent, cheap and easy dessert. The secret is very slow and watchful frying. The brandy, of course, can be either omitted or emphasized. In most Latin American countries the cooks use any authoritative local rum that can be considered the equivalent of brandy. If enough of it is used, the simple dish may be elevated to a festive level.

Socialites in Arequipa, Peru, enjoy a patio luncheon of spicy regional dishes: *ocopa* (a cheese and peanut sauce on potatoes, *Recipe Booklet*), *rocotos rellenos* (stuffed red peppers) and a *pebre* (pepper) stew. To accompany these dishes Peruvians prefer a beverage called *chicha morada (foreground)*, made of cherries, lemons, pineapple and purple corn.

101

Papas a la Huancaina
WHOLE BOILED POTATOES WITH CHEESE AND CHILI SAUCE

NOTE: Before using hot chilies, read the instructions on page 51.

In a large mixing bowl, combine the lemon juice, 1½ teaspoons of dried chili or the *pequín* chilies, ½ teaspoon of salt and a few grindings of black pepper. Add the onion rings, turning them about with a spoon to coat them evenly with the mixture. Cover the bowl and set aside to marinate at room temperature while you boil the potatoes.

Drop the potatoes into a large pot of lightly salted boiling water (enough to cover them completely), and boil the potatoes briskly until they are tender but not falling apart. Meanwhile make the sauce by combining the cheese, cream, turmeric, chopped fresh chili, ½ teaspoon salt, and a few grindings of pepper in the jar of a blender. Blend at high speed for 30 seconds, or until smooth and creamy. (To make the sauce by hand, beat the ingredients together until they are well combined.) In a heavy 10-inch skillet, heat the olive oil over moderate heat. Pour in the cheese and cream sauce, reduce the heat to low, and cook, stirring constantly, for 5 to 8 minutes, or until the sauce thickens.

To assemble, arrange the potatoes on a heated platter and pour the sauce over them. Drain the onion rings and strew the rings and fresh chili strips over the potatoes. Garnish with eggs, black olives and lettuce.

Arroz con Pato
BRAISED DUCK WITH CORIANDER RICE

In a small bowl combine the lemon juice, cumin, ½ teaspoon salt and ⅛ teaspoon pepper. With your fingers brush the pieces of duck on all sides with the mixture. Place the duck on a plate, cover with foil, and let it rest at room temperature for 3 hours, or refrigerated for 6 hours.

In a heavy 4- to 5-quart flameproof casserole or saucepan, heat the oil over high heat until a light haze forms above it. Add the duck and brown it well on all sides, turning it frequently. Drain off and discard all but 2 tablespoons of fat from the casserole. Add the beer, bring to a boil over high heat, meanwhile scraping into it any brown bits from the bottom and sides of the pan. Reduce the heat to low, cover the casserole and cook the duck for 45 minutes, or until a leg shows no resistance when pierced with the tip of a knife. Transfer the duck to a heated plate and cover it with foil to keep it warm.

Pour off the cooking liquid from the casserole, strain, measure and return 3½ cups of it, and discard the rest. Bring to a boil over high heat, then stir in the rice and return to a boil. Reduce the heat to low, cover the casserole and simmer undisturbed for 20 minutes, or until the rice has absorbed all the cooking liquid. Stir in the coriander, peas, ½ teaspoon salt and ⅛ teaspoon pepper. Arrange the duck on the rice; cover the casserole and return it to low heat for a few minutes to heat the duck through. Serve from the casserole, or mound the rice and peas in the center of a serving platter and arrange the pieces of duck on top.

To serve 8

¼ cup fresh lemon juice
1½ teaspoons crumbled, seeded, dried *hontaka* chili, or 3 *pequín* chilies, crumbled
1 teaspoon salt
Freshly ground black pepper
1 large onion, peeled, thinly sliced, and separated into rings
8 medium boiling potatoes, peeled
1 cup coarsely crumbled *queso blanco,* or substitute 1 cup coarsely grated fresh *mozzarella* or Münster cheese
⅔ cup heavy cream
1 teaspoon turmeric
2 teaspoons finely chopped, seeded fresh red or green hot chili
⅓ cup olive oil
1 fresh red or green hot chili, stemmed, seeded and cut lengthwise into ⅛-inch strips
4 hard-cooked eggs, cut lengthwise into halves
8 black olives
Bibb or Boston lettuce leaves

To serve 4

¼ cup fresh lemon juice
½ teaspoon ground cumin seeds
1 teaspoon salt
¼ teaspoon freshly ground black pepper
A 4- to 5-pound duck, cut into 6 to 8 serving pieces and trimmed of all fat
¼ cup olive oil
2 twelve-ounce bottles light beer
1 cup bock beer (if not available, use 1 cup additional light beer)
2 cups raw long-grain rice
1 cup finely chopped fresh coriander
1 cup cooked fresh green peas or thoroughly defrosted frozen peas

The ancient Peruvian dish *ceviche*—marinated raw fish and red onion rings—is served with corn on the cob and sweet potato.

Ceviche

FISH MARINATED IN LIME AND LEMON JUICE

NOTE: Before using hot chilies, read the instructions on page 51.

In a large bowl, mix the lime and lemon juice, ground dried chilies, onion rings, garlic, salt and a few grindings of pepper. Place the fish in a flat glass or ceramic dish (a metal dish or utensil may affect the flavor of the fish) and pour the marinade over it. If the marinade does not cover the fish, add more lemon or lime juice. Cover and refrigerate for 3 hours, or until the fish is white and opaque, indicating that it is fully "cooked."

About 30 minutes before serving, bring about 2 quarts of water to a boil in a 3- to 4-quart saucepan. Drop in the sweet potatoes, cover the pan and cook over moderate heat for 25 minutes, or until tender. Drain the potatoes, peel them, and cut each crosswise into 3 rounds. Meanwhile, bring 2 quarts of water to a boil in a separate saucepan. Drop in the corn and boil it, uncovered, for 5 to 10 minutes, until tender. Drain.

To assemble each serving, shape several lettuce leaves into a cup on a plate. Place a portion of marinated fish in each cup and garnish it with onion rings and strips of fresh chili. Place a sweet potato round at one side of the cup, several corn rounds at the other, and serve at once.

To serve 6

1 cup fresh lime juice
1 cup fresh lemon juice
4 dried *hontaka* chilies, seeded and
    pulverized with a mortar and pestle
2 red onions, sliced ⅛ inch thick
    and separated into rings
¼ teaspoon finely chopped garlic
1 teaspoon salt
Freshly ground black pepper
2 pounds grey sole fillets cut into 1-
    inch pieces, or substitute any other
    firm white delicately flavored fish
3 large sweet potatoes, unpeeled
4 ears fresh corn, shucked and cut
    crosswise into 1½-inch rounds
2 heads Boston or romaine lettuce,
    washed, separated into leaves, and
    chilled
2 fresh hot red chilies, washed, split,
    seeded, deribbed and cut
    lengthwise into ⅛-inch strips

To serve 8 to 10

THE MARINADE
1 cup red wine vinegar
1 tablespoon finely chopped, seeded
    and deribbed fresh hot red chili
4 teaspoons finely chopped garlic
2 teaspoons ground cumin seeds
2 teaspoons salt
Freshly ground black pepper

THE SAUCE
½ cup dried *hontaka* chilies
1 tablespoon annatto *(achiote)* seeds,
    pulverized with a mortar and pestle
1 tablespoon olive oil
1 teaspoon salt

A 4- to 5-pound beef heart, trimmed
    and cut into 1-inch cubes

To serve 8

3 pounds baking potatoes, peeled and
    quartered

THE SAUCE
½ cup finely chopped onions
½ cup fresh lemon juice
1 teaspoon finely chopped, seeded
    fresh hot chili
1 tablespoon salt
⅛ teaspoon freshly ground black
    pepper
A pinch of Cayenne pepper
1 cup olive oil

THE GARNISH
1 pound sweet potatoes, peeled, cut
    in half lengthwise and then
    crosswise into ¼-inch slices
1 pound fresh *yuca*, peeled, sliced
    crosswise and cut into small
    wedges
4 ears of fresh corn, shucked and cut
    into 4 rounds each
8 raw jumbo shrimp in their shells
4 hard-cooked eggs, cut lengthwise
    into halves
16 pitted black olives
½ pound *queso blanco*, fresh
    mozzarella or Münster cheese,
    sliced ½ inch thick and cut into
    triangles about 2 inches long and
    1 inch wide

Anticuchos
SKEWERED SPICED BEEF HEART WITH CHILI SAUCE

NOTE: Before using hot chilies, read the instructions on page 51.

In a large bowl, combine the vinegar, fresh chili, garlic, cumin, salt and a few grindings of pepper. Add the cubes of beef heart. If the marinade doesn't cover the beef heart, add more vinegar. Refrigerate, covered, for 24 hours. Remove the beef heart from the marinade and set them both aside.

Break the dried chilies in half and brush out the seeds. Place the chilies in a bowl, pour ¾ cup of boiling water over them and let them soak for 30 minutes. Drain the chilies and discard the soaking water. Combine the chilies and ¾ cup of the reserved marinade, the annatto, oil and salt in the jar of a blender and purée at high speed for 15 seconds. (To make the sauce by hand, purée the soaked chilies through a food mill into a bowl. Discard any pulp left in the mill. Stir in ¾ cup of marinade, the annatto, oil and salt.)

Light a layer of coals in a charcoal broiler and let them burn until white ash appears on the surface. Or preheat the broiler of the oven to its highest point. String the beef heart cubes on skewers and brush them with sauce. Broil 3 inches from the heat for 3 to 4 minutes, turning the skewers frequently and basting once or twice with the remaining sauce. Serve hot.

Causa a la Limeña
SEASONED MASHED POTATOES GARNISHED WITH SHRIMP AND VEGETABLES

NOTE: Before using hot chilies, read the instructions on page 51.

Preheat the oven to 250°. Drop the potatoes into a large pot of lightly salted boiling water (enough to cover them) and boil them briskly until they are tender. Meanwhile, make the sauce by combining the onions, lemon juice, fresh chili, salt, black pepper, Cayenne pepper and oil, and beat them together with a whisk or fork. Drain the potatoes and mash them to a smooth purée with a fork, potato masher or electric mixer. Beat in the sauce, a tablespoon at a time, and taste for seasoning. Mound the potatoes in the center of a large heatproof platter and cover the platter loosely with foil. Keep the potatoes warm in the preheated oven.

Into each of two 3- to 4-quart saucepans pour about 2 quarts of water. Bring to a boil and drop in the sweet potatoes and *yuca*. Boil briskly, uncovered, for 20 minutes, or until the vegetables are tender. Then remove them from their pans with a slotted spoon and arrange them around the mashed potatoes. Cover the platter again and return it to the oven.

In a heavy 3-quart saucepan, bring 4 cups of water to a boil over high heat. Drop in the shrimp and cook them, uncovered, for 5 to 8 minutes, or until they are firm and pink. Drain them and peel off their shells. If desired, devein them by making a shallow incision down their backs with a small knife and lifting out the black or white intestinal vein.

While the shrimp cook, bring 2 quarts of water to a boil over high heat in a 4-quart saucepan. Drop in the corn and boil, uncovered, for 5 to 10 minutes, until the corn is tender. Drain in a colander.

Remove the platter from the oven and place the corn on it. Alternate the shrimp and cheese triangles in a circular design on top of the potatoes. Add the olives and eggs to the arrangement, and serve at once.

Aceite de Achiote
ANNATTO OIL

In a small saucepan, heat the oil over moderate heat. Drop in the annatto seeds and stir them for 30 seconds. Reduce the heat to low, cover and simmer for 10 minutes. Remove the pan from the heat, let the oil cool and strain it into a jar, cover the jar tightly and refrigerate it. Discard the seeds. Annatto oil will keep for several months, but its flavor will diminish with age.

To make ½ cup

½ cup vegetable oil
¼ cup annatto (*achiote*) seeds

Chancho Adobado
PORK IN ORANGE AND LEMON SAUCE WITH SWEET POTATOES

In a large bowl, combine the vinegar, annatto, cumin, garlic, salt and pepper, and stir to mix thoroughly. Drop in the pork cubes and turn them about until they are coated with the mixture. Cover the bowl and marinate at least 6 hours at room temperature or overnight in the refrigerator.

Remove the pork cubes from the marinade and set the marinade aside. Pat the cubes thoroughly dry with paper towels. In a heavy 10- to 12-inch skillet, heat the oil over high heat until a light haze forms above it. Add the pork cubes and fry them in the hot oil, turning them on all sides until they are golden brown. Pour off and discard the fat in the pan. In its place add the reserved marinade and water, and over high heat bring the liquid to a boil, scraping into it any brown bits clinging to the bottom and sides of the pan. Reduce the heat to low, cover the skillet and simmer the pork for 45 minutes, or until it shows no resistance when pierced with the tip of a knife. Stir the orange juice and lemon juice into the sauce, simmer a moment or two, and taste for seasoning. To serve, arrange the hot sweet potato slices on a large heated platter, and pour the pork cubes and their sauce over them.

NOTE: If the sweet potatoes were cooked before the pork, they may be kept warm in a preheated 250° oven. Or you may transfer the pork from the skillet to a plate with a slotted spoon and reheat the potatoes in the simmering sauce for 2 or 3 minutes before placing them on the platter.

To serve 4

1 cup distilled white vinegar
1 tablespoon annatto (*achiote*) seeds, ground in a blender or pulverized with a mortar and pestle
2 teaspoons ground cumin seeds
2 teaspoons finely chopped garlic
1 teaspoon salt
¼ teaspoon freshly ground black pepper
2 pounds lean boneless pork, cut into 1-inch cubes
2 tablespoons olive oil
2 cups water
1 cup fresh orange juice
½ cup fresh lemon juice
4 sweet potatoes, boiled, peeled and sliced ¼ inch thick

Ají Molido con Aceite
RED CHILI PASTE

NOTE: Before using hot chilies, read the instructions on page 51.

Break the dried chilies in half and brush out the seeds. Place the chilies in a bowl, pour 2 cups of boiling water over them, and let them soak for 2 hours. Drain the chilies and discard the soaking water. Combine the chilies, oil, garlic, salt and boiling stock or water in the jar of a blender and purée at high speed for 1 minute, or until the mixture is reduced to a smooth purée. Scrape into a bowl and cover with plastic wrap. (To make the paste by hand, purée the chilies and garlic in a food mill set over a bowl. Discard any pulp left in the mill. A few tablespoons at a time, beat the boiling stock or water into the purée, then stir in the salt and oil, a tablespoon at a time.) Chili paste can be used as a substitute for fresh hot chilies in many South American dishes. It will keep successfully for 2 to 3 weeks if it is tightly covered and refrigerated.

To make about 2 cups

1 cup tightly packed dried *hontaka* chilies
2 cups boiling water
6 tablespoons olive oil
½ teaspoon finely chopped garlic
¼ teaspoon salt
1 cup boiling beef or chicken stock, fresh or canned, or boiling water

To serve 4

A 3½- to 4-pound chicken, cut in quarters
5 cups cold water
8 slices fresh homemade-type white bread
2 cups milk
⅔ cup olive oil
1 cup finely chopped onions
1 teaspoon finely chopped garlic
¼ cup red chili paste *(page 105)*, or ¼ cup dried *hontaka* chilies, seeded and ground in a blender or pulverized with a mortar and pestle
1 cup shelled walnuts, ground in a blender or pulverized with a mortar and pestle
2 teaspoons salt
¼ teaspoon freshly ground black pepper
2 tablespoons annatto *(achiote)* oil *(page 105)*
¼ cup freshly grated Parmesan cheese
2 pounds boiling potatoes, peeled, sliced ¼ inch thick, freshly boiled and hot
3 hard-cooked eggs, each cut in 6 to 8 lengthwise wedges
12 ripe black olives
1 or 2 fresh hot red chilies, stemmed, seeded, deribbed and cut lengthwise into strips ⅛ inch wide

Two forms of chili—called *ají* in Peru —are used in preparing *ají de gallina*, a kind of chicken fricassee. The dish is a triumph of Creole cooking, which combines Spanish techniques and Indian ingredients. The *ají de gallina* is garnished with hard-boiled eggs, olives and red chilies *(ajíes)*.

Ají de Gallina
CHICKEN IN SPICY NUT SAUCE

NOTE: Before using hot chilies, read the instructions on page 51.

In a heavy 4- to 5-quart saucepan, bring the chicken and 5 cups of cold water to a boil over high heat, and remove all scum from the surface. Reduce the heat to low, cover the pan and cook the chicken for 30 minutes, or until it is tender but not falling apart. Transfer the chicken to a plate, and set the stock aside for another use. When the chicken is cool enough to handle, remove the skin with a small knife or your fingers. Cut or pull the meat away from the bones. Discard the bones, and cut the chicken meat into strips ⅛ inch wide and 1 to 1½ inches long.

Cut the crusts from the bread and tear the slices into small pieces. Place them in a bowl, add 1 cup of the milk and let them soak for 5 minutes. Then, with a fork or your hands, mash the bread and milk to a thick paste.

In a heavy 10- to 12-inch skillet, heat the oil over moderate heat and add the onions and garlic. Cook, stirring frequently, for 5 minutes, or until the onions are soft and transparent but not brown. Add the chili paste or ground chilies, walnuts, salt and pepper, reduce the heat and simmer for 5 minutes. Stir in the annatto oil and bread paste, then gradually add the remaining cup of milk. Cook, stirring constantly, until the sauce thickens. Add the chicken and cheese, and simmer, stirring occasionally, until the cheese melts and the chicken is heated through.

TO ASSEMBLE: Spread the boiled potato slices side by side in a large casserole or deep platter and spoon the chicken and sauce over them. Garnish the top with hard-cooked eggs, olives and chili strips.

NOTE: Peruvian cooks blanch and skin the walnuts—and you may, too, if you have the patience. Drop shelled walnuts into boiling water and let them soak for an hour. Drain and peel them, one at a time.

VI

Sweets
for Every Tooth

In the old city of Puebla, a Mexican boy and his sister display a lively pinwheel of exquisite candies. Although tasting like fruit, the candies consist mainly of sweet potatoes ground into a paste, then colored and flavored artificially. In Latin America many confections are made from local fruits and vegetables.

Latin America is a land of sweets. The Spanish word for sweets is *dulces,* and it somehow does not carry the weight-watching opprobrium of the English word. Anyway, few Latin Americans pay much attention to calorie counting. Those who can afford it nibble elegant candies and pastries at all hours. For those with little money the streets are full of shops and peddlers selling hunks, slices and gobs of wonderful gooey things at very reasonable prices. The poorest people of all chew sections of sugar cane that look like bamboo, an operation that requires persistence as well as excellent front teeth. Perhaps this intensive sweet eating is bad for the teeth and the health, but few Latin Americans get unattractively fat.

Sweets have long been enjoyed in Latin America. The Mexican Indians kept bees for their honey, and the early Peruvians made sweets of squash and sweet potato dried in the sun. But the era of *dulces* really began when sugar cane arrived from the Old World. Columbus planted the first cane and the first large sugar grower was Hernán Cortés, conqueror of Mexico, who planted cane over a considerable area of his estate near Cuernavaca, outside Mexico City. Now the tall green cane grows luxuriantly in every country except Chile. For large-scale commercial production many thousands of acres may cluster around a factorylike *central,* or sugar mill, which crushes the cane through a series of heavy rollers and evaporates the juice to make raw or refined sugar (while burning spent cane, called bagasse, as fuel). But cane is also grown in little patches for local use, the way small farmers of temperate countries grow potatoes.

In many remote villages a picturesque sight is the old-fashioned cane mill. It has two small vertical rollers, one of them corrugated and powered by a horse that walks in a circle at the end of a long pole. The cane is fed between the rollers by hand, a few stalks at a time, and the juice runs down in a thin trickle. It is rather too sweet, but when fresh it has a pleasant taste, and many people, children especially, like to drink it. In the old days the juice was boiled down in a huge iron kettle over a bonfire. Some of these kettles survive but mostly as curiosities; simple pan-like evaporators are much more efficient. They produce heavy syrup that solidifies in molds as blocks of hard brown sugar, so dark it is often called "black." This is eaten without embellishment as a cheap fudge and resembles the sugary part of Louisiana pralines. Many cooks demand "black sugar" in their favorite traditional recipes, insisting that refined sugar is not a proper substitute. The addition of a little black molasses gives the same flavor.

With sugar so abundant, it is no wonder that the Latin Americans candy almost everything. Candied fruits are cheap and plentiful in the markets, including some kinds that are hard to identify. Candied limes are especially delicious, and so are candied strawberries. They shrink to less than half their natural size, are dry enough to keep indefinitely, and retain most of their natural flavor. Mexicans say that strawberries cannot be properly dried and candied like this except at high altitude where the air is thin and evaporation is rapid. Fruits are only a beginning in all this: Sweet potatoes and squash are candied and so is the firm pith that fills the interior of certain kinds of cactus. Candied green walnuts, husks and all, are a Peruvian delicacy traditionally made by nuns. They are tender, black and sticky, with a somewhat resinous flavor, and they are sold wrapped in aluminum foil.

Closely related to candied fruits are the delightful fruit pastes that are found almost everywhere in Latin America. They usually contain nothing but fruit pulp and sugar and can be made semisolid like thick jam or stiff enough to be cut with a knife. All available fruits are used: guavas, quinces, mangoes, pineapples, plums, peaches. An especially popular combination is guava paste that is generally served with a mild kind of white cheese. (In the United States cream cheese is substituted.) This combination is offered as dessert on many restaurant menus.

Dried fruits that tend to be insipid, such as papayas, are helped by a little cinnamon or lime juice. If made fairly solid and dried in the sun, these ubiquitous sweets will keep a long time, but in most households they do not get the chance. Many desserts are based on them, and they are also used as fillings between layers of cake. A fine Argentine dessert, *pastelito de mil hojas* (thousand-leaf pastry), is filled with wine and quince paste *(page 196)*.

An unusual and very inexpensive Brazilian dessert is made of ripe bananas and brown sugar. The bananas, say the Brazilians, should be very ripe and the sugar very brown, but some Americans may prefer white sugar. To prepare this dessert, the Brazilians skin and mash the bananas, mix them with about half their volume of sugar, and add a little ginger, preferably fresh grated ginger root, or clove or cinnamon. The proportions are a matter of taste, but Brazilians like things sweeter and spicier than

A serape-clad Mexican girl tenderly holds a candy chicken and duck that were made chiefly of squash seeds. To prepare these confections, the squash seeds are first washed, then ground into a paste and sweetened with sugar. When the paste has begun to harden, it is molded into various shapes and decorated by hand.

most Americans do. They cook the soft mixture over a very low fire, preferably in an earthenware pot, stirring it continuously to avoid burning. The longer it is cooked the darker it gets as the sugar caramelizes. When it achieves a rich caramel color, they let it cool a little and mold it into a loaf. Served cold and sliced it is an excellent sweet.

A pleasant ingredient of many sweet dishes is *manjar blanco*, a specialty of Peru that is also made in other countries, usually under the name of *dulce de leche* or *leche quemada*. Essentially, it is milk boiled down with sugar and vanilla until it becomes a thick, golden-brown paste with a light caramel flavor. It is fine to eat by itself or on crackers. It can be used as a filling in cake or rolled into balls with chopped nuts. Thin, plain cookies stuck together with it and rolled in shredded coconut become fancy party cookies. All sorts of small delicacies are the better for *manjar blanco*, but it is not easy to make in the traditional way; if the heat is held low to keep the milk from burning, the boiling down takes an inordinate amount of time and stirring, and often the milk burns anyway, in spite of careful tending. A shorter variation, *natillas piuranas (page 118)*, produces an equally delectable dessert.

Luckily there is a handy modern shortcut: Just cover an unopened can of sweetened condensed milk (not evaporated milk) with water and let it simmer, making sure that the water does not boil away. The longer you

111

cook it the darker, thicker and more caramelized the contents become. Three hours of simmering is about right to make an excellent *manjar blanco;* the can is opened and the custardlike contents are ready to eat. Every cook should try this trick, which is easy, cheap and unfailing. Some people add a little vanilla, cinnamon or other flavorings after the cooking is over, but this is not necessary. Plain *manjar blanco* and the *dulces* based on it make a hit with children and adults alike and are better nutritionally than most other sweets.

The standard dessert of all Latin America is *flan,* a caramelized cup custard of Spanish origin that appears on all restaurant menus and is often served in households. (A Venezuelan version of *flan,* flavored with pineapple, is given on *page 118.)* The basic recipe is simple; the custard is made of milk, sugar, eggs and vanilla, like an American cup custard. Sugar is melted in a saucepan and allowed to caramelize until it is golden brown. The custard cups (or a larger mold) are warmed, and a little of the caramelized sugar is poured into the bottom of each cup and sloshed around so that it coats the inside as completely as possible. Then the cups are filled with custard and baked in the oven while standing in a pan of hot water. The Spanish name for this arrangement is *baño de María* ("Mary's bath" in English, *bain-marie* in French). If the custard is to be eaten in the cups, it is sometimes topped with caramel that hardens into a brittle layer like brown ice. If it is prepared in a mold, it should be covered with a layer of brown, delicious caramel after it is unmolded.

There are dozens of variations of this simple recipe. Brown or "black" sugar can be used for the caramel instead of white, and some cooks insist it is far superior. The custard itself is often glorified by adding ground almonds, grated fresh coconut, cinnamon, grated lemon rind, chocolate or coffee. The fanciest *flan* of all contains cut-up fruit and is served with flaming rum or brandy.

A favorite Mexican egg dessert is *huevos reales* (royal eggs—*page 116).* It is usually made of well-beaten egg yolks, a dozen at least, poured into a baking dish and baked until firm in a "Mary's bath." The product is cut into cubes and saturated with a syrup made of sugar, sherry and cinnamon. It is served sprinkled with raisins and pine nuts, and is about as delicious as any dessert can be.

Nuts of all sorts are used extensively in the more luxurious kinds of Latin American cooking. Almonds are preferred, perhaps because they are usually imported and are therefore expensive, but walnuts and pecans are also admired, and pine nuts are widely used in Mexico, where they are gathered wild. A fine traditional Mexican dessert is a thick syrup made of ground-up nuts—any available kind—cooked with milk and sugar. When properly made, which is not easy, it is just short of solid, and has a smooth texture and a wonderful nutty flavor. It is eaten with a spoon or poured over slices of cake.

Many kinds of candy start with almond paste mixed with sugar, like the marzipan of Europe, but the name used for the confection, *turrón,* may also mean a mixture of sugar and ground peanuts formed into hard blocks or bars. This humble sweet is cheap and surprisingly good, although considered a food of the poorest people. It is better balanced nu-

tritionally than most candies, since the peanuts contribute protein and fat to take the dietary curse off the sugar.

Perhaps the most elegant *dulces* of Latin America, to eat, to look at and to hear about, are made in Lima, Peru, in the Convent of the Congregation of the Daughters of the Immaculate Mary. Known for the quality and variety of their sweets (all are handmade), the convent is a charming place located in the old section of town, with a patio full of palms and flowerbeds under which the bodies of the last two Inca emperors, helpless captives of the Spanish conquerors, are believed to be buried. The nuns are as cheerful as the flowers, and delicious scents of chocolate and spice drift out of a spotless kitchen where pretty girls in light-blue uniforms make dainty and imaginative confections for Lima's leading families. Presiding over this amiable scene is Mother Paz, a middle-aged nun known to all Lima as *La Madre de los Dulces*. Her convent brings up orphan girls and teaches them domestic skills and crafts, as well as the art of the confectioners' trade. Their chocolates, bonbons and elaborately iced cakes are so much in demand that the convent no longer depends on contributions for support. Part of this success is due to the magical authority of its ornate wedding cakes. Many a young girl of Lima, and the girl's mother too, feels that her marriage will not be happy unless it is blessed with a cake from the kitchen of *La Madre de los Dulces*.

A young street vendor in Puebla, Mexico, balances a tray laden with delectable wares. The golden-brown tubes at right are *gaznates*, crisp wheat shells deep-fried in sesame oil, then filled with cream and coconut whipped to a bright white froth. The round pink confections at center and the white cylinders at left are meringues. The ladyfingers at center —called *duquesas*, or duchesses—are rice coconut cakes. The vendor and his sister made these confections.

113

Sweets for Sweet Charity's Sake

The art of making confections is as old among Latin American nuns as the art of distilling liquor is among monks; the tradition was imported from Spain soon after the Spanish Conquest. The young nun at the left holds a tray of candy peaches *(duraznos)* made by the nuns of the Santa Monica Convent in Puebla, Mexico. Realistically tinted with vegetable coloring, the peaches are wrapped in cellophane to be sold in confectionery stores. The elaborate wedding cake above is the handiwork of nuns at the Convent of the Congregation of the Daughters of the Immaculate Mary in Lima, who are famous for the cakes and other *dulces* (sweets) they make to support charity schools for girls.

Chayote Relleno
BAKED CHAYOTE SQUASH WITH CAKE AND RAISIN FILLING

To serve 6

3 large *chayotes*, about 5 inches long and 3½ to 4 inches in diameter
3 eggs, lightly beaten
¾ cup sweet sherry
1½ teaspoons ground nutmeg
1 cup seedless raisins
1 cup sugar
4 cups finely crumbled fresh poundcake or spongecake
½ cup slivered blanched almonds

Cut the *chayotes* in half lengthwise and place them in a 2- to 3-quart saucepan. Cover them with cold water, and bring to a boil over high heat. Reduce the heat to low, cover the pan and simmer for 30 minutes, or until the *chayotes* show no resistance when pierced with the tip of a small, sharp knife. Drain the *chayotes* in a large colander. When the *chayotes* are cool enough to handle, remove the seeds with a small spoon. Then scoop out the pulp, leaving a layer of pulp about ⅛ inch thick intact in the shell. In a large mixing bowl, mash the pulp with a fork until it is perfectly smooth. Then beat in, a little at a time, the eggs, sherry and ground nutmeg. Add the raisins, sugar and crumbled cake, and beat again. The filling should have the consistency of mashed potatoes and should hold its shape in a spoon; if it seems too thin, add more cake crumbs.

Preheat the oven to 350°. Fill the *chayote* shells with the filling, mounding the top slightly, and dot with the almonds. Arrange the shells side by side in a buttered baking dish and bake for 15 minutes, or until the top of the filling is golden.

Serve the *chayotes* from the baking dish or arrange them on a platter or on individual serving dishes.

Calabaza Enmielada
HONEYED SQUASH

To serve 6

A 3-pound butternut or Hubbard squash, or 3 one-pound acorn squashes
1 pound Mexican *piloncillo*, broken into pea-size pieces, or 2 cups dark-brown sugar
½ cup water
1 cup heavy cream, stiffly whipped (optional)

If you are using the butternut or Hubbard squash, with a sharp knife cut it in half lengthwise and divide each half, as equally as possible, into 3 pieces. If you are using acorn squash, cut each one in half. In either case, remove all the seeds and cut away any stringy filaments. Pour the water into a 12-inch skillet or shallow flameproof casserole, and in it arrange the pieces of squash side by side. Sprinkle each piece with the *piloncillo* or brown sugar, and bring the water to a boil over high heat. Then reduce the heat to its lowest point, cover the pan and simmer for 1 hour, basting the squash every 10 minutes with the pan liquid. When the squash is tender but not mushy, turn off the heat and let the squash cool in the pan to room temperature.

To serve, arrange the squash on a platter or in individual dessert bowls, and spoon over it a little of its cooking liquid—now a syrup. If you like, top each piece of squash with whipped cream.

Huevos Reales
ROYAL EGGS

To serve 6 to 8

3 egg whites
12 egg yolks
½ cup sweet sherry
2 tablespoons seedless raisins
2 cups sugar
1 cup cold water
A 2-inch piece of stick cinnamon
¼ cup pine nuts

Preheat the oven to 325°. In a large mixing bowl, beat the egg whites with a whisk or a rotary or electric beater until they are stiff enough to form soft peaks. In another bowl, beat the egg yolks until they thicken enough to fall back in a ribbon when the whisk or beater is lifted out of the bowl. Then, thoroughly mix the whites into the yolks, and pour the

Tempting Mexican desserts include stuffed *chayotes (left)*, honeyed squash *(center)* with whipped cream and "royal eggs" *(bottom)*.

mixture into a buttered shallow baking dish about 8½- to 9-inches square. Smooth the top with the spatula.

Place the baking dish in a large shallow roasting pan in the middle of the oven and pour enough boiling water into the pan to come halfway up the sides of the dish. Bake for about 10 to 15 minutes, or until the eggs are firm. Remove the dish from the oven and cool to room temperature. Then cut the baked eggs into 1½-inch squares with a knife dipped in hot water.

Combine ¼ cup of sherry and the raisins in a small bowl and set aside to soak. In a small saucepan, bring the sugar, water and cinnamon stick to a boil over high heat, stirring only until the sugar is dissolved. Boil briskly, undisturbed, over high heat for 5 minutes. Discard the cinnamon stick and pour the syrup into a shallow heatproof dish or pan.

With a spatula, place the egg squares in the dish, one at a time, and when they are almost entirely saturated with syrup, transfer the squares to individual dessert dishes or a deep platter, arranging them side by side in one layer. Strain the remaining syrup through a fine sieve into a small bowl, stir in the remaining ¼ cup of sherry, and pour as much of the mixture as you like over the egg squares. Then sprinkle the tops evenly with the presoaked raisins and the pine nuts.

Quesillo de Piña
PINEAPPLE CUSTARD

To serve 6 to 8

THE CARAMEL
1 cup sugar
½ cup water

THE CUSTARD
3 whole eggs plus 2 egg yolks
A 14-ounce can condensed milk
1½ cups pineapple juice
¼ cup sugar

To line a 6-cup metal or porcelain mold with caramel, it is necessary to work quickly. Remember in handling the caramel that its temperature will be over 300°, so be extremely careful with it. Place the mold on a large strip of wax paper. Then, in a small, heavy saucepan or skillet, bring the sugar and water to a boil over high heat, stirring until the sugar dissolves. Boil the syrup over moderate heat, gripping a pot holder in each hand and gently tipping the pan back and forth almost constantly, until the syrup turns a rich, golden, tea-like brown. This may take 10 minutes or more. As soon as the syrup reaches the right color, remove the pan from the heat and carefully pour the caramel syrup all at once into the mold. Still using the pot holders, tip and swirl the mold to coat the bottom and sides as evenly as possible. When the syrup stops moving, turn the mold upside down on the wax paper to drain and cool for a minute or two.

Preheat the oven to 325°. In a large mixing bowl, beat the eggs and egg yolks with a whisk or a rotary or electric beater until they thicken and turn a light yellow. Gradually pour in the condensed milk, pineapple juice and sugar, and beat until all the ingredients are well combined. Strain through a fine sieve into the caramel-lined mold, and place the mold in a large pan on the middle shelf of the oven. Pour enough boiling water into the pan to come halfway up the sides of the mold. Bake the custard for about 1 hour, or until a knife inserted in the center of the custard comes out clean. Remove the mold from the water, let it cool to room temperature, then refrigerate the custard for at least 3 hours, or until it is thoroughly chilled.

To unmold and serve the large custard, run a sharp knife around the sides, and dip the bottom of the mold briefly in hot water. Then wipe the outside of the mold dry, place a chilled serving plate upside down over the mold and, grasping mold and plate together firmly, quickly turn them over. Rap the plate on a table and the custard should slide easily out of the mold. Pour any extra caramel remaining in the mold over the custard. Serve cold.

Natillas Piuranas
CARAMELIZED MILK PUDDING

Popular throughout Latin America, this type of dessert is prepared in many ways and has many names, such as manjar blanco, dulce de leche and leche quemada.

To serve 6 to 8

A 14-ounce can condensed milk
3 cups fresh milk
½ teaspoon bicarbonate of soda
1 cup dark-brown sugar
¼ cup water

In a 2-quart saucepan, bring the condensed milk, fresh milk and soda just to the boil over high heat, stirring constantly. Immediately remove the pan from the heat. Combine the sugar and water in a heavy 4- to 5-quart saucepan and cook them over low heat, stirring constantly, until the sugar dissolves. Pour in the hot milk and stir well. Cook over low heat for 1 hour and 15 minutes, maintaining a low simmer and stirring occasionally. Watch carefully for any sign of burning and regulate the heat accordingly. The mixture will become an amber-colored pudding. Serve the pudding at room temperature, or refrigerate it and serve it chilled.

A rich caramel coating lends both color and flavor to this pineapple custard, known to Venezuelans as *quesillo de piña*.

VII

Brazil: A Touch of Africa

On a penthouse terrace overlooking Rio's celebrated Copacabana district, elegant Brazilian ladies enjoy their country's elaborate national dish, *feijoada completa*. The *feijoada* combines black beans and a variety of cured and fresh meats, served with rice and hot pepper sauce. The gaudy dish is garnished with manioc meal and accompanied by orange slices and fresh kale.

Brazil is not in the least like the rest of South America. It is different in climate, people, history and language (Portuguese rather than Spanish), and consequently its food is different. Instead of the blend of Spanish and civilized Indian cuisines found in neighboring Andean nations, Brazilian cooking is a fascinating mixture of Portuguese, primitive Indian and West African influences. Brazil, moreover, is the only land in Latin America where Negroes imported as slaves kept a good part of their original culture and used it in the development of the new country.

When the Portuguese colonists settled in Brazil in the early 1500s, they found no glittering cities like those of the Inca Empire. Most of the country was covered with dense tropical forests inhabited by a few naked Indians who lived in small isolated villages. Some of these Indians were gentle and friendly but others were notably ferocious. Their principal food, aside from fish, game and jungle fruit, was manioc, a root crop that was probably domesticated in the Amazon basin in very ancient times. Manioc will grow almost anywhere, and its easy culture made it ideal for the haphazard agriculture of the Brazilian Indians.

There are many kinds of manioc. Some plants produce large roots, woody-looking on the outside, hard and white within, that can be boiled and eaten directly. Known to North Americans as sweet cassava, in Spanish-speaking countries this is called *yuca*. Brazilians call it several names, including *aipím* and *macaxeira*. The roots must be boiled for hours before they are soft enough to eat, and even then they are not very good. They have hardly any taste and almost no nourishment except plain starch.

More widely used is bitter cassava, whose roots contain, besides starch, a considerable amount of deadly poisonous hydrocyanic acid. It is hard to understand how the Amazon Indians ever learned to cope with this perilous vegetable, but learn they did. The women peel the massive roots and patiently grate them into pulp. They put the pulp into a cylindrical basketlike contraption made in such a way that it contracts when pulled out lengthwise. Then they hang the laden basket on a tree branch and attach a heavy weight to its lower end. The weight pulls the basket together squeezing out the poisonous juice. When this step is completed, an Indian woman dries the damp white residue and toasts it slightly over a fire. The result is manioc meal, *farinha de mandioca*. The juice is sometimes saved, boiled to get rid of its poison, and used as a sauce.

This ingenious and unlikely procedure is still followed in Brazil, much mechanized, of course, in civilized places but little changed in principle. *Farinha de mandioca* is manufactured in enormous quantities and used to make many different dishes from soups and stews to breads, cakes and candies. By itself it has no taste at all, but when fried in oil, it turns into a crumbly material with a pleasant toasted flavor. Although generally served as a side dish, when no other reason can be found for serving it, plain untoasted *farinha* appears on the table in a special shaker, a *farinheira*, like the cheese shakers in Italian restaurants. Brazilians sprinkle *farinha* on any dish that has a suspicion of moisture. It acts like bread in sopping up the last drops of juice or sauce. *Farinha* is also ground into a kind of flour that is seldom seen outside Brazil. On world markets *farinha* appears as tapioca, which is made by forcing moist *farinha* through a sieve in a way that forms it into round pellets.

Besides manioc, the Brazilian Indians had other crops, such as corn, sweet potatoes and peanuts, that they presumably got from the distant civilized Indians of the Andes, and from this same source came certain cooking techniques. Tamales wrapped in cornhusks or banana leaves are made in Brazil as well as in Mexico and Peru. But that is about all. The Indians were one of Brazil's important racial strains, and their languages had a considerable effect on the Portuguese now spoken in Brazil, but they made no further contribution to the nation's culture.

Much more important were the Africans, who were brought to Brazil as slaves in early colonial times to work on the great sugar plantations. Unlike the slaves who came to North America, they found themselves in a land very similar to their ancestral home, so that the skills and knowledge that they brought with them were of considerable value. Brazil is much like West Africa in climate, and has the same dense jungles and dry, hot savannas. West African crops grow well in Brazil and thatched huts of the West African type are quite sufficient for the Brazilian climate. So the slaves felt pretty much at home. Their masters set them to raising basic African food crops such as bananas, coconuts and yams, and practicing African crafts of wood- and metalworking. And they quickly learned how to grow manioc and other native crops.

Besides raising most of the food in early Brazil, the Africans did nearly all of the cooking. Portuguese women were too few and too pampered to have much influence on what was done in the kitchens of the great plantation houses. The African cooks took charge and followed their own culinary customs, the best of which were as advanced as those of Portugal. This tradition has continued to the present time. Brazilians have a saying: "The blacker the cook the better the food." Brazilian cooks are usually Negro women whose work has considerable status and who are greatly honored for their skill.

In a curious way the West African religions that came to Brazil with the slaves had a strong effect on the country's cooking. Although most of the slaves became nominal Christians, many of them continued to follow religions they had known in Africa. One of their most important ceremonies was the preparation of ritual meals to feed the gods. This was an amiable kind of sacrifice since most of the food actually went to feed the communicants after the gods had eaten, but the cooks had to be priestesses who approached their tasks with meticulous piety. Everything had to be done according to tradition or the gods might be displeased. Although the sacrificial dishes would not be suited to modern tastes, their preparation required great skill. Often the best cooks in the "great houses" of the sugar plantations were the same priestesses who cooked for the gods. It was only natural that the African raw materials and cooking skills that they used for this purpose should influence the food they prepared for the plantation family.

One of the West African sects, called Candomblé, is still going strong in Brazil, especially in the state of Bahia on the east coast. Its priestesses cook the same dishes for the gods that were cooked centuries ago. This is no quick or easy process. The right ingredients must be collected, some of them African vegetables or obscure herbs and spices. Then come laborious scraping and cutting. Half a dozen women participate under the eye of the priestess, who watches carefully to prevent even the slightest shortcut that might lead the gods to reject the offering. The base of one ritual dish is okra, originally an African vegetable. Each pod is held by one end while the other end is given many lengthwise cuts about an inch deep. The pod is then cut crosswise in thin disks that fall apart. The process takes hours as the okra is reduced to small bits, and each soft, edible seed is cut into two or more pieces.

The final product may serve its religious purpose, but it is not very good from a purely gastronomic point of view. Apparently the African gods of 300 years ago did not eat very well. The ritual meals prepared so carefully for them contain very little except finely cut or mashed vegetables; they are obviously the diet of a poor agricultural people who lacked meat. The dish based on okra is a slimy mess, but its sliminess is considered a virtue, and so it is increased by cutting the pods and seeds exceedingly fine.

The recipe for the best and simplest of the ritual dishes, called *bobó para Ibeiji*, consists of small red beans, peeled sweet potatoes and peeled bananas. All of them are cooked in a little water until soft, and mashed together with the ever-present *dendé* (palm) oil, small dried shrimp and grated onions. The mixture is heated slowly for about five minutes. During this final cooking the food absorbs the water and becomes rather dry and stiff.

Americans are guaranteed not to like this dish; its flavor is flat (unless

In the marketplace in Salvador, a young Brazilian offers prospective buyers a tempting, freshly tapped coconut. To prepare it for drinking, he has cut away the coconut's shell and inserted a straw through which the sweet milk may be sipped.

a lot of red pepper is added), and the unpeeled shrimp make its texture scratchy. To judge by their delicious nonritual cooking, the people who make it probably do not like *bobó para Ibeiji* either. It should be considered a nostalgic relic of earlier times, like the humble hoecakes and hush puppies that are sentimentalized in the southern United States.

A much better kind of *bobó* (derived from the ritual African dish) contains a larger proportion of shrimp, as well as tomatoes, green peppers, manioc root, grated coconut and other flavorsome ingredients. It is not served dry but in a pleasant mushy state *(Recipe Booklet)*. Another excellent descendant of the ritual African dish is *acarajé*, a small dumpling, made of skinless mashed beans, shrimp and onion, that is dropped by spoonfuls into a skillet and fried in deep *dendé* oil. Served with a hot sauce, it is a fine-flavored appetizer that can be found all over Brazil.

The modern cooking of Bahia, where the African influence predominates, is famous throughout Brazil. Gourmets and intellectuals make pilgrimages to Bahia or even set up housekeeping there. The city of Salvador, the capital of the state, is an agreeable if somewhat dilapidated place. The people are friendly and charming, with skins mostly the color of coffee with milk. Admirers of Salvador claim with considerable justification that it has the world's highest proportion of pretty girls.

The first thing that a visitor notices about the food of this pleasant city— like the *bobós* already mentioned—is that many dishes are colored bright yellow-orange. The *dendé* oil gives them this color. Extracted from the plumlike fruit of the West African oil palm, it is widely used in Brazilian cooking, especially in the northeast. The stiff, bristly palms were imported centuries ago and flourish in Brazil as well as in Africa. This oil, which varies from yellow to deep orange or even red, is sold all over Brazil but is hard to obtain in the United States, where it is imported chiefly for soapmaking (it was the original palm oil in Palmolive soap) and for industrial purposes such as cooling hot steel.

Brazilian gourmets decry such uses as a desecration. *Dendé* oil, they insist, gives the final touch of flavor that makes a Bahian dish a delight. This is true, but the flavor of the refined oil, while excellent, is quite subtle. Bahian dishes can be made without it, and the oil's bright color can be simulated by adding a little paprika to them.

Another Bahian ingredient that is hard to find in the United States is *malagueta* pepper, an exceedingly hot spice that some Bahians use as lavishly as Mexicans use chili. Most Brazilians seem to think it is African, but it is actually a relative of chili, a native of the New World that was taken to West Africa long ago and welcomed as a key part of the African cuisine. Many northeast Brazilian recipes call for a large lacing of it, but it can be reduced or omitted to spare tender tongues. Hot red pepper or tabasco pepper can be substituted for it.

Bahian cooking makes great use of fish and shrimp, which are plentiful in Salvador. The shrimp are fresh, but often they are dried in a way that gives them a powerfully "ripe" but surprisingly pleasant flavor. Small dried shrimp are seldom peeled; they are generally ground fine so no part will be wasted. A popular Bahian dish of African origin, *vatapá (page 139)*, is a delicious stewlike concoction containing fish, dried shrimp and sometimes fresh shrimp. It can also be made with meat or fowl instead of fish. Bahian cooks are rather informal as to the main ingredients of their dishes. They often use them interchangeably, believing that the sauce and seasonings are more important. Chicken, turkey and pork appear on the table in sauces that are very like those of fish dishes. This does not mean, however, that Bahian cooking is monotonous. There is an endless list of sauces using different combinations of vegetables, spices, herbs and other seasonings. Every Bahian cook takes pride in doing everything in her own special style, and some of them guard their secrets like precious jewels.

Many Brazilian recipes contain coconut or coconut milk. It is not definitely known whether coconut palms grew anywhere in the New World before the arrival of Europeans. The nuts in their large, buoyant, waterproof husks are equipped to make long sea journeys on ocean currents, and perhaps they crossed the Atlantic before Columbus, but if they did, they certainly were not important in the diet of the Indians. It is more likely that coconuts came from Africa later, along with the slaves. Whatever their origin, the graceful coconut palms now march in long parades along the curving beaches of Brazil, and the nuts are used in countless ways.

The nuts are bought in the market with the husks already removed, as in the United States, but they are usually fresher and contain more liquid. The first step in dismembering the coconut is to punch two holes in the soft "eyes" (from which the infant palm seedling emerges) and pour out the sweet, cloudy fluid. Then the nut is put in the oven for a few minutes. The heat makes the shell come loose when it is cracked, leaving the nut meat free. The cook pares off the dark rind and grates the meat finely. She heats it with a little milk or water and then squeezes out the moisture in a cloth bag or sieve, extracting "thick milk," the rich emulsion of coconut oil that is called for in some recipes. When water or the natural coconut fluid is added to the grated coconut for a second squeezing, it yields "thin milk" which has a coconut flavor but not as much emulsified oil. This laborious process is still in use, and whole coconuts are conspicuous in Brazilian markets, but the thick milk can now be bought readyprepared. Freshly grated coconut is also sold, and it can be taken home in quantity and frozen for later use. So when a modern Brazilian cook or housewife wants to make a delicacy that calls for a coconut product, she need not face a tedious struggle.

Grated coconut and coconut milk are used with surprising frequency, especially in Afro-Brazilian dishes. Besides being cooked with rice to make a delightful sweet pudding and being used for flavoring in candies, cakes and cookies, coconut is also called for in recipes for highly seasoned fish or shrimp stews where its mild flavor is all but overwhelmed. Brazilian gourmets insist, however, that the dishes would be worthless without it.

The influence of African cooking, with its dendé oil, red pepper, bananas and coconuts, touches all Brazil, gradually diminishing toward the south. In Rio de Janeiro, 750 miles southwest of Salvador, it is still strong, but other cooking traditions make themselves felt. Rio was the capital of the country until 1960 when the federal government moved to Brasília, 600 miles inland. But during Rio's sway as the capital, its upper-class cuisine absorbed cooking ideas from Portuguese colonial rulers and foreign embassies. Many hotels and wealthy homes in Rio serve French or international dishes almost exclusively, and even North American food of the humbler sort is not unknown. Hot dogs, hamburgers and American-style sandwiches are featured along Rio's famous Copacabana Beach.

But Rio is still Rio, perhaps the loveliest city on earth, and it has a character too distinctive ever to slide into uniformity. A lot of mundane work is done in Rio, which still performs many of the national government's functions, but to the casual visitor's eye the city is a South Sea island—the biggest in the world—that just happens to be moored to the land. The beautiful beaches sweep into the downtown district, which lies on a sparkling, island-dotted bay, and many of the nearest suburbs have their beaches too. A charming sight in Rio is girls in minimal bikinis strolling through crowded city streets toward a beach a few blocks away.

The cooking of Rio is elaborate, as befits such a cosmopolitan, rich and luxurious city, but there the meals have fewer courses than those in the Spanish-speaking countries. Even a formal dinner may have as few as four courses: soup, fish or shrimp, meat or chicken, and dessert. No one is likely to go hungry, however, for many of the dishes have secondary dishes served along with them, as Americans serve vegetables with the meat course. Most of these auxiliary plates are substantial, being based on rice, manioc meal or cornmeal, and some of them are as complicated as the dish that they accompany.

One important family of these side dishes is called *farofas,* which are based on manioc meal. Butter *farofa (page 135)* is manioc meal fried with butter, egg and seasonings to make a delectable, crumbly companion dish for meat, fish or poultry. Other *farofas* contain olives, raisins, cheese, prunes, bacon, chopped meat, carrots or other vegetables. Besides being served as side dishes they are used as stuffings for chicken or turkey.

Another kind of accompanying dish is called *pirão,* which means, literally, porridge. It may be made either of rice or cornmeal. If whole rice is used, it is boiled until mushy and mashed into a smooth paste. If rice flour or cornmeal is used, no mashing is needed. The mixture is pressed into a buttered mold and allowed to cool and solidify. Perhaps the best *pirão* is made with coconut milk and rice flour *(page 139);* it does not look like much but is a delightful taste surprise. Another good one contains cornmeal and cheese and a bit of nutmeg. It is cut in small square slices, covered with egg and bread crumbs and deep-fried as a crisp side dish to serve with meat, like Britain's Yorkshire pudding.

No Brazilian, or other Latin American for that matter, admires the way that North Americans generally cook rice: plain and white with the grains stuck together. Rice is one of Brazil's basic foods, and the consumers insist that it be glorified. This can be done in many ways; perhaps the simplest and most popular is to fry the dry grains with a thinly sliced onion in a little lard or oil over a low fire. The rice should be stirred, and the onion must not burn. A cut-up tomato is stirred in. Then after adding boiling salted water or stock, the rice is brought to a boil, stirred a few times, and left covered for 20 to 30 minutes over very low heat. The rice absorbs the water, and when it is pressed into a mold and tipped out again, the grains are soft and so dry that they barely hold together. Each grain retains its independence, and has its share of the onion and tomato flavor.

Rice cooked in more or less this way may appear on any Brazilian table, but it is also the first step toward other preparations, some of which rank as main dishes. Cooked rice is layered in a baking dish with almost anything edible—shrimp, ham, chicken, cheese, and tomato sauce—and baked with a covering of grated cheese. In this way a skilled cook can compose a wonderful orchestration of many flavors. A similar dish is made of cooked rice with peas and bread crumbs added to a goodly amount of stewed meat in its gravy. When the proportions are figured correctly, the mix is firm enough to be pressed into a mold. Greasing the inside of the mold with butter and sprinkling it with bread crumbs helps unmold the rice in an unbroken form.

A different and popular way to cook rice is first to make a stew of beef, pork or sausage with onions, other vegetables, and herbs and seasonings. Uncooked rice is added, boiled and stirred for 10 minutes. Then the covered pot is left over a very low flame until the rice is cooked. Water may be added if needed, but the final product should be dry enough to be molded into a loaf.

Along with rice and manioc, the third great staple food of Brazil is beans. Much more than Boston, Brazil is the land of the bean. Everyone eats them frequently; servants are said to flee any household where beans are not available whenever the urge to eat them strikes. Brazil's devotion to beans exceeds even that of bean-loving Mexico, whose national dish, *mole poblano de guajolote*, contains no beans. Brazil's own national dish, *feijoada completa (page 134)*, is based on beans and named in part after them, the word *feijão* being Portuguese for beans.

Beans are the salvation of the Brazilian diet, which is not well balanced and would be impossibly low in protein without them. Many kinds of beans are grown, but most Brazilians prefer small, shiny black ones that cook to a mush that is also almost black. For the poorer people the standard and sufficient meal is black beans cooked very soft with rice on the side and manioc meal sprinkled thickly over both.

Beans are generally cooked until tender; then some are removed and fried in a small amount of lard with grated onion and garlic. After this they are mashed and returned to the pot. The cooking continues slowly for about half an hour more. This produces a moist mixture of soft but still firm beans embedded in a mashed bean sauce, a savory dish as beloved in Brazil as *frijoles refritos (page 72)* in Mexico. If manioc meal is added until the mixture thickens, the result is *tutú de feijão,* which is served on a platter and may be garnished with fried onion, bacon and sausage. Beans are also baked with meat, and sometimes they are cooked with coconut milk, a dish that is called *feijão de coco.*

The Brazilian national party dish, *feijoada completa,* is a meat-and-bean combination that is an outgrowth of the workingman's humble daily beans, but it can be very fancy indeed. Brazilians are not laggards when it comes to display; a full-dress *feijoada completa* looks like a triumph of a horn of plenty. If it is served for a small group of guests, there is a practical limit to its lavishness, but the dish is also served to large, festive gatherings. When the celebration is an expensive one, the meats in the dish take first place while the cheaper beans are overshadowed.

In the traditional *feijoada,* the meats must include dried beef and a smoked tongue, but other meats are usually added, including fresh beef, pork, lean bacon, ordinary bacon, various kinds of sausage, corned spareribs and pig's feet. The dried or salted meats are freshened by soaking overnight, and all meats are simmered until tender. Sometimes the dried beef, which is often made from old, tough, semiwild cattle, does not get really tender; it merely turns into bundles of fibers. But a guest at a lusty *feijoada* does not worry about such details. If he does not like dried beef with the consistency of Manila rope, he has many other meats to choose from. While he is making this choice, he probably will belt down several shots of *cachaça* (Brazilian sugar-cane brandy) to put him in a mood for large-scale festive eating.

There are many detailed recipes for *feijoada completa,* but the presentation always follows the same strict traditional rules. The meats are laid out on a large platter (or on several platters for a major occasion) with the smoked tongue always in the center. Around it the other meats are arranged in symmetrical, decorative patterns, the smoked meats at one side, the fresh meats at the other. All of them are moistened with bean liquor. The beans themselves are served in a great tureen or other large-sized container. Also on the table are mounds of cooked rice, manioc meal and green heaps of shredded kale or collard greens as well as many bottles of colorless, fiery *cachaça,* or pitchers of *batida paulista (Recipe Booklet)—cachaça* mixed with lemon juice and sugar. Also provided are bowls of hot sauces and dishes heaped with sliced oranges. There is a theory that when the stomach seems so full that it cannot hold a single additional bean, a touch of orange and *cachaça* persuades it to expand and accept more.

Feijoada completa is obviously a heavy, hearty dish, a relic of pioneering days when men worked hard and dangerously and looked forward to eating themselves into a drowsy stupor. But for modern men (and sturdy women) whose stomachs are in good working order, it still has an atavistic appeal, like a Texas barbecue, which it somewhat resembles. It is recommended to American housewives whose husbands have vigorous friends who will enjoy eating as heartily as Brazilian backlands cowboys.

Though the *feijoada completa* is hailed throughout Brazil as the national dish, it is really too simple to be typical of Brazilian cookery, which features painstaking preparation, decorative appearance and complexity of flavor. A resourceful cook can prepare a duck or chicken in a way that requires a hint of dozens of ingredients and a full page of description. Even a simple item like *canja,* chicken soup *(Recipe Booklet),* may contain unexpected items such as diced ham. Stews, which Brazilians adore, may contain almost anything. *Carurú,* for instance, is basically a stew of shrimp, but it also calls for green pepper, onion, parsley, tomato, okra, manioc meal, coconut milk and *dendê* oil. The oil gives it a remarkable flavor and a texture that no non-Brazilian would expect to find in a shrimp stew *(page 138).*

Some Brazilian dishes are triumphs of culinary skill that are almost im-

possible to achieve without long practice. At festive dinners a roast turkey, for instance, might be decorated with fine golden-yellow threads or surrounded by little beehive piles of the same material. This is *fios de ovos* (egg threads), which are made by trailing thin streams of egg yolk into boiling sugar syrup. One especially decorative dish calls for the yolks of 36 eggs and the whites of three. They are mixed carefully in a gentle way that introduces no air bubbles. The resulting yellow liquid is strained to remove the delicate membranes that surround the yolks.

Words can hardly tell how to take the next step correctly. The sugar syrup, which is flavored with vanilla or rose water, must be at just the right density and temperature. A little of the egg yolk is poured into a special funnel that has three widely spaced openings. As the egg yolk runs out in three fine streams, the cook guides it gently around the edge of the saucepan that holds the hot syrup. If she does this properly, the yolk congeals into solid, flexible threads that do not break or stick together. They are skimmed off and plunged for a moment into cold, sweetened water. Later they are arranged in decorative shapes or strands. Egg threads are a pleasant confection with a slightly sweet taste and an interesting texture, but they are most impressive as evidence that a household has an unusually skillful cook.

Aside from such tours de force as egg threads, perhaps one of the most unusual Brazilian dishes is *cuscuz (page 140),* which illustrates the national

Pungent spices—essential ingredients of Brazilian cooking—bedeck a vendor's stand in Rio. In the foreground are a mild chili called *pimenta de cheiro (center),* and *pimenta malagueta (left),* the famous pepper brought to Brazil by African slaves. On the right in the foreground is ginger root. Beyond these spices lie garlic *(left),* onions *(right)* and coconuts slashed open to show their firm white meat. The bottles hold a prepared, extra-hot chili.

habit of accepting foreign ideas and elaborating them beyond recognition. *Cuscuz* (the word has many spellings) was originally an Arabian or North African dish made chiefly of steamed rice, wheat meal, sorghum or other Old World grain. It is not certain whether the Portuguese adopted it during their early trading and warfare with North Africa or whether the Moors carried it across the Sahara to West Africa, to be brought from there to Brazil by the slaves. However it may have arrived, *cuscuz* was changed and glorified in Brazil, and it eventually fathered many different dishes.

In modern Brazil there are two main kinds of *cuscuz*. In the northern states the dish is a dessert made of tapioca, fresh-grated coconut, coconut milk, sugar, salt and water. Steaming is not necessary. The ingredients are mixed with the boiling water, put in a mold and left in the refrigerator overnight. They make a solid cake that is turned out, sliced and decorated with more coconut milk and grated coconut. It is very sweet, very "coconutty" and very good.

The other kind of *cuscuz*, which is called *cuscuz paulista* from São Paulo in southern Brazil, is an excellent way of cooking a wide variety of foods. It is usually made with cornmeal specially prepared so that it clings together in small crumbs. This material can be bought in Brazilian markets, but in the United States it can be made in the kitchen by toasting cornmeal slightly in the oven. Some cooks insist that manioc meal must be added, but it is not necessary. The main thing is to give the cornmeal an open, crumblike texture so the steam can penetrate and cook it. *Cuscuz paulista* can be a simple mixture of the prepared cornmeal mixed with shortening and perhaps a few vegetables or shreds of cooked meat. But it can also be fancy indeed, with chunks of fish, meat, lobster and even raisins and nuts.

The steaming of the dish is done in a *cuscuzeiro,* a sort of round-bottomed aluminum colander supported on a wire frame. American colanders with plenty of holes in them will do just as well. The cook starts by lining the bottom and sides of the *cuscuzeiro* with the most decorative things that she intends to use, such as sliced tomatoes, sliced hard-boiled eggs, olives cut in halves or shrimp sliced lengthwise. If she has an artistic eye, as most Brazilian cooks do have, she produces pretty patterns in bright colors. When she has plastered the first layer solid with the moist cornmeal mixture, she adds a second layer of vegetables and meat. The layers are alternated until the *cuscuzeiro* is full. Sometimes a little herb-flavored oil is poured on the center so it can seep downward. The top is often covered first with chopped collard greens and then with a napkin. Then the *cuscuzeiro* is put in a large covered kettle in boiling water that reaches about one inch below the colander. The water must not touch the bottom of the *cuscuzeiro;* its steam passes through the holes and cooks the cornmeal without making it soggy.

When the steaming is complete, the *cuscuzeiro* is taken out of the kettle and allowed to cool for a few minutes. Then it is turned upside down on a platter. The *cuscuz* emerges in all its glory, the bright patterns of egg and tomato decorating its mounded outside, and its inside stuffed with all sorts of good things held together by flavorful cornmeal so it can be nicely sliced. No dish makes a bigger impression when brought to the table.

A Spicy Heritage of Africa

Even though four centuries have passed since the first African slaves were brought to Brazil, the cooking of Bahia—on the eastern coast—still strongly reflects the African influence. Bahian cooks still favor rich, piquant dishes, like the *vatapá* seafood stew *(page 139)* made with *dendé* oil—the orange-colored, subtle-flavored oil of the West African oil palm—and fiery red *malagueta* pepper. And modern Bahian cooks still depend heavily on bananas and coconuts—foods that were known to their ancestors long before they left Africa.

African spiciness marks the savory sauce *mólho de acarajé* *(1)*, the shrimp-based dishes *abará* *(2)* and *acarajé* *(3)*, and the fish cooked in banana leaves, *peixe em moqueca* *(4)*, *vatapá* *(5)* combines shrimp, sea bass, halibut, ginger, cashew nuts, onion, garlic and other ingredients with *dendé* oil and *malagueta* pepper. Desserts such as *cuscuz de tapioca* *(6)* and *doce de coco* *(7)*, are coconut-based, while *carurú* *(8)* is a mixture of okra, shrimp and coconut seasoned with red hot pepper and ginger.

In Bahia, a native woman prepares *peixe em moqueca* by rolling sardines into banana leaves, an Indian technique adopted by the Africans after their arrival in Brazil. The leaf-wrapped fish are placed on a brazier over coals and cooked half an hour.

The Bahian woman above is making *abará,* another African import that came to be made with banana leaves. She is spooning a mixture of cowpeas, shrimp spiced with pepper and *dendé* oil into the leaves, which will then be cooked over the brazier.

Familiar African ingredients—shrimp and cowpeas— are mixed together and carefully cooked by the woman at the top, opposite, to prepare *acarajé.* Unlike *abará* the mixture is fried crisp and brown by the spoonful, as shown in the close-up at the bottom, opposite.

CHAPTER VII RECIPES

To serve 8 to 10

A 3-pound smoked beef tongue
1 pound corned spareribs, if available
½ pound jerked or dried beef, in 1 piece
½ pound *chorizo* or other smoked spiced pork sausage
½ pound fresh breakfast-type pork sausage
1 fresh pig's foot, if available
3½ quarts water
4 cups dried black beans
¼ pound lean bacon, in 1 piece with the rind removed
1 pound lean beef chuck, in 1 piece
½ pound Canadian-style bacon, in 1 piece
2 tablespoons lard
1½ cups coarsely chopped onions
1 tablespoon finely chopped garlic
3 medium tomatoes, peeled, seeded and coarsely chopped (*see salsa cruda, page 44*), or substitute 1 cup chopped, drained, canned Italian plum tomatoes
2 bottled tabasco peppers, drained, seeded and finely chopped
1 teaspoon salt
½ teaspoon freshly ground black pepper

Farofa de ovo (opposite)
Couve à mineira (opposite)
Mólho de pimenta e limão (opposite)
Arroz brasileiro (opposite)
5 large oranges, peeled and thinly sliced or cut into chunks

Feijoada Completa
SMOKED AND FRESH MEAT WITH ACCOMPANIMENTS

THE MEATS: Place the tongue, spareribs and jerked beef in separate pots, and cover the meats with cold water. Soak them overnight.

Precook the meats in the following fashion: Drain the tongue, cover it with fresh water, and bring to a boil over high heat. Partially cover the pan, reduce the heat to low, and simmer the tongue for 3 to 4 hours, or until it is tender and shows no resistance when it is pierced with the point of a small, sharp knife.

The tongue should be kept covered with water at all times; if it boils away, add more boiling water. Remove the tongue from the water and let it cool slightly. Then skin it with a sharp knife, cutting away all the fat, bones and gristle at its base.

Drain the jerked beef, cover it with fresh water and bring to a boil. Reduce the heat and simmer uncovered for 30 minutes; drain and set aside.

Drain the spareribs, add the smoked sausage, fresh sausage and pig's foot, and cover with fresh water. Bring to a boil, reduce the heat to low, and simmer uncovered for 15 minutes. Drain and set the meats aside.

THE BEANS: In a heavy 12-quart casserole or a large soup pot, bring 3 quarts of water to a boil over high heat. Drop in the beans and boil them briskly for 2 minutes. Turn off the heat and let the beans soak for 1 hour. Then add the jerked beef, spareribs, pig's foot and lean bacon. Bring to a boil, reduce the heat to low, cover and simmer for 1 hour. Check the water in the pot from time to time. It should cook away somewhat, leaving the beans moist and slightly soupy; but if the beans are getting too dry, add some more boiling water.

Add the chuck to the pot, and continue cooking the beans and meat for 1 hour. Finally, add the smoked and fresh sausage and Canadian bacon, and cook for 30 minutes. Skim the fat from the surface of the beans, add the peeled tongue and remove the pot from the heat.

THE SAUCE: In a heavy 8- to 10-inch skillet, melt the lard over moderate heat. Add the onions and garlic, and cook, stirring frequently, for 5 minutes, or until the onions are soft and transparent but not brown. Stir in the tomatoes, tabasco peppers, salt and black pepper, and simmer for 5 minutes. With a slotted spoon, remove 2 cups of beans from the casserole and add them to the skillet. Mash them thoroughly into the onion mixture, moistening them with 2 cups of the bean liquid as you mash. Stirring occasionally, simmer the sauce over low heat for 15 minutes, or until it becomes thick. With a rubber spatula scrape the sauce into the pot and cook over low heat, stirring occasionally, for 20 minutes.

TO ASSEMBLE: Remove the meats from the pot. Slice the beef tongue, jerked beef, lean bacon, chuck, Canadian bacon, spareribs and pig's foot into serving pieces, and separate the smoked and fresh sausages. Transfer the beans to a serving bowl. Traditionally, all the meats are presented on one large, heated platter with the sliced tongue in the center, the fresh meat on one side, the smoked meats on the other. Present the beans, *farofa, couve, mólho, arroz* and orange slices in separate bowls or platters.

Farofa de Ovo
TOASTED MANIOC MEAL WITH EGG

In a heavy 8- to 10-inch skillet, heat the butter over moderate heat, tipping the pan to coat the bottom evenly. Drop in the onion slices and cook them, stirring constantly, for 5 minutes, or until they are soft and transparent but not brown. Reduce the heat to low and—still stirring constantly—pour in the egg. The egg will coagulate in seconds. Slowly stir in the manioc meal and cook, stirring frequently, for 8 minutes, or until the meal becomes golden. Watch carefully for any sign of burning. Stir in the salt and parsley. Serve hot or cooled to room temperature. The *farofa* may be garnished in either case with olives and hard-cooked eggs.

To serve 8 to 10

2 tablespoons butter
½ large peeled onion, thinly sliced
1 egg, lightly beaten
1⅓ cups manioc meal
1 teaspoon salt
1 tablespoon finely chopped parsley
4 pimiento-stuffed olives, cut crosswise into ¼-inch slices (optional)
2 to 4 hard-cooked eggs, cut in half lengthwise (optional)

Couve à Mineira
SHREDDED KALE GREENS

Wash the kale or collard greens under cold running water. With a sharp knife, trim away any bruised or blemished spots and cut the leaves from their tough stems. Shred the leaves into ¼-inch strips. In a large pot, bring 4 quarts of water to a boil over high heat. Drop in the greens and cook them uncovered for 3 minutes. Then drain them in a colander, pressing down on the greens with a spoon to extract all their liquid. In a heavy 10- to 12-inch skillet, melt the bacon fat over moderate heat, and when it is hot, but not smoking, add the greens. Cook, stirring frequently, for 30 minutes, or until the greens are tender, but slightly crisp. Don't let them brown. Stir in the salt and serve at once. If the greens must wait, cover them with foil, and keep them warm in a preheated 250° oven.

To serve 8 to 10

5 pounds kale greens, or substitute 5 pounds collard greens
¾ cup bacon fat
1½ teaspoons salt

Mólho de Pimenta e Limão
PEPPER AND LEMON SAUCE

In a small bowl, combine the peppers, onions, garlic and lemon juice, and stir until they are well mixed. Marinate, uncovered, at room temperature for an hour before serving, or refrigerate, covered, for as long as 4 hours.

To make about 1 cup

4 bottled tabasco peppers, drained and finely chopped
½ cup finely chopped onions
¼ teaspoon finely chopped garlic
½ cup fresh lemon juice

Arroz Brasileiro
RICE WITH TOMATOES AND ONION

In a heavy 3- to 4-quart saucepan, heat the oil over moderate heat for 30 seconds, tipping the pan to coat the bottom evenly. Add the onion and cook, stirring constantly, for 5 minutes, or until it is soft and transparent but not brown. Pour in the rice and stir for 2 to 3 minutes, until all the grains are coated with oil. Do not let the rice brown. Add the stock, water, tomatoes and salt, and return to a boil, still stirring. Cover the pan and reduce the heat to its lowest point. Simmer for 20 minutes, or until the rice has absorbed all the liquid. If the rice must wait, drape the pan loosely with a towel and keep it warm in a preheated 250° oven.

To serve 8 to 10

¼ cup olive oil
1 large onion, thinly sliced
3 cups raw long-grain rice
3 cups boiling chicken stock, fresh or canned
3 cups boiling water
2 medium tomatoes, peeled, seeded and coarsely chopped (*see salsa cruda, page 44*), or substitute ⅔ cup chopped, drained, canned Italian plum tomatoes
1 teaspoon salt

Overleaf: The feijoada completa
1 Orange slices
2 Brazilian rice
3 Collard greens
4 Pepper-and-lemon sauce
5 Egg *farofa*, garnished
6 Black beans
7 *Batida paulista* (rum-lemon drink)
8 Fresh beef
9 Tongue
10 Corned spareribs
11 Smoked sausages
12 Jerked beef
13 Fresh pork sausages
14 Lean bacon

4

5

12

13

14

8

7

6

Feijoada Completa

To make about 1 cup

1 cup water or fresh milk
Freshly grated coconut *(below)*

Leche de Coco
COCONUT MILK

In a small saucepan, heat the water or milk over low heat until small bubbles form around the edge of the pan. Place the freshly grated coconut in a large, fine sieve set over a mixing bowl and pour the water or milk over it. Without disturbing it, let the liquid drip through the coconut for about 15 minutes. Then, with the back of a large spoon, press down hard on the coconut to extract all its liquid before discarding it. Refrigerate the coconut milk tightly covered until ready to use.

NOTE: This technique is always used precisely, whatever the ratio of grated coconut to water or fresh milk called for in a specific recipe.

To make about 3½ cups

A fresh coconut, about 2½ pounds

Coco Rallado
FRESHLY GRATED COCONUT

NOTE: When buying a coconut, shake it to make sure it is full of milk.

Preheat the oven to 400°. Puncture 2 of the 3 smooth, dark eyes of the coconut by hammering the sharp tip of an ice pick or screw driver through them. Drain all of the coconut milk into a measuring cup. There should be about ½ cup. Set the milk aside.

Bake the empty coconut in the oven for 15 minutes, then transfer it to a chopping block. While the coconut is hot, split the shell with a hammer. The shell should fall away from the meat; if it doesn't, cut off any bits still clinging to the shell. Pare off the brown outer skin of the coconut meat with a swivel-bladed peeler or small, sharp knife, and cut the coconut meat into 1-inch pieces. Place these in the jar of a blender with ½ cup of coconut milk, and blend them at high speed for 1 minute, or until finely grated. (Alternatively, grate the coconut, piece by piece, through a hand grater and stir in ½ cup of coconut milk.)

To serve 4

3 pounds raw shrimp in their shells
3 tablespoons butter
2 tablespoons coarsely chopped
   onion
2 tablespoons coarsely chopped green
   pepper
2 large tomatoes, peeled, seeded and
   coarsely chopped *(see salsa cruda,
   page 44)*, or substitute ¾ cup
   chopped, drained, canned Italian
   plum tomatoes
½ pound fresh okra or a thoroughly
   defrosted 10-ounce package frozen
   okra, cut into 1-inch pieces
¼ pound dried shrimp, pulverized
   with a mortar and pestle
2 tablespoons manioc meal
1½ cups coconut milk, made from
   1 coconut and 1½ cups water or
   milk according to the directions
   above
⅓ cup *dendé* oil, if available
⅓ cup dry-roasted peanuts, wrapped
   in a towel and crushed with a
   rolling pin
2 tablespoons finely chopped fresh
   coriander *(cilantro)*
3 cups hot cooked rice (made from
   1 cup raw long-grain rice)

Carurú
SHRIMP WITH OKRA AND PEANUTS

Shell the shrimp. With a small, sharp knife, devein them by making a shallow incision down their backs and removing the black or white intestinal veins with the tip of the knife.

In a heavy 12-inch skillet, melt the butter over moderate heat and in it cook the shrimp for 2 or 3 minutes, turning them frequently, until they are firm and pink. With a slotted spoon, transfer the shrimp to a bowl and set aside. Add the onion to the butter remaining in the pan and cook, stirring frequently, for 5 minutes, or until the onion is soft and transparent but not brown. Add the green pepper, tomatoes, okra and dried shrimp. Stir the manioc meal into the coconut milk, and pour the mixture into the pan. When the ingredients are well combined, cover the pan, reduce the heat to low, and simmer for 25 minutes, or until the okra is tender.

Return the shrimp to the skillet and cook, stirring, for about 5 minutes, or until the shrimp are heated through. Stir in the *dendé* oil, crushed peanuts and coriander, taste for seasoning, and serve at once over a mound of hot cooked rice. Traditionally the shrimp is served with *môlho de pimenta e limão (page 135)* presented separately in another serving bowl.

Pirão de Arroz com Leite de Coco
RICE AND COCONUT-MILK PUDDING

In a heavy 2- to 3-quart saucepan, scald 3 cups of the coconut milk by warming it over moderate heat until tiny bubbles form around the edge of the pan. Combine the remaining 1 cup of coconut milk with the rice flour and salt in a small bowl and, stirring constantly, pour it gradually into the scalded milk. Reduce the heat to low and cook, stirring, until the mixture is thick and smooth.

Pour the pudding into a lightly buttered or oiled 1-quart metal or porcelain mold or into 6 individual 6- to 8-ounce custard molds and cool it to room temperature. Then refrigerate for at least 4 hours, or until the pudding is firm.

The pudding may be served directly from the mold (or molds) in which it chilled or it may be unmolded in the following fashion: Run a thin, sharp knife around the inside edge of the mold and dip the bottom of the mold in hot water for a few seconds. Place an inverted plate over the top of the mold and, grasping the plate and mold firmly together in both hands, quickly turn them upside down. Rap the plate sharply on the table. The pudding should slip out of the mold easily. If it doesn't, repeat the whole process.

Pirão de arroz com leite de coco is traditionally served as an accompaniment to *vatapá (below)* or *bobó (Recipe Booklet)*.

To serve 6

4 cups coconut milk, made with 2 fresh coconuts and 4 cups milk, according to directions opposite
¾ cup rice flour
1 teaspoon salt

Vatapá
FISH AND SHRIMP IN GINGER-FLAVORED PEANUT SAUCE

In a heavy 10- to 12-inch skillet, heat the oil over moderate heat until a light haze forms above it. In it, lightly brown the fish and shrimp in 2 or 3 batches, being careful not to crowd the pan and not to let the fish and shrimp overcook. As you proceed, transfer the cooked seafood to a plate with a slotted spoon. Set the fish and shrimp aside.

Add the chopped onions to the oil remaining in the skillet and cook over moderate heat, stirring frequently, for 4 or 5 minutes, or until the onions are soft and transparent but not brown. Add the tomatoes and the tabasco pepper, reduce the heat to low, cover the skillet and cook for 10 minutes. Stir in the grated coconut, then add the 2½ cups of water or milk, the peanuts, dried shrimp, coriander, ginger, salt and a few grindings of black pepper. Bring to a boil over moderate heat, reduce the heat to low and simmer, covered, for 15 minutes. Stir in the rice flour and water mixture and cook, stirring constantly, until the mixture thickens slightly.

With the back of a spoon, force the sauce through a fine sieve set over a large bowl, pressing down hard on the contents of the sieve to extract all of their liquid before discarding them. Return the strained sauce to the skillet, and cook over moderate heat, stirring frequently, until the sauce is thick enough to coat the spoon lightly. Add the fish and shrimp and the *dendé* oil, and simmer for 2 or 3 minutes, or until the fish and shrimp are heated through.

To serve, transfer the entire contents of the skillet to a large, deep heated platter. If you like, you may accompany the *vatapá* with the *pirão de arroz com leite de coco (above)*.

To serve 6

4 tablespoons olive oil
2 pounds sea bass fillets and 1 pound halibut fillets, cut crosswise into 2-inch-wide pieces, or substitute any other combination of firm white fish
1 pound raw shrimp, shelled and deveined
½ cup finely chopped onions
2 medium tomatoes, peeled, seeded and coarsely chopped *(see salsa cruda, page 44)*, or substitute ⅔ cup chopped, drained, canned Italian plum tomatoes
1 bottled tabasco pepper drained, seeded and finely chopped
1 coconut, freshly grated *(opposite)*
2½ cups water or milk
¼ cup dry-roasted peanuts, wrapped in a towel and crushed with a rolling pin
¼ cup dried shrimp, ground in a blender or pulverized with a mortar and pestle
1 tablespoon finely chopped fresh coriander *(cilantro)*
1 tablespoon finely grated fresh ginger, or 1 teaspoon ground ginger
1 teaspoon salt
Freshly ground black pepper
1 tablespoon rice flour dissolved in 2 tablespoons cold water
2 tablespoons *dendé* oil, if available

To serve 8

A 3½- to 4-pound chicken, cut into
  6 to 8 serving pieces
¼ cup distilled white vinegar
¼ cup fresh lemon juice
¼ cup olive oil
½ cup coarsely chopped onions
¼ teaspoon finely chopped garlic
¼ cup finely chopped fresh parsley
1 teaspoon coriander seeds
1 teaspoon dried savory
½ teaspoon finely chopped fresh
  mint
1 teaspoon salt
¼ teaspoon freshly ground black
  pepper
1 large tomato, peeled, seeded and
  coarsely chopped (*see salsa cruda,*
  page 44), or substitute ½ cup
  chopped, drained, canned Italian
  plum tomatoes
1 cup chicken stock, fresh or canned
½ pound *chorizo* or other smoked,
  spiced pork sausage, sliced ⅛ inch
  thick
4 cups white cornmeal
1 teaspoon salt
1 cup boiling water
1 cup melted butter (2 quarter-pound
  sticks)
¼ cup finely chopped fresh parsley
3 bottled tabasco peppers, drained,
  rinsed in cold water and finely
  chopped
3 medium tomatoes, peeled and sliced
  about ⅛ inch thick
A 10-ounce can hearts of palm,
  drained and sliced into rounds ⅛
  inch thick
3 hard-cooked eggs, cut crosswise
  into ⅛-inch slices
12 pimiento-stuffed olives, cut
  crosswise into ⅛-inch slices
1 cup cooked fresh green peas, or 1
  cup thoroughly defrosted frozen
  peas
3 seedless oranges, peeled and cut
  crosswise into ⅛-inch slices

Cuscuz de Galinha

MOLDED STEAMED CHICKEN, CORNMEAL AND VEGETABLES

THE CHICKEN: Arrange the chicken in one layer in a large shallow flame-proof casserole or skillet. In a small enameled or stainless-steel saucepan, combine the vinegar, lemon juice, ¼ cup of the oil, the onions, garlic, parsley, coriander seeds, savory, mint, 1 teaspoon of salt and the black pepper, and bring to a boil over high heat. Pour the hot vinegar marinade over the chicken, turning the pieces to coat them evenly. Cover the casserole tightly with aluminum foil or plastic wrap, and marinate the chicken for 3 hours at room temperature or 6 hours in the refrigerator, turning the pieces occasionally to keep them well moistened on all sides.

Over high heat, bring the chicken and marinade to a boil in the casserole. Reduce the heat to low, and simmer, uncovered, for 10 minutes. Stir in the chopped tomato and chicken stock and return to a boil. Reduce the heat to low, cover the casserole, and simmer for 30 minutes, or until the chicken is tender but not falling apart. Transfer the chicken to a plate, and remove the casserole from the heat.

As soon as the chicken is cool enough to handle, remove the skin with a small, sharp knife or your fingers. Cut or pull the meat away from the bones. Discard the skin and bones, and cut the chicken meat into strips about ⅛ inch wide and 1 to 1½ inches long. Strain the reserved cooking stock through a fine sieve set over a mixing bowl, then return it to the casserole. Drop in the chicken strips and set the casserole aside.

THE SAUSAGE: In another skillet, heat 2 tablespoons of oil over high heat and add the sausage slices. Turning the pieces constantly, brown them quickly but lightly on both sides, then remove them from the pan and spread them out on paper towels to drain.

THE CORNMEAL: Spread the cornmeal out in a large ungreased skillet and cook it over moderate heat, stirring it constantly with a wooden spoon for about 5 minutes. Watch carefully for any sign of burning and regulate the heat accordingly. When the cornmeal is a pale golden color, stir into it one teaspoon of salt and slowly pour in the cup of boiling water, stirring constantly. Cook over low heat, for 2 minutes, until all the moisture is absorbed. Then remove the skillet from the heat and mix in the cup of melted butter and the ¼ cup of parsley. Stir it little by little into the reserved skillet of chicken and stock and when they are well combined add the reserved sausage slices and the chopped tabasco peppers. Test the cornmeal mixture by rolling a spoonful of it between the palms of your hands. It should form a loose ball. If the cornmeal is too dry and crumbles, add a little chicken stock or water to the pan and mix until the cornmeal particles adhere. (Be careful not to add too much liquid; the cornmeal should be moist but not pasty.)

TO ASSEMBLE: Butter or oil the inside of a 9- to 10-inch fine-holed colander and center a large slice of tomato on the bottom of it. Arrange some of the sliced hearts of palm, hard-cooked eggs, tomatoes and olives in an attractive pattern around it, covering the sides as completely as possible. Spoon in a third of the meat and cornmeal mixture and, with a spoon, smooth it and pack it down gently. Scatter a layer of peas on top and on it arrange half the reserved hearts of palm, eggs, tomatoes and olives. Spoon another third of the cornmeal mixture into the colander, pack

For Brazil's *cuscuz de galinha*, chicken, cornmeal and 24 other ingredients are steamed in a mold, then garnished with orange slices.

it down, and cover with the remaining peas and other ingredients. Spoon in the remaining cornmeal mixture, pack it down lightly, and cover with a large piece of foil. Tuck the ends of the foil under the top rim of the colander to hold it securely in place.

TO COOK AND SERVE: Place the colander in a deep pot, large enough to enclose it completely. Pour enough water into the pot to come within 1½ inches of the bottom of the colander. Bring the water to a boil over high heat, cover the pot tightly, and steam over low heat for 50 minutes, replenishing the water in the pot with boiling water if it boils away.

To unmold and serve the *cuscuz*, place a serving plate upside down over the top of the colander and, grasping both sides firmly, turn the plate and mold over. (If the handles of your colander stand up above the rim, be sure to choose a plate small enough to fit inside them. If the handles project from the sides of the colander, you can use any size serving plate you like.) Rap the plate on a table and the *cuscuz* should slide out of the mold. If any of the vegetable or egg garnish sticks to the colander, pry the pieces loose with the tip of a knife and replace them on the mold. If some of the garnish appears too crushed, substitute fresh slices of egg or vegetable. Serve the *cuscuz* hot, accompanied by sliced oranges.

VIII

Colombia, Venezuela: Spain in the Andes

Only a few years after Columbus discovered America, the Spaniards were exploring the Caribbean coasts of modern Colombia and Venezuela. They did not like what they found, which was mostly tropical jungles that stood tall and forbidding behind nearly every shore. But the explorers were not discouraged. Beyond the hostile coasts they saw great mountains, and they heard or imagined a story about a golden man, El Dorado, an Indian king who covered his body with gold dust and bathed ceremonially in a sacred pool.

In search of El Dorado and his presumed abundance of gold the Spaniards struggled through horrible jungles, climbed mountains as steep as gable roofs, pushed their way up pestilential rivers. They never found much gold, but among the Andean ranges that extend into Colombia and Venezuela they did find temperate, fertile valleys whose climates were as pleasant as any on earth. In these mountain paradises, cut off from the rest of the world, distinctive local cultures slowly established themselves. They were not strongly Indian. The Indians of Colombia and Venezuela, unlike those of Mexico and Peru, were neither numerous nor highly civilized. They were quickly absorbed by the Spanish conquerors whose customs they affected only in minor ways. The new life that developed in the high valleys did not completely conform with traditional Spanish ways either, for it was deeply affected by its isolation. Until well into the 20th Century many of the mountain cities could be reached only on muleback over hair-raising trails, so old-fashioned, local frontier customs persisted stubbornly. Another pervading influence was that of the tropics.

Although the Andean valleys were definitely temperate, some of them even chilly, the hot jungle lowlands lay only a few miles away, and produced tropical crops and fruits in abundance. The easy availability of these hot-country foods had considerable effect on the food and cooking of the mountain people. For instance, a housewife of modern Bogotá, the capital of Colombia, may know a dozen ways to cook green bananas though they are not grown commercially in her high, cool valley. Avocados are another tropical product that has long played a part in traditional Bogotá cooking. As in Mexico, they are added, generally in small slices, to all sorts of soups and stews, which they enrich and improve.

Bogotá and Caracas, the capital of Venezuela, have more than two million people each, and both are strikingly modern in appearance. They are, in fact, almost brand-new. Bogotá was largely destroyed in 1948 by a popular revolt whose unusual savagery earned it a special word in Spanish: *bogotazo;* and the city was rebuilt in contemporary glass and concrete with hardly a trace surviving of its colonial past. Caracas, lavishly enriched by easy money from Venezuela's fabulous oil fields, is even more modern. It looks rather like Miami Beach with a mountain background. Neither city has much in the way of an easily accessible native cuisine. In both cities most of the leading restaurants serve foreign or international food of indifferent quality. A visitor must look elsewhere—in humbler restaurants, private homes or smaller cities—in order to find the authentic native dishes of Colombia and Venezuela.

The staff of life among the poorer people of both countries is the *arepa*, a primitive sort of cornbread of Indian origin. The standard *arepa* is made by simply mixing corn flour, either white or yellow, with a bit of salt and enough water to make a stiff dough. This heavy-as-lead mass is formed into balls or patties nearly an inch thick and toasted on a slightly greased griddle. The result is not good. The inside of the *arepa* is not cooked at all and sometimes hardly warmed. It is nothing but moistened corn flour, and the outside is not cooked enough to acquire any pleasant crusty flavor. Nevertheless, *arepas* are eaten in large quantities by the poor, because they are very cheap, but also by more prosperous people, for whom they have the attraction of tradition.

Few foreigners like this primitive food, which is not nearly as good as the Mexican tortilla, but the humble basic *arepa* can be glorified. In the course of time quite a number of very attractive corn-flour dishes have developed out of it. A good example is the Venezuelan *bollos pelones (Recipe Booklet)*, which is made by stuffing balls of *arepa* dough with a mixture of seasoned ground or finely diced meat. The resulting *bollos* can be simmered in soup or in sauce like dumplings or fried in deep fat until their crusts are golden brown. Cooked either way they are excellent and not at all like their ancestor, the depressing original *arepa*.

Ingenious Latin American cooks do wonders with a combination of corn flour mixed with egg yolks to make it hold together and to give it a lighter texture. They make it into small balls, rods or rings that are fried in deep fat until they are crisp and light all the way through. They add sugar and sometimes spices or cottage cheese, or work the dough around strips of cheese before they fry it. If the frying is done properly, the prod-

144

uct is golden brown, toasty and delicious. Corn flour is little admired in the United States, but Latin American cooks appreciate it and know how to handle it to the best advantage.

Like most Latin Americans, the Colombians and Venezuelans make good use of fresh, immature corn kernels scraped off the cob and puréed (sometimes in a blender). This simple material, mixed with a little salt and perhaps sugar and an egg, but with no wheat flour, makes marvelous deep-fried fritters. To make pancakes with a wonderfully fresh and interesting flavor the corn kernels are first sautéed and added to a mixture of eggs, flour, butter and seasonings *(tortillas de maiz, Recipe Booklet)*. Young corn is also the main ingredient of many fine soups.

The highest and coolest mountain valleys, especially the 8,500-foot one where Bogotá is located, produce good white potatoes, which are native to the Andes farther south, and many traditional Bogotá dishes feature potatoes or use them as important ingredients. *Papas chorreadas (page 152)* are basically boiled potatoes, but the savory sauce of scallions, tomatoes, cheese, coriander and cream poured over them makes a gorgeous dish. For those who like *picante* (hot) foods, a judicious addition of chili makes them even better.

Transportation between the mountain valleys of the Colombian-Venezuelan Andes is fairly easy now, but before the time of airplanes and auto highways the people of each valley were forced to keep to themselves, and in their isolation many of them developed characteristic dishes using locally produced ingredients. For instance, the Cauca Valley and neighboring valleys in the western part of Colombia, where the two important cities of Medellín and Cali are located, have a well-defined local cuisine of which its inhabitants are belligerently proud.

Since the Cauca Valley is lower and warmer than Bogotá, its regional dishes do not feature white potatoes, which do not thrive in semitropical climates. Instead, its soups and stews almost always contain *yuca* (sweet cassava), a firm, white, almost tasteless root that grows luxuriantly and produces an enormous amount of starchy food. Plantains are used a great deal too. At these middle altitudes, where bananas and plantains are likely to be growing in everyone's backyard, the leathery leaves of the plants come into their own as cooking aids. Much use is made of them to wrap various mixtures of corn and other ingredients for boiling or steaming. These savory packets are called *hallacas (page 150)* in Colombia and Venezuela, but they are very similar to the tamales of Mexico and *humitas* of western South America. Invented by the Indians in ancient times, they are now eaten by millions of people with little or no Indian ancestry. If banana plants grew in North American backyards, it is almost certain that North American cooks would also use their leaves in this charming way. Almost any food tastes a great deal better if it comes wrapped individually in green banana leaves.

Colombian and Venezuelan cooks are noted for the many ingenious tricks they use to cope with tough meat. Large parts of Colombia, and of Venezuela too, lie south and east of the Andes in the great valley of the Orinoco River. The level plains *(llanos)* covered with tall grass have long been famous for cattle, but the beef that these hardy animals yield has

A fish stew, *sancocho*, cooks over a beach fire on the island of Margarita off the coast of Venezuela. Into this pot went chunks of red snapper and pumpkin with several native root vegetables, lemons and tomatoes. The *sancocho* was then allowed to simmer for several hours.

often been as tough as leather. Though its quality has recently improved, Colombian cooks still tenderize the tougher cuts by the drastic but effective techniques developed in early times.

When North Americans have been confronted with exceedingly tough beef, they generally have ground it into hamburger, pounded it to a pulp or boiled it to tasteless shreds. Colombian cooks do all these things, but they also cut tough meat into quarter-inch or smaller cubes. These can be sautéed, formed into patties and broiled, or simmered in stews and soups. The cubes are too small to be unpleasantly tough, but the meat in them is still natural meat. It has not lost its character in the meat grinder the way hamburger does.

Another tenderizing method sometimes used is to simmer a chunk of tough meat for two or three hours, then roast it with frequent basting for several hours more. After this treatment, the toughest meat becomes reasonably tender without being made tasteless by too many hours of boiling and without being desiccated by too long a time in the oven.

The beef of grass-fed tropical cattle has little fat, so it is often larded by sticking small knives through it and filling the cuts with strips of bacon or pork fat. The fat permeates the too-lean beef and makes it less dry, more flavorsome and seemingly more tender. Sometimes a tough bottom round roast called a *muchacho* (boy) is filled in this way with large amounts of whole carrots and onions as well as bacon or pork. Cloves of garlic are inserted here and there for extra flavor, and often the roast swells to twice its original size. If the meat is especially tough, it may be simmered for a while before roasting. When a *muchacho* is carved, a slice looks like an open network of meat with the meshes filled with cooked vegetables, and it is surprisingly tender and good. Tough legs of lamb (and mountain-climbing sheep can produce very tough ones) are treated the same way, often with a great deal of garlic, which seems to have a delicious affinity for lamb.

The great bulk of the people of Colombia and Venezuela live in the temperate mountain valleys, but the hot, tropical lowlands along the Caribbean coast have their own peculiar way of life centered around old cities such as Santa Marta and Cartagena in Colombia and Maracaibo in Venezuela. The people are different. Some of them are almost pure African, and they have found it easy to adapt themselves to the intensely tropical climate, which often matches the hottest and wettest parts of Africa.

The coastal rain forests that frightened, but did not daunt, the early Spanish explorers are a sight to see. Some of them have been cleared and replaced by cultivation, but others have never been cut. Sometimes the trees are tall and stately, with hardly a branch below 100 feet, and the crowns are so dense that only a little light struggles through to the ground. Great vines twine and loop through the forests like serpents, and over the ground parade streams of ants carrying fragments of green leaf. The air on the forest floor is windless and still except for the cries of distant birds.

Such tall, uncluttered open forests are rare; much more common are lower-growing jungles where the undergrowth is so dense that nothing bigger than a snake can get through it without a struggle. Some plants have

At an elegant, Spanish-style *finca* near Bogotá, Don Fermín Sanz de Santamaría, scion of a distinguished Colombian family, and his wife and daughters prepare to enjoy a sumptuous buffet. Spread out on the table before them are dishes frequently served on festive occasions: a roast suckling pig, a soup called *ajiaco bogotano (page 152)*, stuffed avocados, sautéed plantains *(foreground)* and a refreshing fruit drink *(sorbete de curuba)* made from a fruit native to Latin America.

146

poisonous, stinging leaves, and the trunks of slender palms bristle with needle-pointed thorns many inches long.

In such jungles live people, usually strongly Indian or African, who have adapted their lives to their stern necessities. They clear small fields to plant *yuca,* plantains, corn and beans. For meat they eat anything they can catch, including monkeys, tapirs and all sorts of birds except parrots, which are considered too tough. A favorite dish with the jungle people, and with many other rural Colombians and Venezuelans, is ants. At certain times of year, March and April in some places, the anthills that riddle the soil send out their winged males and females to found new colonies. These hopeful, innocent insects, which are called *culonas* (big bottoms), are easily caught in quantity as they emerge. They are nutritious and are considered a delicacy, though they taste mostly of the fat or oil in which they are fried.

The better-off people of lowland Colombia and Venezuela do not live, of course, on monkeys and ants, but their cooking does take advantage, as it should, of tropical opportunities. The city markets sell strange meat killed in the jungle. Peccary meat is like lean and stringy pork, but venison from the small, delicate tropical deer is excellent. Turtles and strange-looking fish caught in the slow, warm rivers make delicious eating, and so does the curassow, a large, black, noisy bird considered the finest game bird of South America. It is named for, and pronounced like, Curaçao, the Dutch island 40 miles north of Venezuela. When anyone who cares about unusual food finds himself in a tropical, jungle-surrounded city, he should make an effort to sample the local game.

The tropical lowlands people are, of course, heavy eaters of cooked bananas and plantains in all their innumerable forms. These are boiled, grilled, fried, put into stews and soups. Sometimes they have a banana flavor; often they do not. A very good Venezuelan tidbit for an hors d'oeuvre is *tostones,* slices of plantain that are fried, pounded thin, and fried again until they are crisp. Ripe plantains are also made into cakes known as *tortas de plátano, (page 154).* which are served with meat dishes *(page 154).* They are slightly sweet and spiced with cinnamon and serve as an excellent change from potatoes.

The greatest pride and joy of tropical lowland cooking is the coconut. The tall coco palms stand in graceful ranks along the shores and riverbanks, and their nuts are used in innumerable ways. Grated coconut or coconut milk is added to stewed meats, giving the sauce a surprising but attractive flavor *(page 138).* Coconut oil is used for frying, and coconuts are made into soup and ice cream, both of them excellent.

The best use of coconut is in sweet dishes, for coconut and sugar have a well-known affinity. In any place where coconuts are in good supply, they show up in many kinds of candies, puddings, cakes and desserts. Grated coconut flavors fritters that are served with heavy syrup; fresh coconut cream poured over the top can make the dullest cake or pastry a delight. A famous Venezuelan dessert, *bien me sabe de coco (Recipe Booklet),* is cake that has been moistened with muscatel wine and topped with coconut cream. In this dish and many others, the taste of coconut is one of the pleasantest memories of tropical eating.

A fresh *hallaca*, made of corn dough with chicken, beef and pork stuffing, rests on a banana leaf in which it cooked.

Hallacas Centrales
STEAMED BANANA LEAVES WITH CHICKEN AND MEAT FILLING

To make about 25

THE DOUGH

3 cups dried white corn and 6 cups of cold water, or substitute three 1-pound-13-ounce cans of hominy
½ cup lard
1 teaspoon annatto *(achiote)* seeds
1 teaspoon salt

THE FILLING

A 1½- to 2-pound chicken, cut into quarters
2 cups cold water
½ cup olive oil
1 pound boneless loin of pork, cut into ⅓-inch cubes
1 pound beef chuck, cut into ⅓-inch cubes
1¼ cups finely chopped green peppers
1¼ cups finely chopped onions
1 tablespoon finely chopped garlic
4 medium tomatoes, peeled, seeded and coarsely chopped *(see salsa cruda, page 44)*, or substitute 1⅓ cups chopped, drained, canned Italian plum tomatoes
6 tablespoons capers, drained and rinsed in cold water
⅓ cup sugar
1 tablespoon ground cumin seeds
1 tablespoon salt
1½ teaspoons freshly ground black pepper
½ cup finely chopped fresh parsley

¼ pound fresh pork fat, cut into ¼-inch dice
¾ cup seedless raisins
25 pimiento-stuffed olives
3 whole banana leaves plus 25 ten-inch squares of white parchment paper, or substitute 50 ten-inch squares of white parchment paper

THE DOUGH: If you are using dried corn, combine it with the water in a 4-quart saucepan and bring to a boil over high heat. Reduce the heat to moderate and cook, uncovered, stirring frequently, for 20 minutes. Drain off any excess water. Put the corn through the finest blade of a meat grinder and then put it through a food mill or a coarse sieve. If you are using hominy, drain it well and put it through a food mill. Melt ¼ cup of lard over moderate heat in a small skillet, add the annatto seeds and cook for 3 minutes. Strain the lard through a sieve and discard the seeds. With a spoon or your fingers, combine the remaining ¼ cup of lard with the corn. Add the strained lard and 1 teaspoon salt, and knead the dough for 10 minutes, or until it is very smooth.

THE FILLING: In a 4-quart saucepan, combine the chicken and 2 cups of water, and bring to a boil over high heat. Reduce the heat to low, cover and cook for 30 minutes, or until the chicken is tender but not falling apart. Transfer the chicken to a plate and set the stock aside for another use. Remove the skin from the chicken with a small knife or your fingers. Cut or pull the meat away from the bones. Discard bones, and cut the meat into strips ⅛ inch wide and 1 to 1½ inches long.

In a heavy 12-inch skillet, heat the oil over high heat until a light haze forms above it. Add the pork and beef cubes, and cook, stirring frequently, until the meat is lightly browned on all sides. Transfer the meat to a plate. Reduce the heat to moderate, and add the green peppers, onions and garlic to the oil remaining in the pan. Cook, stirring frequently, for 5 minutes, or until the vegetables are soft but not brown. Add the tomatoes and cook for 15 minutes until the tomato juices evaporate and the sauce becomes a thick purée. Return the meat to the pan, add the capers, sugar, cumin, 1 tablespoon salt and black pepper, and reduce the heat to low. Simmer, uncovered, stirring occasionally, for 30 minutes. Stir in the chicken strips and parsley, and set the pan aside off the heat.

In a small skillet, cook the pork fat over moderate heat, stirring frequently, until it has rendered most of its fat. Do not let the pork brown. Using a fine sieve, drain the bits of pork fat and set them aside.

TO ASSEMBLE: Shape 3 tablespoons of the dough into a ball and place it in the center of a banana-leaf square or piece of parchment paper. With the fingers press the dough into a rectangle about 6 inches wide and 7 inches long diagonally on the leaf as shown in the pictures opposite. Place 3 tablespoons of meat filling on the center of the dough and dot it with 2 or 3 pieces of pork fat, 4 or 5 raisins and 1 olive. Construct the *hallaca* following the directions on the opposite page. Both the banana-leaf and paper-covered *hallacas* can be wrapped for the second time in paper.

TO COOK: When all the *hallacas* are filled, wrapped and tied, place them seam side down in several layers in a large colander. Place the colander in a deep pot and pour enough water into the pot to come to just below the bottom of the colander. Bring the water to a boil over high heat, cover the pot and reduce the heat to low. Steam the *hallacas* for 1

1 To assemble a *hallaca*, smooth dough onto a banana-leaf square.

2 Spread filling in the center of the flattened dough and add the garnish.

3 Fold the sides of the leaf (against the grain) over the filling.

4 Bring the ends of the leaf up over the filling on the seam side.

5 Lap the two ends over each other to enclose the filling securely.

6 Press the seams closed gently, trying not to tear the banana leaf.

7 Center the *hallaca* on a paper square; bring two sides of paper up together.

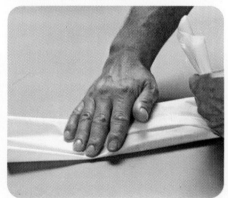

8 Make a ½-inch fold along the edge and fold again over the *hallaca*.

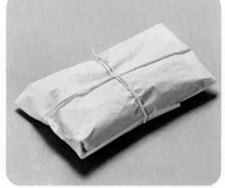

9 Close the ends over the seam side and tie snugly with kitchen cord.

hour, keeping the water at a slow boil and replenishing it with additional boiling water as it cooks away. With kitchen tongs, transfer the *hallacas* to a heated platter. They may be served at once or refrigerated overnight with no loss of flavor. Reheat by steaming them again for 30 minutes.

TO PREPARE THE BANANA LEAVES: If you are using banana leaves, cut away and discard the center ribs of the leaves with scissors, and carefully tear the leaves into 10-inch squares, following the veins of the leaf. (The leaf shreds easily if pulled against the vein.) Wash the squares in cold water, rubbing them with a cloth or sponge in the direction of the vein pattern. Dry the pieces gently with paper towels.

151

To serve 8

2 tablespoons butter

4 scallions, including 2 inches of
    green top, cut into 1-inch lengths

½ cup finely chopped onions

5 tomatoes, peeled, seeded and
    coarsely chopped (*see salsa cruda,
    page 44*), or 1⅔ cups chopped,
    drained, canned Italian plum
    tomatoes

½ cup heavy cream

1 teaspoon finely chopped fresh
    coriander (*cilantro*)

¼ teaspoon dried oregano

Pinch of ground cumin seeds

½ teaspoon salt

Freshly ground black pepper

1 cup freshly grated fresh *mozzarella*
    or Münster cheese

8 large potatoes, peeled and boiled

To serve 6

A 3- to 3½-pound chicken, cut into
    6 to 8 serving pieces

A 1-pound beef shinbone, sawed into
    2-inch pieces

2 quarts cold water

1 large onion, peeled

1 small bay leaf

⅛ teaspoon ground cumin seeds

⅛ teaspoon dried thyme

1 tablespoon salt

¼ teaspoon white pepper

4 medium boiling potatoes, peeled
    and sliced ¼ inch thick

3 ears corn, cut into 2-inch rounds

1 cup plus 2 tablespoons heavy cream

2 tablespoons capers, drained and
    rinsed in cold water

1 avocado, peeled, pitted and thinly
    sliced (*see guacamole, page 45*)

To serve 4

A 2-pound flank steak, trimmed of
    all fat

1½ teaspoons salt

Freshly ground black pepper

3 tablespoons olive oil

1 cup coarsely chopped onions

½ cup finely diced celery

½ teaspoon finely chopped garlic

5 cups water

1 teaspoon ground cumin seeds

Papas Chorreadas
POTATOES WITH SPICED CHEESE, TOMATO AND ONION SAUCE

In a heavy 8- to 10-inch skillet, heat the butter over moderate heat. When the foam subsides, add the scallions and onions, and cook them, stirring frequently, for 5 minutes, or until the onions are soft and transparent but not brown. Add the tomatoes and cook, stirring, for 5 minutes. Add the cream, coriander, oregano, cumin, salt and a few grindings of pepper, and, stirring constantly, drop in the cheese. Cook, stirring, until the cheese melts. Traditionally, *chorreada* sauce is served over boiled potatoes (or cooked string beans) and often accompanies *sobrebarriga (below)*.

Ajiaco Bogotano
CREAMED CHICKEN AND POTATO SOUP WITH AVOCADO AND CAPERS

In a heavy 5-quart casserole, combine the chicken, shinbone and water. The water should cover the chicken by about an inch; if necessary add more water. Bring to a boil over high heat, skimming off the scum that rises to the surface. Add the onion, bay leaf, cumin, thyme, salt and pepper. Reduce the heat to low, cover and cook for 30 minutes, or until the chicken is tender. Transfer the chicken to a platter. Pick out and discard the shinbones and onion, strain the stock through a fine sieve and return it to the casserole. Remove the skin from the chicken with a small knife or your fingers. Cut or pull the meat away from the bones; discard the skin and bones. Cut the chicken meat into strips ¼ inch wide and 1 to 1½ inches long. Return the stock in the casserole to a boil over moderate heat, and drop in the potatoes. Cover and cook for 30 minutes, or until the potatoes are soft, then mash them against the sides of the pan with a spoon until the soup is thick and fairly smooth. Add the corn and chicken, and simmer, uncovered, for 5 to 10 minutes, depending on the tenderness of the corn. To serve, pour 3 tablespoons of cream and 1 teaspoon of capers into each of 6 deep soup bowls. Ladle the soup into the bowls and float the sliced avocado on top.

Sobrebarriga
ROLLED FLANK STEAK WITH ONIONS AND CUMIN SEEDS

Preheat the oven to 350°. Season both sides of the steak with 1 teaspoon of the salt and a few grindings of pepper. Then roll the steak with the grain in jelly-roll fashion, and tie it at both ends and in the middle with kitchen cord. In a heavy 3- to 4-quart flameproof casserole, heat 2 tablespoons of the oil over high heat until a light haze forms above it. Add the rolled steak and brown it on all sides. Regulate the heat so that the steak browns quickly without burning. Transfer the steak to a plate and, to the fat remaining in the casserole, add ½ cup of the onions, the celery and garlic. Cook over moderate heat, stirring frequently, for 5 minutes, or until the vegetables are soft but not brown. Return the steak and any juice on the plate to the casserole, add the water and bring to a boil over high heat. Cover the casserole, place it in the oven and braise the steak 2 hours, or until it shows no resistance when pierced with the tip of a knife. Remove from the oven and increase the heat to 400°.

In a 6- to 8-inch skillet, heat the remaining tablespoon of oil over moderate heat and add the remaining ½ cup of onions. Stir in the cumin and ½ teaspoon of salt and cook for 3 minutes. Spread the onions on top of the steak. Return the casserole to the oven and bake, uncovered, for 15 minutes, or until the onions are lightly browned. Slice the steak into ¼-inch rounds and arrange them attractively on a heated platter. Pour the pan juices over them and serve immediately. The steak is often accompanied by *papas chorreadas (opposite)*.

Pabellon Criollo
STEAK IN TOMATO SAUCE WITH BLACK BEANS, RICE AND PLANTAINS

To serve 4 to 6

THE BLACK BEANS: Combine the black beans and 5 cups of cold water in a heavy 4- to 5-quart flameproof casserole. Bring to a boil over high heat, reduce the heat to low and simmer, uncovered, for 2 hours. In a heavy 8- to 10-inch skillet, heat 2 tablespoons of oil over moderate heat. Add ½ cup of chopped green pepper, 2 tablespoons of onions, ½ teaspoon of garlic and 1 teaspoon of salt. Cook for 3 minutes, stirring constantly, and then, with a rubber spatula, scrape the mixture into the simmering beans. Add the coriander and cook for 15 minutes, or until the beans are tender. Discard the coriander. Cover the casserole and put it aside.

THE STEAK AND SAUCE: Heat the broiler to its highest point and broil the steak 4 inches below the heat for about 5 minutes on each side. Watch for any sign of burning and regulate the heat accordingly. When finished, the steak should be medium rare. With a knife or your fingers, cut or pull the meat into pieces ¼ inch wide and ½ inch long. In a heavy 12-inch skillet, heat ⅓ cup of oil over moderate heat. Add 1 cup of onions and 1 teaspoon of garlic and cook about 5 minutes, stirring occasionally. When the onions are soft and transparent but not brown, add the tomatoes, cumin and 1 teaspoon salt. Reduce the heat to low and cook, uncovered, for 30 minutes, stirring frequently, until the tomato juices evaporate and the sauce becomes a thick purée. Drop in the strips of beef, mix them well with the sauce, cover the skillet and put it aside.

THE RICE: Preheat the oven to 250°. In a heavy 3- to 4-quart casserole, heat ¼ cup of oil over moderate heat until a light haze forms above it. Add the onion and pepper halves, and cook them for 5 minutes, turning them frequently, until they color lightly. Add the rice, and stir constantly for 2 or 3 minutes to coat the rice with oil. Do not let the rice burn. Pour 4 cups of boiling water over the rice, add the salt, and bring to a boil. Stir once or twice, then cover the pan and reduce the heat to low. Simmer undisturbed for 20 minutes, or until the rice is tender and has absorbed all the liquid. Remove the cover and discard the onion and pepper. Drape the casserole with a towel and keep the rice warm in the oven.

THE PLANTAINS: Heat ½ cup of oil in a heavy 10- to 12-inch skillet over moderate heat. Drop in the plantain pieces and cook them for 2 or 3 minutes on each side until they are tender and golden brown.

TO ASSEMBLE: Return the beans and beef to low heat and cook only long enough to heat them through. Spoon the beef into the center of a large heated platter. Surround it with alternating mounds of rice and black beans. Decorate the platter with plantain slices and serve at once.

THE BLACK BEANS
1½ cups dried black beans,
  thoroughly rinsed in cold water
5 cups cold water
2 tablespoons olive oil
½ cup finely chopped green pepper
2 tablespoons finely chopped onions
½ teaspoon finely chopped garlic
1 teaspoon salt
3 fresh coriander sprigs (*cilantro*)

THE STEAK AND SAUCE
2 pounds lean top sirloin of beef or
  boneless sirloin steak, cut ½ inch
  thick
⅓ cup olive oil
1 cup coarsely chopped onions
1 teaspoon finely chopped garlic
6 medium tomatoes, peeled, seeded
  and coarsely chopped (*see salsa
  cruda, page 44*), or substitute 2 cups
  chopped, drained, canned Italian
  plum tomatoes
½ teaspoon ground cumin seeds
1 teaspoon salt

THE RICE
¼ cup olive oil
½ large peeled onion
½ large green pepper, seeded,
  deribbed and left in 1 piece
2 cups raw long-grain rice
4 cups boiling water
2 teaspoons salt

THE PLANTAINS
½ cup flavorless vegetable oil
2 large ripe plantains, peeled, each
  cut crosswise in half and lengthwise
  into 6 or 8 slices

A Venezuelan larded pot roast is accompanied by a ripe plantain cake (*center*), a companion that is not as unlikely as it seems. The tangy cheese in the cake gives it a flavor that makes it an excellent complement to this highly seasoned meat dish.

To serve 4

7 tablespoons butter
2 very ripe plantains, peeled, cut in
    half crosswise and cut lengthwise
    into ¼-inch slices
2 cups grated *queso blanco,* or
    substitute 2 cups grated Münster
    cheese
3 tablespoons sugar
1 teaspoon ground cinnamon
3 egg whites
3 egg yolks
1 tablespoon flour or dried bread
    crumbs

Torta de Plátano Maduro

RIPE PLANTAIN CAKE

In a heavy 8- to 10-inch skillet, melt 3 tablespoons of the butter over moderate heat. When the foam subsides, drop in the sliced plantains and cook, turning frequently, until the slices are golden brown on both sides. Transfer the plantains to a double thickness of paper towels to drain. In a small bowl, mix the grated cheese, sugar and cinnamon and set aside.

In a large bowl, beat the egg whites with a whisk or a rotary or electric beater until they are stiff enough to form unwavering peaks on the beater. In a separate bowl, beat the egg yolks until they are thick and lemon colored, then with a spatula fold the whites into the yolks.

Preheat the oven to 350°. Grease the bottom and sides of a deep

154

1-quart baking dish or mold, then sprinkle in 1 tablespoon of flour or bread crumbs, tipping the dish to spread the flour or crumbs as evenly as possible. Turn the dish over and rap it sharply to remove any excess.

Ladle about a quarter of the egg mixture into the dish, and spread it with the back of a spoon. Cover with a layer of plantains—using about one third of the slices. Sprinkle with ⅔ cup of the cheese mixture and dot with 1 tablespoon of butter. Repeat the layers two more times, ending with the egg mixture. Dot with the last tablespoon of butter and place in the middle of the oven. Bake for 35 minutes. Serve hot directly from the baking dish, or let the cake cool for 5 minutes or so and unmold it onto a platter in the following fashion: Run a knife around the edge of the dish and dip the bottom in hot water for a few seconds. Cover the dish with an inverted platter and, grasping dish and platter together, turn them over. Hot or cold, this is a traditional accompaniment to meat dishes.

Asado Antiguo a la Venezolana Mechado
LARDED BEEF POT ROAST WITH CAPERS

To serve 8 to 10

Lard the beef in the following fashion: Chill the pork strips in the freezer for 10 minutes or so to stiffen them. First make a hole by inserting the point of the larding needle 2 inches into one short end of the meat; pull the needle back an inch or so and lay a pork strip in its groove. Then gradually force the needle through the length of the beef roast until the pork strip emerges from the other end. Pressing the end of the strip where it entered the meat, carefully pull out the needle, leaving the pork in the meat. Repeat with the rest of the pork strips, spacing them at about 2-inch intervals. Trim off the protruding ends of the larding strips. Then, with the tip of a small skewer or knife, push one caper at a time into the beef around the strips of pork at both ends.

Combine the vinegar, grated onion, garlic, salt and pepper, and press and rub the mixture firmly into the outside surfaces of the beef. Cover with foil, and let it stand at room temperature for at least 6 hours—or overnight in the refrigerator. When you are ready to cook the meat, heat the olive oil over high heat in a heavy 4- to 6-quart casserole until a light haze forms above it. Sprinkle the meat evenly with the *panela* or brown sugar and press the sugar into the meat with the fingers. Place the meat in the pot. Regulate the heat so that the meat colors quickly and evenly without burning, turning it every few minutes to brown it on all sides. When the meat is a deep-mahogany color, pour the water into the pan and bring it to a boil, scraping up any brown sediment clinging to the bottom and sides of the pan. Cover the casserole tightly, reduce the heat to its lowest point and simmer the meat for about 2 hours, or until it shows no resistance when pierced with the tip of a small, sharp knife.

To serve, remove the meat from the casserole and carve it against the grain into neat ¼-inch slices, each of which should be patterned with tiny bits of larding pork. Arrange the slices on a heated platter and cover it with foil to keep the meat warm. Bring the cooking liquid in the casserole to a vigorous boil and boil it rapidly, uncovered, until it thickens to the desired consistency. Taste the sauce for seasoning and either pour it over the sliced meat or serve it separately.

6 to 8 strips larding pork, cut ⅛ inch wide and 2 inches longer than length of the meat

4 pounds bottom round of beef, in one piece

3 tablespoons capers, drained and rinsed

2 tablespoons white distilled vinegar

¼ cup finely grated onions

½ teaspoon finely chopped garlic

1 teaspoon salt

¼ teaspoon freshly ground black pepper

¼ cup olive oil

1 tablespoon coarsely grated *panela,* or substitute 1 tablespoon dark brown sugar

2 cups water

IX

Coffee and Stronger Drink

Latin America's celebrated beverage, coffee, is enjoyed in steaming cupfuls over large parts of the globe. Every year Latin America exports more than four billion pounds of coffee, almost half of the world's total production.

Latin America is the land of coffee. Except in the southernmost countries, coffee is served at every meal and often between meals too. The fragrance of brewing coffee—sometimes of roasting coffee beans—drifts from kitchens, offices, stores and country farmhouses. The poor peasant has his coffee, which he may have grown and processed himself, and the rich man in the capital city often has a favorite brand that comes from a particular plantation. This source will almost always be in his own country, for coffee patriotism is a strong emotion. A Colombian would not dream of drinking or even saying a good word about Brazilian coffee, and if he is a native of a coffee-producing part of Colombia he is apt to look down on all coffee that does not come from his own immediate area, even that grown in other regions of his own country.

Latin America accounts for over half of the world's coffee crop, but the small, elegant trees that produce this beverage came originally from Africa. Coffee was taken to Arabia and became the "wine of Islam," filling the need for a stimulant among Muslims, whose religion forbade alcoholic drinks. It reached Europe in the early 1600s but not until the 1720s was the first coffee tree planted in Latin America. According to one story, a young French naval officer, Gabriel Mathieu de Clieu, brought a single seedling to the island of Martinique, keeping it alive with part of his own meager water ration. This tree was the ancestor of most of the billions of coffee trees now growing in Latin America.

Coffee is a beautiful crop. The trees are neat and graceful, with dark-green glossy leaves. If left to themselves they grow about 20 feet tall, but they are usually kept pruned below 10 feet or so to make picking easier. In southern Brazil they are planted in long, straight rows in great open orchards, but in Colombia and Central America the trees generally grow on cool mountain slopes among taller trees that shield them from the glare of the tropical sun. These plantations have a pleasantly informal look. Mountain streams rush through them and footpaths wind among the decorative little trees.

Once, twice or even three times per year, according to climate, coffee trees cover themselves with fragile, white flowers with a jasminelike scent. A plantation at the height of bloom perfumes the air for several miles downwind. About two months after the petals fall, berries appear and the fruits grow slowly for six to seven months, when they turn from green to dark red and look like smallish cherries. New flowers keep opening, so that a single branch of a coffee tree often shows red "cherries," green ones and flowers simultaneously.

In Brazil and some other countries the ripe cherries are allowed to dry on the trees and are then stripped off the branches along with many immature ones, but for the best grades of coffee the berries must be picked laboriously one by one as soon as they turn red. Beneath the skin of the berry is a thin layer of sweet yellow pulp usually surrounding two large beans that are flattened where they face each other. Each bean is protected by a tough outer hull and several inner skins. A few of the cherries contain single rounded beans that are called "male." *Café macho* is considered superior, probably because any kind of maleness *(machismo)* has great prestige in Latin America, and connoisseurs pay a premium price for male beans that have been separated by hand or by a special machine from the commoner female ones. Most people in the coffee business think there is no difference.

The finest coffee is prepared for market by an elaborate "wet" process. The ripe cherries are washed first, then they are put through a machine that rubs off the outer skin and most of the pulp. Afterward they are soaked in tanks where fermentation removes the rest of the pulp and loosens the thin inner skins that surround the beans. A final washing occurs before the beans are dried, sometimes in drying machines—which takes approximately a little over a day—sometimes in the sun on concrete drying floors, a process that takes four to eight days. Finally they go through another machine that removes the inner skins of the beans and leaves them olive green.

Before the green beans can acquire the taste and fragrance of coffee, they must be roasted. This is generally done in large factories, but coffeegrowers, who are all coffee connoisseurs, usually scorn such mechanization. Even small growers who have only a few thousand trees prefer to process their own beans and roast them before each meal, usually in a clay or iron frying pan heated cautiously over a small pile of glowing charcoal. The roasting must not be hurried, and the beans must be stirred constantly to give them all the same brownness. They lose about one sixth of their weight during the roasting, swell up considerably and give off a marvelous perfume. Coffee made from fresh-roasted beans that have hardly had time to cool off is a memorable taste experience, and it is even better when the grower tells you proudly that his beans came from trees on a specially favored mountain slope that produces the very best coffee in the entire world.

Most coffee sold in coffee-producing countries is of much lower quality than the pampered beans that growers save for their friends. By government decree the best coffee is reserved for export, leaving only low-quality beans for domestic consumption. Venezuela, for instance, produces a famous coffee whose beans are pale blue, the prized *café azul de Caracas*. But the Venezuelan public drinks *café nacional*, a blend of lower grades, and never sees a bean of delectable blue coffee.

Many old-fashioned Latin Americans who are not growers roast their coffee daily, a process that requires a good deal of skill and patience, and some of them still pound the beans to powder in a wooden mortar. All the modern gadgets for brewing coffee are available, but the traditional method, which seems to produce the best results, is to put powdered coffee in a conical cloth bag and pour boiling water through it. The brew is always stronger than normal American coffee, which Latin Americans scorn as little better than dishwater. The standard recipe is one tablespoon of powdered coffee to each *cafecito* (demitasse). It is usually drunk black, sometimes with as much sugar as coffee, and is called *tinto*, a word that means red wine in the Spanish of Spain but which in this case probably derives from *tinta*, the word for ink.

A confirmed coffee drinker in Colombia or Brazil has a cup of black coffee as soon as he gets out of bed and keeps drinking it all day long—at meals, during working hours, at coffee shops and coffee stands in the streets. There are no coffee breaks in Latin American offices; in order to satisfy the customers, the halts would take up nearly all the working time. Instead, a woman circulates among the desks dispensing *tintos*. Twenty cups a day is considered moderate consumption.

For breakfast, coffee is generally served as *café con leche*, that is, as hot milk flavored with sugar and coffee. In most countries the milk is put in the cup first, then the sugar. Finally very strong coffee is added until the color is dark enough. In Peru, coffee appears on the table as an ink-black essence in a glass cruet. A spoonful or so of this powerful stuff is enough to make *café con leche* out of a cup of warm milk. For people who want black coffee of reasonable strength, hot water is provided to dilute the strong coffee essence.

In most coffeegrowing countries instant coffee is despised as flavorless, but its use is growing in a shamefaced way. In Chile, which grows no coffee, the instant variety is almost the only coffee available, and very bad it is, and usually very weak. If the customer complains and demands "coffee coffee," he merely gets stronger instant coffee. In Peru, instant coffee is considered semirespectable, but one widely sold brand, Nescafé, is nicknamed *No es café*, which means "It is not coffee."

Many countries have their special ways of preparing and drinking coffee. In Mexico and Argentina, for instance, the green beans are often roasted with sugar, which turns to caramel and covers them with a dark, shiny coating. The resulting brew is very dark and tastes as much of caramel as of coffee, but when added to hot milk it makes a pleasant drink. Another

Continued on page 162

159

Tender Care for Coffee on a Finca in Colombia

Few crops require such tender care as coffee. On the 15-acre *finca* of José Gonzalez in the Colombian Andes, for example, coffee is produced almost entirely by hand. Gonzalez and his helpers plant the seeds individually in sandy soil. When the seedlings *(below)* are 40 to 50 days old, they are transplanted into earth-filled plastic bags *(right)*. Each plant must be watered daily, dosed with fertilizer and fungicides, and weeded with meticulous care. After six months, the trees are planted in groves *(opposite, top)*, where they are interspersed with taller shade trees. Even then they must be weeded, sprayed, fertilized and pruned for about four years before the berries can be harvested. And when the berries finally are picked *(opposite, bottom left)* they must be gathered by hand to make sure that few green ones slip through *(opposite, bottom right)*.

160

Mexican trick is to boil coffee with cinnamon. The product as generally made is odd and not very good, but if only a very faint hint of cinnamon is added to well-prepared coffee, the drink has a flavor that is both unusual and agreeable. Some Latin Americans insist on brown sugar to sweeten their coffee. This is worth trying too.

Nearly all coffee sold in the United States is "blended," which means that the packager has used as much cheap Brazilian coffee as he thinks he can get away with and as little as possible of the costly shade-grown beans from Colombia and Central America. The more expensive brands use more of this extra-fragrant coffee, but since most brands are sold in large quantities and must be uniform, the blender is usually forced to mix coffee of many types in small amounts. Accustomed to this sameness, the buyers of blended coffee have no idea how widely coffee can vary and how delicious it can be. It is worthwhile to visit a dealer in unblended coffee and buy small bags of beans that come from a high, cool mountain in Colombia or a parklike valley in Costa Rica or a peasant's back yard in Haiti. They will all be different in flavor, and some of them should prove much more interesting than the monotonous brews produced by commercial blending.

While coffee is its most famous drink, Latin America has also developed a wide variety of alcoholic beverages. They range from excellent to dreadful. The good ones are well worth trying, while most of the bad ones can easily be avoided by the simple expedient of drinking nothing that costs less than 10 cents a portion.

The civilized Indians of Mexico and the Andes did not contribute appreciably to the world's assortment of good alcoholic drinks. Neither of the indigenous Indian drinks—the *pulque* of Mexico (the fermented sap of the *maguey*, or century plant) and the *chicha* of South America (a sour, cloudy corn beer)—has much to recommend it. But when the Spaniards arrived bringing wine grapes and the technique of distillation, the situation changed for the better. Latin America now has a long list of native drinks, some of which are favored all over the world.

The drink best known in the outside world is probably tequila, which is made in Mexico out of the starchy root stock of a relative of the *maguey* plant called the *Agave azul tequilana*. The roots are ground up, mixed with water, fermented and distilled twice. Tequila (the name comes from the town in Jalisco, a state in western Mexico, where the beverage is made) is normally colorless, but some varieties are aged in a way that gives them a light straw color. Tourists who visit Mexico and drink too much tequila, which is very cheap, like to think it has the kick of a pile driver, but actually it is no stronger than whiskey. It has a pleasant flavor all its own, not at all like the rotten-apple taste of *pulque*, and many Americans living in Mexico come to prefer it to whiskey. Another distilled drink, mescal, is made out of a similar plant, and its taste is not very different from that of tequila.

Both tequila and mescal are drunk straight, but they are at their best in a cocktail called the Margarita *(page 172),* which is made with lime juice, sugar and a dash of Cointreau or Triple Sec. Usually the rim of the glass is moistened and pressed lightly into a dish of coarse salt so a frosting of

salt clings to it. Those who do not like salt can brush it off, but for the true aficionado it adds something extra.

Mexicans believe tequila has an affinity for salt. Traditionally it is served in a small, slim glass beside a saucer with a piece of lime and a little salt. The idea is to combine contrasting flavors at the same instant. According to one system, the drinker puts a pinch of salt on the back of his left hand, preferably in the hollow between the two tendons that run to the thumb. He tosses the salt into his mouth, and with his right hand drinks the tequila, bottoms up. Then he quickly sets down the glass, picks up the lime and sucks it. The whole sequence should take less than two seconds, but to learn the trick requires a lot of tequila drinking.

Tequila is sometimes served in a much larger glass along with another glass of cloudy pink liquid called *caldo de camarón* that is made of dried shrimp, garlic, onions, chili and, of all things, carrots. The drinker takes a large swallow of tequila; then to cool its alcoholic burn, he takes a sip of *caldo de camarón*. Its chili burn is worse, so he cools his throat with tequila. Then he cools the tequila with *caldo de camarón*, and so on, until the tequila runs out. A similar effect is achieved by substituting *sangrita*—called "little blood" for its color—a mixture of tomato, orange and lime juices, mixed with onion, salt, pepper and chili for the *caldo de camarón*.

Each coffee berry contains a pair of beans or seeds wrapped in four protective layers. After the ripe berries have been picked and washed, José Gonzalez cranks them through a husker *(above)* to remove the first of these protective coverings. Then the berries must be soaked in water—in a process called "fermentation"—to rid them of a sticky, pulpy coating. After another washing, they are spread out to dry, and then they are fed into a huller, which breaks two more layers and exposes the two beans.

This mode of drinking is not recommended for weaklings, and inexperienced Americans are advised to stick to Margaritas, which are very palatable and less explosive.

For most modern Mexicans the commonest alcoholic drink is the local beer *(cerveza* in Spanish), which is uncommonly good, so good that some of the best brews are exported extensively to the United States. Mexican beer, however, has little that is truly Mexican about it. Most breweries are run by Germans or follow German traditions, as they do in the United States. This is also true in the rest of Latin America, where beer is drunk in vast quantities. It may be made from native grains, but it is as German as if it were brewed in Munich.

In many parts of Latin America the "wine of the country" is rum, which was invented in the Caribbean region and is made out of sugar cane. Some rums are made from fresh cane juice that is fermented and distilled. Other kinds are made from the sweet scum of the sugar-boiling vats or from diluted molasses. The cheapest cane spirit is plain alcohol, which is called *aguardiente* in most places. It is sometimes diluted, but is sometimes so strong that it can be burned in an automobile engine instead of gasoline. The best kinds of drinking rum are distilled, aged, flavored and colored by traditional methods as complicated as those that the Scots apply to their whisky.

These methods produce an extraordinary variety of rums, many of which are unfamiliar to Americans. The common strong drink of Brazil, for instance, is colorless *cachaça*. It is made from sugar cane, but the Brazilians do not consider it rum. They like to have its name translated as "sugar brandy," and indeed it tastes more like brandy than rum. In genteel surroundings it is generally mixed and shaken with lemon or lime juice and sugar—and called *batida (Recipe Booklet)*—but on more robust occasions *cachaça* is tossed off straight. Other rums are smooth, dark and "rummy," with a strong molasses flavor. Still others have light and attractive flavors that do not suggest molasses. In all of the sugar-raising countries the best local rums are well worth trying. They are generally so inexpensive that half a dozen of them can be sampled for the price of one small glass of imported whiskey.

Most of the bottled soft drinks of Latin America are much too sweet and have an unpleasant chemical taste to outsiders, but Brazil's *guaraná* is an exception. It contains a small amount of caffeine and looks rather like ginger ale, but tastes like some unusually tangy and interesting fruit. There is no fruit in it, however; it is based on the seeds of a jungle plant. *Guaraná* can be bought anywhere in Brazil, and many a thirsty man who has absorbed all the beer and sickish-sweet cola drink that he can stand has thanked heaven for it. To my palate, no commercial soft drink in the United States is nearly as good.

Coffee is the favorite hot drink of nearly all Latin America, but in Uruguay, Paraguay, Argentina, parts of Chile and Brazil it has a native rival in *yerba maté*, made from the dried leaves of a shrub belonging to the holly family that grows wild on the upper reaches of the Paraguay River. Drunk hot or cold, it is rather like tea. It contains stimulating caffeine as tea and coffee do, but the most remarkable thing about it is the way it is

Skillfully gulping a fountain of local wine, an exuberant gaucho celebrates the grape harvest in Mendoza, Argentina.

A gaucho sips the Argentine beverage *maté* through a metal tube *(bombilla)* from a gourd. The caffein-laden, tealike drink is made by steeping in boiling water the dried leaves of the South American holly tree.

drunk. The *yerba*, or dried leaves, are put in a gourd about as big as an orange, and the gourd is filled with boiling water. When it has steeped for a while, the liquid is sucked out with a *bombilla*, a wooden or metal tube with a perforated spoonlike strainer at the lower end. One charge of *yerba* will retain its strength for several refills of hot water. Sugar and even cream are sometimes added, but not by real connoisseurs. Among the fashionable folk of the large cities *maté* is going out of style, but it is still popular with most of the people, especially in country districts. A good part of its charm comes from the sociable tradition of passing a freshly filled gourd from person to person. Even in humble families the gourds are beautifully decorated, sometimes silver mounted, and the *bombillas* are often finely made of silver.

In the really tropical countries of Latin America grapes do not grow well, and wine is therefore an imported luxury drunk chiefly by the rich. Mexico produces some wine, but the quality is not dependable. The Argentines are great wine drinkers, and most of their wine is grown domestically near Mendoza, close to the Chilean border on the eastern slope of the Andes where the climate is favorable. Although the quality of this wine is said to be improving, it is still poor. Only Chile has large vineyards that produce really good wine.

In Chile's central valley, centered on Santiago, the climate is "mediterranean." That is, it is dry and hot in summer and cool and rainy in winter. This is the climate in which wine was first grown on the shores of the Mediterranean Sea, and grape vines brought to Chile by the early Spaniards thrive as if they were back home in Southern Europe. Vineyards now cover much of the beautiful Valley of Chile, and their excellent wine is exported to many parts of the world. Many types of wines are produced, including light, dry "Rhine wine" made from Riesling grapes and robust, well-fortified Chilean sherry. But the best Chilean wines do not imitate any European model. They do not need to; they are first rate in their own right.

Northern Chile is mostly desert and grows almost nothing, but in southern Peru a few small rivers struggle down from the Andes and irrigate thin strips of fertile land. The climate is anything but mediterranean. The wind that blows off the sea is usually moist and cool, and the sky is often cloud-covered, but rain hardly ever falls, either winter or summer. Grapes thrive nevertheless, and varieties have been developed that yield excellent wine in quantities too small to export. The vineyards themselves are at a low altitude, but one brand of wine is taken high in the Andes for aging. Its makers claim it gains a uniquely fine quality by maturing in a cave 12,000 feet above sea level.

Besides good wine, the cramped vineyards of Peru produce a kind of brandy that is like nothing else in the world. It is called *pisco* after the little port of Pisco from which it was first exported. It is generally colorless (so are all distilled spirits unless they are artificially colored), and the best kinds have a light, flowery fragrance that is truly delightful. Not all brands are good, however. The demand far exceeds the supply, and adulteration is common.

Good *pisco* is excellent when drunk straight and slightly warmed, like cognac, but Peruvians often mix it with a thick brown local bitters called *algarrobina* that is supposed to be good for almost any ailment. The best mix, however, is the famous *pisco* sour *(page 172)*, which is made of *pisco*, lime juice, sugar and a foam-making agent such as gum arabic or white of egg. This last ingredient is considered very important; unless a *pisco* sour is served in a glass half full of hissing foam it does not exhibit its true, wonderful fragrance.

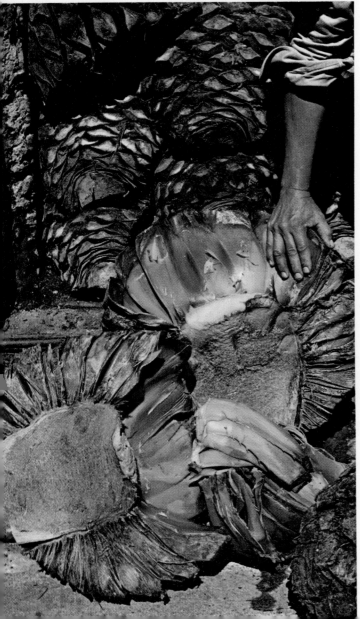

A Fiery Drink
from a Well-spiked Plant

Mexico's powerful liquor, tequila, comes from a plant called the *Agave azul tequilana,* which grows in long, carefully cultivated rows *(top)* in the state of Jalisco. Named after the town of Tequila, where it has been brewed for more than 200 years, the beverage is the fermented, distilled juice of the agave's huge, pineapplelike base, the *cabeza.* Only mature agave plants, eight to 12 years old, are harvested to obtain the juice. The plants are first uprooted and shorn of their leaves. Then the *cabezas* are conveyed to a distillery where they are trimmed, split in half *(bottom left)* and steamed, a process that converts them into brownish lumps *(bottom right)* full of sugary liquid. This liquid is crushed out of the *cabezas* and allowed to ferment in vats for about three days. Then the resultant brew is distilled to provide 80- to 100-proof tequila. This colorless, harsh spirit is taken with lime and salt *(page 171)* or used in cocktails like the Margarita *(page 172).* Other brands of tequila, aged in wood after distillation, are smooth enough to be downed straight.

169

How to Drink Tequila

In Mexico City a group of gentlemen riders dressed in *charro* costumes—colorful cowboy suits with big sombreros—take part in rodeos on Sundays. During practice sessions, the *charros* often pause for tequila. They take it with lime and salt *(opposite)*, but an orange slice or lime-rubbed cucumber may be substituted for the lime, or they may simply use a limed and salted piece of white *jicama* (a tuber). On this page, a *charro* shows one way to drink tequila. First he puts some salt in the space between his left thumb and index finger *(left)*, holds a lime with the same hand and grasps the glass in his right. Then he licks the salt *(below, left)*, swallows the tequila *(immediately below)* and sucks the juicy lime *(bottom)*.

Yugeño
PERUVIAN BRANDY WITH ORANGE JUICE

To make 1 cocktail

1½ ounces fresh orange juice
1½ ounces *pisco* (Peruvian brandy)
3 or 4 ice cubes

A 4-ounce cocktail glass, chilled

Combine the orange juice, *pisco* and ice cubes in a mixing glass, and place a bar shaker on top of the glass. Grasping the glass and shaker firmly together with both hands, shake them vigorously 9 or 10 times. Remove the shaker, and place a strainer over the mixing glass. Then pour the *yugeño* into a chilled cocktail glass.

Margarita
TEQUILA WITH LIME JUICE

To make 1 cocktail

1 slice lime
Coarse (kosher) salt
½ ounce fresh lime juice
1½ ounces tequila
½ ounce Triple Sec
3 to 4 ice cubes

A 4-ounce tumbler or cocktail glass, chilled

Rub the inside rim of the chilled tumbler or cocktail glass with the slice of lime. Pour salt into a saucer or cup and dip in the glass so that a thin layer of salt adheres to the moistened rim.

Combine the lime juice, tequila, Triple Sec and ice cubes in a mixing glass and place a bar shaker on top. Grasping the glass and shaker firmly together with both hands, shake them vigorously 9 or 10 times. Remove the shaker, place a strainer on top of the mixing glass, and pour the Margarita into the salt-rimmed tumbler or cocktail glass.

Pisco Sour
PERUVIAN BRANDY WITH LEMON JUICE

To make 1 cocktail

1 tablespoon egg white
1½ teaspoons superfine sugar
3 ounces *pisco* (Peruvian brandy)
1½ teaspoons fresh lemon juice
3 to 4 ice cubes

A 4-ounce cocktail glass or tumbler, chilled

Combine the egg white and sugar in a mixing glass, and stir with a bar spoon to dissolve the sugar. Add the *pisco*, lemon juice and ice cubes. Place a bar shaker on top of the mixing glass and, grasping the glass and shaker firmly together with both hands, shake them vigorously 9 or 10 times. Remove the shaker, place a strainer on top of the mixing glass and pour the Pisco sour into a chilled cocktail glass or tumbler.

Sangrita
SPICED TOMATO, ORANGE AND LIME JUICE WITH TEQUILA

To make 6 cocktails

2 cups tomato juice, fresh or canned
2 ounces fresh orange juice
3 ounces fresh lime juice
2 tablespoons finely chopped onion
½ teaspoon finely chopped, seeded, fresh hot chili, or ½ teaspoon finely chopped, drained, canned *serrano* chili, or 2 dried *pequín* chilies, crumbled
½ teaspoon salt
12 ounces tequila

6 four-ounce tumblers, chilled
6 two-ounce shot glasses

NOTE: Before using hot chilies, read the instructions on page 51.

Pour the tomato juice, orange juice and lime juice into a pitcher. Stir the juices together until they are well combined, then refrigerate them until they are thoroughly chilled. Just before serving, stir the chopped onion, chopped chili and salt into the chilled juice. Pour the juice mixture into the chilled tumblers and the tequila into the shot glasses. Present the juice and the tequila together.

For a frothier drink, pour the chilled juice into a mixing glass. Add the onion, chili, salt and 3 or 4 ice cubes. Place a bar shaker on top of the glass, grasp the glass and shaker firmly together, and shake them vigorously 9 or 10 times. Remove the shaker, place a bar strainer on top of the glass and pour into the chilled tumblers.

Popular Latin American drinks are deployed under the watchful eye of a brave bull. *Left to right:* the *yugeño,* Margarita, *pisco* sour, a glass of tequila, and a *sangrita*—a chili pepper concoction drunk with tequila.

X

Argentina and Chile: The Temperate South

A classic Argentine dish, *carbonada criolla*—beef chunks, corn and peaches, served here in a pumpkin shell decorated with candles —is displayed before the church of Nuestra Señora del Pilar, one of the oldest and most beautiful churches in Buenos Aires. Flanking the dish are other traditional Argentine foods *(from the left): pan casero* (wheat bread), *pastelitos de mil hojas* (quince pastries), *humitas* (corncakes) and *empanadas* (meat-filled pastries).

On the southeast coast of South America lies the world's richest expanse of agricultural land. This is the humid Pampa, a level or gently rolling grassland on both sides of the Río de la Plata estuary, including Uruguay and most of central Argentina. It has an almost ideal rainfall and a temperate climate. The grass is green and grows the year round, and flowers are almost always in bloom. The soil is deep and wonderfully fertile; there are no barrier mountains, no hurricanes, no earthquakes. No part of the earth of comparable size has so many natural advantages.

Before the arrival of Spanish colonists in the 16th Century the only inhabitants of this favored land were a few fierce, nomadic Indians who had achieved nothing resembling civilization. Perhaps the advanced Indians of the Inca Empire, who were strongly established in the mountainous northwestern corner of Argentina, came down to the Pampa once in a while to look around, but they did not colonize the area. The thick sod that covered it was too tough for their methods of cultivation, and they had no cattle to fatten on its rich pasture.

For the Spaniards the humid Pampa proved a horn of plenty. The cattle they brought from Europe multiplied enormously and provided all the meat they could eat. When horse- or ox-drawn ploughs had turned the heavy sod, all the temperate climate crops and some of the semitropical ones grew in lavish abundance. Argentina and Uruguay had their troubles, most of them man-made, but as far as food was concerned they soon became lands of plenty and remain so today.

Most of the people of Argentina and Uruguay are of European ancestry, mainly Spanish and Italian, but this does not mean that their food lacks its own special character. Both countries were colonized a long time ago, and the settlers quickly adapted their cooking to living conditions in the new, raw but wonderfully rich land. One result that the modern visitor notices immediately is the startling amount of meat that the people eat. In Argentina particularly, beef is really the staff of life. Many people eat it at every meal, and they sometimes eat little else. The Argentines complain that the government exports the best beef to help its balance of foreign exchange, but what remains is abundant and of excellent quality by North American standards. Uruguay is primarily a sheep-raising country and therefore eats somewhat more lamb and mutton, but it produces plenty of beef too. In both countries the smell of broiling steak can be called the national aroma.

Beef and other meats are commonly broiled or roasted, but they are also cooked in more elaborate and unusual ways. An excellent product of Argentine ingenuity is the meat roll called *matambre (page 190)*, which means "kill hunger." A special cut of flank steak, it is marinated overnight in vinegar and various seasonings. The steak is then spread out flat, covered with spinach, over which are laid hard-boiled egg halves, whole carrots and onion slices—the ingredients vary. The meat is then seasoned, rolled up like a jelly roll and tied with string. The meat roll is usually poached, although it is sometimes roasted. It can be eaten hot, but is generally sliced into decorative spiral cross sections and served cold. In most countries *matambre* would be considered the main course of a considerable meal, but the Argentines consume quantities of it as an appetizer before settling down to serious eating. *Matambre* is also popular in Uruguay, where it is often sewed up in cheesecloth before poaching. This method is more trouble, but it keeps all the filling in place.

Another tempting specialty that the Argentines toy with before starting their main meal is *empanadas (page 195)*. These are small pies or turnovers usually filled with chopped meat, raisins, olives and onions. Some special varieties are named for Argentine cities, such as Santa Fe or Tucumán, and others are products of an individual cook's creativity. It is hard to tell before you bite into an *empanada* what you will find inside, but the filling, like most Argentine food, is usually delicious.

In the old days, preparing *empanadas* for appetizers, picnic lunches or between-meal snacks was a regular task in every proper kitchen. Now they can be bought ready-made, and the markets offer a happy compromise in the form of disks of dough rolled thin and cut to the proper size. Many cooks take them home and use them to enclose any leftover meat or other suitable filling that happens to be on hand. There is no more pleasant way to make good use of leftovers.

In much of Argentina and Uruguay many of the dishes are purely European or only slightly modified by native influence. But the far-reaching effect of Andean Indian cooking is still felt, and it is naturally strongest in the mountainous northwest and in other country districts that are not dominated by recently arrived European immigrants. One sign of Indian influence is the wide use of squash and pumpkin, those most ancient Indian crops. The Argentines are very fond of the nutritious, yellow-

fleshed winter squash, and instead of using it only rarely as a mashed vegetable or a pie filling, as Americans do, they make many interesting dishes out of it. These include squash soup, squash fritters and a sort of baked squash pudding that is rather like squash pie without the crust. Another good use of squash is to enrich and decorate stews. Pieces of squash are put into the pot early enough in the cooking so that they turn into a yellow mush that thickens the stew and gives it an interesting color. Perhaps the most appealing squash dish, as well as a very good one, is *carbonada criolla*—an elaborate beef stew that is actually baked in a squash, using the strong-shelled vegetable as a casserole *(page 193)*.

Another Indian dish that has worked its way into Argentine cooking is *humitas (page 194)*, which is generally made of unripe corn kernels. The corn usually is mildly flavored with lightly fried chopped onions, peppers, tomatoes, salt, sugar, cinnamon, red pepper and sometimes cheese. The proportions vary according to the cook's taste, and any of these ingredients may be omitted to vary the dish.

Under the careful supervision of a silver-belted cook known as *parrillero*, gaucho-style chunks of meat are roasted over a smoldering wood fire at an Argentine cookout. Impaled on iron rods that are slanted to prevent the juice from dripping on the fire, the cuts are slowly cooked for about four hours. Shown from left to right are a pair of beef ribs, two lambs and four flanks of beef.

The simplest sort of *humitas* is merely one of these mixtures cooked slowly with milk until the corn grains are tender. It may be served by itself as a side dish to balance a monster meal of meat, or the cooked mixture may be cooled, made into one large loaf or many small loaves, covered with biscuit dough and baked. The most elaborate presentation, *humitas en chala,* is the most traditional and the most Indian. The grated, flavored corn is wrapped by spoonfuls in cornhusks *(chalas),* tied with light string or fiber, and boiled or steamed for two hours. This is almost the same way the Aztecs of ancient Mexico made their tamales, and it proves the long reach and persistence of Indian influence.

Some of the most picturesque food traditions of Argentina and Uruguay derive from the gauchos, the nomadic, part-Indian herdsmen who roamed the Pampa in the old days, living on half-wild cattle. They usually caught those skittish animals with a *bola,* an Indian weapon consisting of three balls of stone or iron held together at a central point by three leather thongs. When a mounted gaucho whirled it around his head and slung

Matambre (kill hunger), an Argentine beef roll stuffed with vegetables and hard-boiled eggs, dates from stagecoach days, when travelers would take *matambres* along to sustain them on their journeys through the vast Pampa. The recipe for the *matambre* at left is given on page 190.

it toward his prey, the balls spread widely. If one of the thongs touched the fleeing animal, all three balls wrapped tightly around it, rendering it helpless until the gaucho galloped up and cut its throat with a knife. The gauchos killed only the cattle they needed for meat and there was enough for all. They usually hung the hides on a bush for the landowner, if there was one. The hide could be exported and in earlier times was the only salable part of the beast.

The great Charles Darwin, author of the theory of evolution, visited Uruguay and Argentina in 1832 when he was a young, adventurous naturalist. He rode with the gauchos and described their carnivorous eating customs. In a comparatively civilized part of Uruguay he had supper with a gaucho landowner named Don Juan Fuentes. "The supper," he reported in *The Voyage of the Beagle,* "consisted of two huge piles, one of roast beef, the other of boiled, with some pieces of pumpkin; besides this latter there was no other vegetable, not even a morsel of bread."

This was a comparatively varied diet. For gauchos living out on the

Pampa, the boiled beef and pumpkin were considered unnecessary luxuries. Later in his book Darwin describes a night he spent in the open with those hardy characters. "We halted for the night: at this instant an unfortunate cow was spied by the lynx-eyed Gauchos, who set off in full chase, and in a few minutes dragged her in with their *lazos* [lassos], and slaughtered her. We here had the four necessities of life 'en el campo,' pasture for the horses, water (only a muddy puddle), meat and firewood. The Gauchos were in high spirits at finding all these luxuries, and we soon set to work on the poor cow."

Darwin does not tell how his friends cooked the cow, but to judge from other accounts they probably toasted strips of meat over the fire on spits of green wood or on the points of their long knives. This is an ancient cooking method favored by meat-eating primitives, and it works acceptably for people with sound teeth and powerful digestions. But even the gauchos preferred to make their meat more tender by roasting it slowly, and they did so whenever they had enough time and firewood.

Nearly half a century later the English writer W. H. Hudson, author of *Green Mansions,* spent some years of his youth on the Pampa. Not much had changed since Darwin's visit. In *The Purple Land,* Hudson describes the enormous kitchen of a Uruguayan ranch house, with a fire smoldering on a clay platform fenced with cow bones stuck in the earthen floor. Meat was boiling in a great iron pot hung by a chain from the roof, and more meat was roasting on a spit six feet long. Nothing was served except meat, which the diners carved from the roast with their knives. The greatest delicacy produced by this simple cookery was a fat, freshly killed heifer roasted in large pieces with the hide still on the meat. Hudson tried this dish and pronounced it the best roast meat he had ever eaten.

The wild, free life of the gauchos is only a memory in modern Argentina and Uruguay. Cattle still teem on the Pampa, but they are the mild-mannered, square-built animals that have been bred to yield the best commercial cuts of beef. They lead pampered lives in great fenced pastures, and the herdsmen who tend them are no wilder than they. But in spite of these inroads of civilization, the traditional gaucho way of roasting meat over a wood fire has been preserved and is a continuing passion with Argentines and Uruguayans of all classes. Even in built-up parts of Buenos Aires, a modern city of close to nine million people, the smell of wood smoke and roasting meat still perfumes the breeze from the Pampa.

At fairs, political rallies and outings of good-sized organizations, the meat is often roasted in the age-old way without modification. Whole sheep are split like kippered herring and impaled front end up on an iron rod that has a crosspiece to keep the carcass flat. Then the rod is thrust into the ground, leaning toward the fire at an angle of about 20° from the vertical to prevent the meat from dripping into the fire and to let the grease baste the meat as it runs down. The best fires for this sort of roasting are fed with hard *quebracho* (meaning "break ax") wood, from northern Argentina, cut in short lengths. If ignited properly, this fire will burn for a long time with great heat but little flame. The carcass is turned from time to time to make it roast evenly on all sides. The upper part, being thinner, is normally done first and is cut off in pieces to feed those guests too hungry to wait for the more succulent hindquarters.

Goats and young pigs are roasted in much the same way as sheep, and so are large slabs of beef and whole sides of beef ribs. The most admired meat of all is still *carne con cuero*, beef roasted with the hide on. If asked to do so in advance, Argentine butchers will supply beef "with hide" for an extra price.

Roasting in this primitive way requires skill, constant attention and plenty of time. If an open-fire *asado* (meat roast) is to be ready by midday, the fire must be lit at dawn and the different kinds of meat set around it at different times so that all will be done simultaneously when the guests have assembled. Traditionalists insist that the result is worth all the effort. Even if the meat is a trifle burned in some places and almost raw in others, its flavor brings to mind the glorious age of the wild, free gauchos roaming the open Pampa.

Only the most determined *asado* lovers still cook their meat in this troublesome way. Argentine cooks now commonly use a *parrilla*, or grill, to hold the meat over a bed of coals. The simplest kind, about three feet long and two feet wide, is made by welding iron bars to an iron frame. Herdsmen, hunters and other outdoor people usually carry some such grill for use in the open, but many town-dwelling Argentines also have such a grill and set it up on weekends in their small backyards, supporting the corners a few inches above the ground on bricks or concrete blocks. More prosperous families have elaborate structures of brickwork with raised grills at convenient waist level. Some large houses have indoor grills with hoods and chimneys to carry off the smoke.

Cooking on these grills is a far more elaborate art than is normally practiced at North American backyard barbecues. Several kinds of meat—beef, lamb, chicken—are usually cooked simultaneously, along with a great variety of sausages, liver and kidneys. Argentines eat without camouflage a number of "innards," such as intestines, that do not appeal to many North Americans; to discomfort Yankees, Argentines enjoy pointing out that these parts of the animal are not wasted by North American packing plants, which grind up these organs, color them with blood so they look more like meat, and turn them into bologna and hot dogs. The Argentines prefer to eat them undisguised, and indeed they are excellent when properly grilled.

Professional cooks are available for elaborate *asados*, but often the host prefers to do the cooking himself. With a long, three-pronged fork he busily turns the meat and innards, brushes them with brine, or moves them to hotter or cooler parts of the grill. The bed of coals needs constant tending, for it should not be allowed to flare up too much from fat dripping into it. The guests gather around, complaining how hungry they are or claiming that the meat is already burned. The Argentines are not a quiet people, and they are loudest at an *asado*. The host fends them off by feeding them sausages and *empanadas* and giving them quantities of strong red wine to drink. As the grilling approaches its climax, the noise level rises. At last the great moment comes when the host begins serving the meat, crisp and brown on the outside, bright red on the inside, and more plentiful than all the guests can eat.

Continued on page 184

Chilean flags lend a patriotic touch to a cowboy's Independence Day dinner of *empanadas* and wines at a rodeo near Santiago.

A Festive Salute to Independence

On September 18, 1810, after nearly 300 years of Spanish rule, Chile declared herself free and plunged into eight years of bitter fighting to secure her independence. The beginning of the war for national freedom is honored in Chile, as it is in the United States, by nationwide celebration. On September 18, a two-day festival known as the Fiestas Patrias—feast of the country—begins. Highlight of the celebration is a rodeo, staged by Chilean *huasos* (cowboys) in brightly striped ponchos, some of them—like those of the man on the opposite page —in the colors of the Chilean flag. Between events at the rodeo, the *huasos* refresh themselves at *ramadas*, temporary structures set up outside the arena. They feast on *empanadas*— meat pies—and *cazuelas de cordero* (the lamb soup shown at left, below). And to accompany these delicacies they drink *chicha* (partly fermented grape juice) and local wines, often from a *cacho* (cow's horn), as demonstrated by the *huaso* at left, above.

A steak and sauce dish, greatly admired in Argentina, which shows its continental heritage, is even more spectacular. It is cooked at the head of the dinner table before the eyes of ravenous guests so the host can feel the glory of creation. The starting point is 12 *bifes* (sections of *filet mignon* one inch thick). They are sautéed in butter in a vast frying pan over a three-burner alcohol stove until both sides are slightly browned. Then they are spread with mustard and sprinkled with three-quarters of a cup of dry sherry mixed with a third of a cup of port. The wine should wash a part of the mustard down among the *bifes,* which are then cooked slowly for five minutes over a low flame, moving them often to prevent sticking. Salt should be added if the salt in the butter is not enough. Then one and a half pints of heavy cream mixed with one tablespoon of cornstarch is poured over the *bifes,* and they are cooked slowly for three minutes more to let the rich sauce thicken. Another cup of sherry and port mixed in the same proportion is added just before serving.

This dish is fun to watch in preparation, and it produces tantalizing odors. If a little preliminary food such as *matambre* or *empanadas* has been provided, the 12 *bifes* doused with wine, butter and cream are enough for six Argentine appetites.

Argentina's neighbor to the west, Chile, is also a temperate country where Spanish is spoken. Chile, too, was once a part of the same Spanish colonial empire. But in other ways the two countries are not at all alike, either in history, people, climate or way of life. Chile has no broad, horn-of-plenty Pampa, and it lacks the easy abundance of Argentina. It is a "string bean" country, 2,600 miles long, crowded into the narrow strip between the crest of the Andes and the Pacific Ocean. Its northern third is utter desert where rain hardly ever falls; its southern third is cold, storm-swept mountains where rain falls almost all the time. But between these unpleasant climatic extremes is some of the loveliest country on earth. The long, fertile valley leading south from Santiago between two mountain ranges looks like California. Its lowlands are covered with irrigated fields or vineyards, and the glittering, snow-capped Andes stand tall in the distance. Farther south the country is wetter and greener and covered with forests, and the lake district inland from Valdivia looks rather like Switzerland and has a similar climate.

When the conquering Spaniards arrived in the 16th Century, central Chile was inhabited by extremely tough and warlike Indians, the Araucanians, who refused to be conquered or exterminated. They yielded reluctantly, holding out for centuries and slowly mixing with the Spanish invaders. Most modern Chileans have some Indian blood, but the mixture is so old and so well blended that there is no noticeable cleavage between Indian and non-Indian parts of the population. The typical Chilean, whatever his ancestry, is vigorous, cocky, scrappy and notably proud of himself and his country.

The Chileans no doubt would like to eat as much beef as their Argentine neighbors do, but Chile is not a cattle country, and beef is comparatively scarce. So popular Chilean dishes feature seafood, the humble bean and meat in moderate quantities. The leading national dish, eaten by all classes, is *porotos granados,* a delightful way of preparing beans *(page 189)*. It is almost certainly of Indian origin since it contains the three most typical Indian foodstuffs: beans, corn and squash. But in a characteristically Chilean way the dish also contains non-Indian ingredients such as garlic and onion.

As a bean-eating country, Chile has an advantage. Its mild climate permits beans to be grown during most of the year, so they can usually be found in the markets in the ripe but not yet dry state. Most bean recipes call for these *porotos,* which are sometimes called cranberry beans in the United States. Dried beans can be soaked and used instead, but they are not nearly as good. In *porotos granados,* the corn kernels should be young and tender. If they are not, they should be cooked until they are soft. The cooking of the squash for this dish should be timed so that the pieces partially dissolve, creating a thick and decorative yellow sauce.

A peculiarity of Chilean cooking is the common use of a sauce called *color,* an orange-red flavoring mixture made by heating garlic and paprika in melted fat or cooking oil. Some cooks keep several kinds on hand, one of them hot with chili, the others milder. *Color* will keep indefinitely, and it is a handy way to add flavor and eye appeal to many dishes.

Another popular Chilean flavoring is *pebre (page 193),* a sauce made of onions, vinegar, olive oil, garlic, chili and coriander. It goes well with almost any meat dish and is far superior to the bottled sauces and catsup that North Americans are so fond of. In some households *pebre* is as hot as if it were Mexican; in others it has hardly any chili in it.

In Chile, as in other South American countries with Indian heritage, much use is made of unripe corn, the grains cut off the cob or scraped off it with a grater or dull blade. Many kinds of corn are used, some of them resembling American sweet corn. Other varieties have foot-long ears four or five inches in diameter with kernels bigger than nickels. So when a Chilean recipe calls for one *choclo* (ear of corn), it may mean the equivalent of several American ears. The corn may be used in the sweet, "milk" stage, or when almost mature but not yet dry. By selecting different kinds of corn at different stages of growth, a cook can give a corn dish a wide variety of flavors.

One of the best, most popular Chilean corn dishes is *pastel de choclo,* a meat pie with a topping of ground fresh corn instead of pie crust *(Recipe Booklet).* Beef alone or beef and chicken are normally used. Other meats or fish are sometimes substituted. Several kinds may be used, and tough meat may be ground or cut in quarter-inch cubes. Olives and raisins may be added if the cook is in the mood. The dish is sometimes hot with pepper or chili (which the Chileans, like the Peruvians, call *ají)* but this is not mandatory. Most Chilean cooking is not peppery. In private homes *pastel de choclo* is generally baked in one large casserole, but restaurants like to serve it in small casseroles, one to each customer.

Whatever it may contain, a *pastel de choclo* stands or falls with its corn topping, which should be firm, but not tough, and slightly sweet. Sugar is sprinkled over the top before it is baked. When the dish is baked properly, the topping has a wonderful thin light-brown skin, and the breadlike material under it has a flavor that contrasts pleasantly with the meat.

Chileans probably eat more seafood than any other Latin Americans,

Seafood stalls like this one line the streets of Angelmó, a waterfront section of Puerto Montt in southern Chile. Strung from the top of the stand are dried *navajuelas* (the brownish shellfish in foreground), *piures* (the coral-red dried shellfish) and dried mussels (flanking the doorway). The shelf holds dried mussels, while the table below bears smoked sawfish and haddock.

Opposite: On Tenglo Island, off southern Chile, a lavish clambake called a *curanto* is prepared. The feast includes lobsters, crabs, mussels, oysters, potato patties, peas, beans and various meats, among which is a whole suckling pig. The food is laid in a pit lined with hot rocks, covered with leaves and baked several hours.

and the seafood here is better, fresher, cheaper and more plentiful than anywhere else. The cold Peru Current sweeping northward from the Antarctic teems with all sorts of edible creatures, and the numerous harbors, bays and inlets along the coast are rich in shellfish. Some of these delicacies are not known elsewhere; others are so similar to northern hemisphere species that they may safely be called by familiar English names.

The best place to appreciate the great variety of Chilean seafood is in Santiago's central market, where hundreds of sea products can be seen. Some booths specialize in abalone. They are not exactly like the California variety but taste almost the same. They are just as tough, too, and a familiar sound in the market is the thud of mallets mashing chunks of abalone meat into thin tenderized sheets. Chilean abalone is cheap enough to be eaten in the poorest homes.

Other booths in the fish market offer shellfish that have been opened for strolling connoisseurs. Some of them are familiar: crab and lobsters, as well as clams or clamlike creatures that look and taste rather like cherrystones and littlenecks. Others are not familiar at all. Very popular with Chileans are monstrous sea urchins. They look like the sea urchins found on North American beaches, but are much larger, averaging four inches or more in diameter. Their edible parts are five thick strips of bright yellow-orange flesh that look about as edible as oil paint. Another delicacy, called *pibre*, looks like a solid chunk of rock with moss growing on it. Actually the "rock" is a mass of creatures related to sea urchins, their shells fused together. Their flesh, which can be exposed by very skillful cracking, is brilliant red. Both kinds taste bitter, but Chilean seafood fanciers like them raw with quantities of excellent Chilean wine.

More appealing to foreigners are Chilean mussels and scallops, both of which are large, abundant and excellent. They are sometimes eaten raw with lemon or with chili or vinaigrette sauce, but the Chileans have ways of cooking them that are worth trying on their North American equivalents. The Chilean scallop stew *(Recipe Booklet)* is a substantial dish whose many ingredients combine nicely with the rather pronounced flavor of the scallops. Mussels are sometimes cooked in the same way, and another fine way to serve them is to heat the well-washed shellfish in a very little water until the shells open. The meats are then removed, and butter, garlic, parsley and other herbs are added to the strained broth. Then the mussel meats are added along with hard, brown cubes of fried bread. The trick is to add the cubes just before serving so they do not become soggy.

The most admired fish in Chile is the *congrio*, which has no exact North American equivalent. The name means conger eel in the Spanish of the dictionaries, but in Chile it stands for two kinds of long fish with skimpy tails. The flesh of both is excellent and can be cooked in a great variety of ways, some of them very elaborate. One of the best is a souplike stew called *caldillo de congrio (Recipe Booklet)*. It is made by stewing *congrio* steaks, which are almost circular, in an earthen pot with potatoes, tomatoes, onions, herbs and spices. It is extremely good to eat and can be made with almost any firm North American fish that is big enough to provide reasonably boneless steaks. The vegetables acquire a wonderful flavor, and the sauce that collects in the pot is a delight.

To serve 4 to 6

⅓ cup olive oil
A 3- to 3½-pound chicken, cut into
  6 to 8 serving pieces
1 cup dry white wine
1 cup distilled white vinegar
1 cup hot water
2 medium onions, peeled, halved and
  cut in wedges ⅛ inch thick
3 carrots, scraped and cut diagonally
  into slices ⅛ inch thick
1 small leek, including 1 inch of the
  green, washed thoroughly and cut
  into rounds ⅛ inch thick
1 tablespoon salt
A bouquet of 1 celery top, 2 parsley
  sprigs, 2 bay leaves, 2 whole
  cloves and ¼ teaspoon thyme,
  wrapped together in cheesecloth
1 lemon, cut lengthwise into halves
  and then crosswise into ⅛-inch
  slices

Escabeche de Gallina
COLD PICKLED CHICKEN

In a heavy flameproof 4- to 5-quart casserole, heat the olive oil, tipping the casserole to coat the bottom evenly and turning the heat down to moderate if the oil begins to smoke. Pat the chicken dry with paper towels and brown it in the oil, a few pieces at a time. Start the pieces skin side down and turn them with tongs. Add the wine, vinegar, water, onions, carrots, leek, salt and bouquet, and bring to a boil over high heat. Reduce the heat to low, cover the casserole, and simmer undisturbed for 30 minutes, or until the chicken is tender but not falling apart. Remove the bouquet, and arrange the chicken pieces in a deep serving dish just large enough to hold them snugly in one layer. Pour the cooking liquid with the vegetables over the chicken. Decorate the top with the lemon slices, and cool to room temperature. Cover the dish and refrigerate for at least 6 hours, or until the cooking liquids have jelled. Serve on chilled plates, as the first or the main course.

Two of the most tempting cold buffet dishes in Chile are *escabeche de gallina* (pickled chicken garnished with lemons, onions and carrots, *right*) and *fruta de mar* (fruit of the sea, *opposite*). The latter is made from two or more varieties of Chile's superb, abundant shellfish—in this case crab and shrimp —served on a bed of rice and corn, mixed and highly seasoned.

Porotos Granados
CRANBERRY BEANS WITH SQUASH AND CORN

To serve 6

Rinse the beans under cold running water and combine them with 5 cups of water in a heavy 5-quart casserole. Bring to a boil, reduce the heat to low and let the beans simmer, half-covered.

In a heavy 8- to 10-inch skillet heat the oil over moderate heat. Add the onions and garlic, and cook, stirring occasionally, for 5 minutes, or until the onions are soft and transparent but not brown. Stir in the tomatoes, basil, oregano and a few grindings of pepper, raise the heat and boil briskly, stirring, until the mixture becomes a thick purée. Add the purée and the squash to the simmering beans. Cover and cook over low heat for 1½ to 2 hours. When the beans are tender, stir in the corn, and simmer 5 minutes. Season with salt, and transfer the beans to a serving bowl. Serve hot in soup plates. If you like, serve *pebre* sauce *(page 193)* with the beans, topping each portion with a spoonful of sauce.

NOTE: If fresh cranberry beans are unavailable, substitute 1½ cups of dried cranberry or navy beans. Rinse them, bring to a boil in 6 cups of water, and boil for 2 minutes. Turn off the heat and let the beans soak for an hour. Add the purée and squash and proceed with the recipe.

3 cups shelled fresh cranberry beans
5 cups cold water
¼ cup olive oil
1½ cups coarsely chopped onions
½ teaspoon finely chopped garlic
6 medium tomatoes, peeled, seeded, chopped *(see salsa cruda, page 44)*
1½ teaspoons dried basil
1 teaspoon dried oregano
Freshly ground black pepper
1 pound winter squash, peeled, seeded and cut into 1-inch cubes (about 2 cups)
½ cup fresh corn kernels, cut from 1 large ear of corn, or substitute ½ cup thoroughly defrosted frozen corn kernels
1 teaspoon salt

To serve 8 to 10

2 two-pound flank steaks
½ cup red wine vinegar
1 teaspoon finely chopped garlic
1 teaspoon dried thyme

THE STUFFING
½ pound fresh spinach
8 scraped cooked whole carrots, about
    6 to 8 inches long and no more
    than 1 inch in diameter
4 hard-cooked eggs, cut lengthwise
    into quarters
1 large onion, sliced ⅛ inch thick
    and divided into rings
¼ cup finely chopped fresh parsley
1 teaspoon crumbled *pequín* chili or
    crushed, seeded, dried *hontaka* chili
1 tablespoon coarse salt
3 cups beef stock, fresh or canned
1 to 3 cups cold water

To make about 1½ cups

½ cup olive oil
¼ cup red wine vinegar
½ cup finely chopped onions
1 teaspoon finely chopped garlic
¼ cup finely chopped fresh parsley
1 teaspoon dried oregano
¼ teaspoon Cayenne pepper
1½ teaspoons salt
1 teaspoon freshly ground black
    pepper

Matambre
STUFFED AND ROLLED FLANK STEAK

Ask your butcher to butterfly the steaks, or do it yourself in the following fashion: With a long, very sharp knife slit the steaks horizontally from one long side to within ½ inch of the other side. Open the steaks, place them between 2 sheets of wax paper, and pound them with the side of a cleaver to flatten them further. Trim away all gristle and fat.

Lay one steak, cut side up, on a 12-by-18-inch jelly-roll pan. Sprinkle it with half the vinegar, then scatter half the garlic and thyme over it. Cover the meat with the other steak, also cut side up, and sprinkle it with the remaining vinegar, garlic and thyme. Cover the pan and let the steaks marinate for 6 hours at room temperature or overnight refrigerated.

Preheat the oven to 375°. Lay the steaks end to end, cut side up, so that they overlap by about 2 inches. Pound the joined ends together with the flat of a cleaver to seal them securely. Wash the spinach under running water, drain it and trim off the stems. Spread the leaves evenly over the meat, and arrange the carrots across the grain of the meat in parallel rows about 3 inches apart. Place the eggs between the rows of carrots. Scatter the onion rings over them and sprinkle the surface evenly with parsley, chili and salt. Carefully roll the steaks with the grain, jelly-roll fashion, into a thick, long cylinder. To tie the *matambre*, cut a kitchen cord into a 10-foot length. Wrap one end of the cord around the steaks about 1 inch from the edge of the roll and knot it securely. Then, holding the cord in a loop near the knot, wrap the remaining length of cord around the steaks about 2 inches from the edge of the roll and feed it through the loop. (See the picture opposite, in the center of the bottom row.) Now tighten the cord to keep the loop in place. Repeat until the roll is tied at 1-inch intervals. Bring the remaining cord across the length of the bottom of the roll (catching it in one or two loops) and up over the opposite end. Tie it around the first loop. Trim off any excess cord.

Place the *matambre* in a 12-quart casserole or roasting pan and pour in the stock. Add enough cold water to come a third of the way up the roll. Then cover tightly and place in the middle of the oven for 1 hour. To serve hot, remove the *matambre* from the pan to a board and let it rest for 10 minutes. With a sharp knife remove the strings and cut the *matambre* into ¼-inch slices. Arrange the slices on a heated platter and moisten them with a little pan liquid before serving. Or the *matambre* may be thoroughly chilled, and served in similarly cut slices. In Argentina, the *matambre* is generally poached in stock or water to cover it completely; it is then removed from the pot, pressed under weights until the juices drain off, refrigerated and served cold as an hors d'oeuvre.

Chimichurri
ARGENTINE SPICED PARSLEY SAUCE

In a bowl, combine the oil and vinegar, and beat them together with a whisk or fork. Stir in the onions, garlic, parsley, oregano, Cayenne, salt and black pepper, and taste for seasoning. To develop its flavor, let the sauce stand at room temperature for 2 or 3 hours before serving. *Chimichurri* is a traditional sauce for grilled and roasted meats.

A Sharp Knife and Sure Touch to Butterfly Steaks

1 To butterfly steaks for *matambre*, slice into each one horizontally from one side, using your sharpest knife.

2 Continuing to slice horizontally, slit the steak almost in half, cutting to within ½ inch of the far side.

3 Open the steak out flat when you finish the cutting—its shape will be similar to that of a butterfly.

Filling, Rolling and Tying the Steaks

4 After marinating the butterflied steaks, place them end to end, overlapping them by about 2 inches.

5 Spread both steaks with the *matambre* stuffing: spinach leaves, carrots, hard-cooked eggs, onion rings, parsley, chili and salt. Then, beginning at either of the short ends, roll the steaks with the grain, jelly-roll fashion.

6 Roll the steaks together carefully and as compactly as possible until they form a long, thick cylinder.

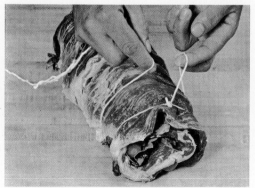

7 Tie the rolled steaks with one long cord, looping it at 1-inch intervals (*see recipe, opposite page*).

8 Cook the *matambre* in a heavy casserole or roasting pan just large enough to hold it snugly.

Argentina's colorful *carbonada criolla* is a complete meal of beef and vegetables served in a squash or pumpkin shell.

Carbonada Criolla

BAKED PUMPKIN WITH BEEF, VEGETABLE AND PEACH FILLING

Preheat the oven to 375°. Scrub the outside of the pumpkin under cold running water with a stiff brush. With a large, sharp knife, cut down into the top of the pumpkin to create a lid 6 or 7 inches in diameter. Leave the stem intact as a handle. Lift out the lid and, with a large metal spoon, scrape the seeds and stringy fibers from the lid and from the pumpkin shell.

Brush the inside of the pumpkin with the soft butter and sprinkle the cup of sugar into the opening. Tip the pumpkin from side to side to make the sugar adhere to the butter. Then turn the pumpkin over and gently shake out the excess sugar. Put the lid back in place.

Place the pumpkin in a large shallow roasting pan and bake in the oven for 45 minutes, or until tender but somewhat resistant when pierced with the tip of a small, sharp knife. The pumpkin shell should remain firm enough to hold the filling without danger of collapsing.

Meanwhile, heat the oil over moderate heat in a heavy 6- to 8-quart casserole until a light haze forms above it. Add the cubes of meat and brown them on all sides, turning them frequently with a large spoon. Regulate the heat so the meat browns quickly without burning. Then with a slotted spoon, transfer the meat to a platter.

To the fat remaining in the pan, add the onions, green pepper and garlic, and cook over moderate heat, stirring constantly, for about 5 minutes, or until the vegetables are soft but not brown. Pour in the fresh beef stock or canned beef stock and water and bring to a boil over high heat, meanwhile scraping in any brown bits clinging to the bottom and sides of the pan. Return the meat and any of its accumulated juices to the pan and stir in the tomatoes, oregano, bay leaf, salt and a few grindings of black pepper. Cover the pan, reduce the heat to low, and simmer undisturbed for 15 minutes. Then add the sweet potatoes and white potatoes, cover the pan and cook for 15 minutes; add the zucchini slices, cover the pan again and cook for 10 minutes. Finally add the corn rounds and peach halves and cook, still covered, for 5 minutes longer.

Pour the entire contents of the pan carefully into the baked pumpkin, cover the pumpkin with its lid again, and bake for another 15 minutes in a 375° oven. To serve, place the pumpkin on a large serving platter and, at the table, ladle the *carbonada* from the pumpkin onto heated, individual serving plates.

Pebre

CHILEAN HOT SAUCE

NOTE: Before using hot chilies, read the instructions on page 51.

In a mixing bowl, combine the oil, vinegar and water, and beat them together with a whisk or fork. Stir in the coriander, onions, chili paste (or chopped fresh chili), garlic and salt, and taste for seasoning. Let the sauce stand at room temperature for 2 or 3 hours to develop its flavor before serving.

Pebre is a traditional accompaniment for meats and also may be served with *porotos granados (page 189)*.

To serve 6

A 10- to 12-pound pumpkin, or other large winter squash
½ cup butter (1 quarter-pound stick), softened
1 cup sugar
2 tablespoons olive oil
2 pounds lean beef chuck, cut into 1-inch cubes
1 cup coarsely chopped onions
½ cup coarsely chopped green pepper
½ teaspoon finely chopped garlic
4 cups fresh beef stock, or 2 cups canned beef stock combined with 2 cups cold water
3 medium tomatoes, peeled, seeded and coarsely chopped (*see salsa cruda, page 44*), or substitute 1 cup chopped, drained, canned Italian plum tomatoes
½ teaspoon dried oregano
1 bay leaf
1 teaspoon salt
Freshly ground black pepper
1½ pounds sweet potatoes, peeled and cut into ½-inch cubes (about 4½ cups)
1½ pounds white potatoes, peeled and cut into ½-inch cubes (about 4½ cups)
½ pound zucchini, scrubbed but not peeled, and cut into ¼-inch slices (about 1½ cups)
3 ears corn, shucked and cut into rounds 1-inch wide
4 fresh peaches, peeled, halved and pitted, or substitute 8 canned white peach halves, drained and rinsed in cold water

To make about 1¾ cups

2 tablespoons olive oil
1 tablespoon red or white wine vinegar
½ cup water
½ cup finely chopped fresh coriander (*cilantro*)
½ cup finely chopped onions
1 tablespoon red chili paste (*page 105*), or 1 teaspoon finely chopped, seeded and deribbed fresh hot chili
¼ teaspoon finely chopped garlic
½ teaspoon salt

To serve 6

1 cup fresh corn kernels, cut from 2
    ears of corn, or 1 cup thoroughly
    defrosted frozen corn kernels
2 medium tomatoes, peeled, seeded
    and coarsely chopped (*see salsa
    cruda, page 44*), or substitute ⅔
    cup chopped, drained, canned
    Italian plum tomatoes
3 tablespoons white wine vinegar
2 tablespoons olive oil
1 tablespoon coarsely chopped fresh
    coriander (*cilantro*)
¼ teaspoon finely chopped, seeded
    fresh hot chili
½ teaspoon salt
Freshly ground black pepper

THE SAUCE
1 whole egg (or 2 egg yolks)
1 cup olive oil
¼ cup lemon juice
1 teaspoon tomato paste
½ teaspoon finely chopped, seeded
    fresh hot chili
½ teaspoon dry mustard
½ teaspoon salt
¼ teaspoon white pepper
3 cups cooked long-grain rice, cooled
    to room temperature (made from
    1 cup uncooked rice)

THE SEAFOOD
2 or 3 small live lobsters, boiled, cut
    in half and cooled; or 3 pounds
    live crabs boiled and cooled; or 3
    pounds shrimp, boiled, shelled and
    cooled; or a combination of
    lobster, crab and shrimp

To serve 4 to 6

4 cups fresh corn kernels, cut from
    about 8 large ears of corn, or
    substitute 4 cups thoroughly
    defrosted frozen corn kernels
⅓ cup milk
2 eggs
2 teaspoons paprika
½ teaspoon salt
Freshly ground black pepper
¼ cup butter
½ cup coarsely chopped scallions
¼ cup coarsely chopped green pepper
⅓ cup freshly grated Parmesan cheese

Fruta de Mar
COLD SEAFOOD WITH CORN AND RICE SALAD

NOTE: Before using hot chilies, read the instructions on page 51.

In a small saucepan, bring 1 quart of water to a boil over high heat. Drop in the corn kernels, return to a boil, and cook, uncovered, for 3 minutes, stirring frequently. Drain the corn thoroughly and return it to the saucepan. Stir in the tomatoes, vinegar, 2 tablespoons of olive oil, the coriander, ¼ teaspoon of fresh chili, ½ teaspoon of salt and a few grindings of pepper; let the mixture rest at room temperature for 1 hour.

Drop the whole egg into the jar of a blender, cover the jar, and blend at high speed until the egg is thick and creamy. Without stopping the machine, remove the cover and gradually pour in 1 cup of olive oil in a slow stream. When the sauce is very thick, add the lemon juice, tomato paste, ½ teaspoon of fresh chili, mustard, ½ teaspoon of salt and white pepper, and blend for 5 seconds.

(To make the sauce by hand, warm a large mixing bowl in hot water, dry it quickly but thoroughly, and drop in the egg yolks. With a wire whisk or a rotary or electric beater, beat the yolks vigorously for about 2 minutes, or until they thicken and cling to the whisk or beater. Add a teaspoon of the lemon juice and the dry mustard, salt and white pepper. Then beat in the oil, ½ teaspoon at a time; make sure each addition is absorbed before adding more. By the time ½ cup of oil has been beaten in, the sauce should be like very thick cream. Add the rest of the oil by teaspoonfuls, beating constantly. Beat in the remaining lemon juice, and the tomato paste and chopped chili.)

To assemble, combine the reserved corn mixture and the cooled rice and heap them in a mound in the center of a large platter. Arrange the cold seafood attractively on or around the rice, and serve the sauce separately in a small bowl.

Humitas
PURÉED CORN WITH SCALLIONS, GREEN PEPPER AND CHEESE

Combine the corn and milk in the jar of a blender and blend at high speed for 30 seconds. Add the eggs, paprika, salt and a few grindings of black pepper and blend for 15 seconds longer, or until the mixture is thick and smooth.

(To make the corn mixture by hand, purée the corn through a food mill set over a bowl. Discard the pulp left in the mill. Add the milk, eggs, paprika, salt and pepper, and mix vigorously with a spoon or whisk until the mixture is thick and smooth.)

In a heavy 10-inch skillet, melt the butter over moderate heat. When the foam subsides, add the scallions and green pepper, and cook, stirring, for 4 or 5 minutes, or until the vegetables are soft but not brown. Pour in the corn mixture, reduce the heat, and simmer, uncovered, stirring frequently, for 5 to 7 minutes, or until the mixture thickens somewhat. Stir in the grated cheese and, as soon as it melts, remove the skillet from the heat. Serve as an accompaniment to meat dishes.

NOTE: This *humitas* mixture is sometimes wrapped in cornhusks and steamed like tamales to make a dish called *humitas en chala*.

Empanadas de Horno

BAKED MEAT-FILLED TURNOVERS

NOTE: Before using hot chilies, read the instructions on page 51.

First prepare the filling in the following fashion: In an 8- to 10-inch skillet, combine the onions, olive oil and ½ cup water, and boil over high heat until the water is completely evaporated. Add the meat and cook, stirring constantly, until it is browned on all sides. Stir in the raisins, chili, paprika, cumin, salt and a few grindings of pepper. Set the filling aside.

Preheat the oven to 400°. To make the dough, combine the flour, salt and butter in a large bowl. Use your fingers to rub the flour and butter together until they blend and look like coarse meal. Pour the water over the mixture all at once and gather the dough into a compact ball.

Roll the dough out on a lightly floured surface, making a rough circle about ⅛ inch thick. As you roll, lift up the dough from time to time and sprinkle a light dusting of flour under it to prevent the dough from sticking. With a cookie cutter 5 inches in diameter or an empty can of similar size, cut out 5-inch circles. (Or using a plate or saucer 5 inches in diameter as a pattern, cut out the circles with a knife or pastry wheel.) Gather the scraps of dough together into a ball and roll out again. Cut out similar 5-inch circles.

Place about 1½ tablespoons of the meat filling in the center of each circle, leaving at least ½ inch of dough exposed around it. Top the filling with 1 piece of egg and 2 pieces of olive, and moisten the exposed dough with a finger dipped in water. Fold the *empanada* in half to form a crescent, and press the edges firmly together. Following the pictures below, shape the edges of the *empanadas*. Arrange the finished *empanadas* on an ungreased baking sheet. If they must wait, cover them with aluminum foil or plastic wrap and refrigerate them.

Bake the *empanadas* on the baking sheet in the middle of the oven for 5 minutes, or until they are lightly browned. With a spatula, transfer them to a heated platter and serve at once.

To make 12 to 14 turnovers

THE FILLING

½ cup finely chopped onions
1 tablespoon olive oil
½ cup water
½ pound boneless sirloin steak, cut into ¼-inch cubes
2 tablespoons seedless raisins, soaked in 1 cup boiling water for 10 minutes and drained thoroughly
1 teaspoon dried *hontaka* chili, seeded and crumbled, or 2 small *pequín* chilies, crumbled
½ teaspoon paprika
¼ teaspoon ground cumin seeds
½ teaspoon salt
Freshly ground black pepper

THE PASTRY

2 cups all-purpose flour
1 teaspoon salt
¼ pound plus 2 tablespoons butter, cut into ¼-inch cubes
⅓ cup cold water
2 hard-cooked eggs, each cut into 8 wedges lengthwise
6 pitted green olives, quartered

To shape an *empanada*, first curve the ends of the turnover gently to form a crescent *(1)*. Then turn ½ inch of one corner edge up toward the top of the arc at about a 45° angle *(2)*. Fold over another ½ inch of the edge to make a rough triangle over the first fold *(3)*. Repeat this folding around the edge, pressing each fold tight, as you proceed, to create a "rope" along the arc of the *empanada (4)*.

To make about 20 cookies

1 cup all-purpose flour
½ teaspoon salt
3 egg yolks
1 whole egg
2 tablespoons brandy
2 tablespoons water
1 teaspoon melted butter
1 cup confectioners' sugar
½ cup heavy cream
1 cup *natillas piuranas* (*page 118*)

To make 18

THE PASTRY
4 cups all-purpose flour
11 tablespoons butter (1 quarter-
    pound stick plus 3 tablespoons),
    chilled and cut into small pieces
¼ teaspoon salt
2 teaspoons fresh lemon juice
2 egg yolks
1 cup ice water
½ cup butter (1 quarter-pound
    stick), melted and cooled
½ cup flour
1½ cups canned or packaged quince
    paste combined with ⅔ cup
    muscatel wine

THE SYRUP
1 cup sugar
¼ cup water
½ teaspoon vanilla extract

Vegetable shortening for deep-frying

Alfajores Santafecinos
FROSTED CARAMEL-FILLED COOKIES

Preheat the oven to 350°. Pour the flour and salt into a large mixing bowl, make a well in the center, and drop in the egg yolks, the whole egg, brandy, water and melted butter. With your fingers gradually mix the ingredients together, continuing to mix until the dough can be gathered into a compact ball. Remove the dough to a lightly floured surface and knead it vigorously for 10 minutes, or until it is smooth and elastic.

Let the dough rest for 10 minutes, then roll it into a large circle about ¹⁄₁₆ inch thick. With a 1½-inch cookie cutter or the rim of a glass, cut out as many rounds as you can from the dough. Gather the scraps together into another ball, roll out again, and cut into similar rounds, repeating until all the dough has been used. Place the rounds 1 inch apart on one or two lightly buttered cookie sheets, prick each one two or three times with the tines of a fork and bake for 10 minutes, or until the cookies are lightly browned. With a spatula transfer them to a cake rack to cool.

Pour the sugar into a small bowl and gradually mix in the heavy cream. The icing should coat the spoon lightly. If it seems thin, add a few spoonfuls of sugar; if it is thick, add a little more cream. With a pastry brush, coat the tops of half the cookies with a thin layer of icing and let them dry for 10 minutes. Meanwhile, spread the remaining cookies with a ¼-inch layer of *natillas piuranas*. Pair the cookies like sandwiches, with the icing on top and the *natillas piuranas* in the center.

Pastelitos de Mil Hojas
THOUSAND-LEAF PASTRY

THE PASTRY: In a large mixing bowl, combine the flour, 11 tablespoons of butter and the salt. With your fingertips, rub the flour and butter together until they blend and look like flakes of coarse meal. Gradually mix in the lemon juice and add the egg yolks, one at a time. Then, working the dough with your fingers continuously, add the water, ¼ cup at a time. When all the water has been absorbed and the dough is quite smooth, place it on a lightly floured surface. Knead it by pressing it down, pushing it forward, then turning it back on itself. Repeat this kneading process for about 10 minutes, until the dough is smooth and elastic.

Cover the dough with a dry towel and let it rest for 20 to 30 minutes. Now, with a lightly floured rolling pin, roll the dough into a rough square about 32 inches long and 32 inches wide. Brush it evenly with some of the melted butter and sprinkle the butter lightly with a small dusting of flour. Smooth the flour over the surface of the dough with the palms of your hands until the flour absorbs the butter and the surface looks dry. Fold the dough in half, creating a rectangle 16 by 32 inches. Butter and flour the top of the dough as before, spreading the flour carefully with your hands until it absorbs the butter. Bring the short ends of the dough together, creating a square 16 by 16 inches. Repeat the entire process twice again, producing a final square 8 by 8 inches. Now roll the dough into a 16-inch square, using the remaining flour to prevent it from sticking to the board.

With a small knife or pastry wheel and a ruler, trim to a perfect 15-

inch square. Measure; cut the square into 36 two-and-one-half-inch squares.

In the center of each of 18 squares, place about 1 teaspoon of the quince filling. Lightly moisten the dough around the filling with cold water. Pair the filled squares with the remaining squares in such a way as to form individual 8-point stars, pressing the dough around the filling firmly to secure it. Pinch the stars into flowerlike shapes as shown in the diagrams below.

THE SYRUP: Combine the sugar and water in a small saucepan. Stir until the sugar is thoroughly dissolved and bring to a boil over high heat, stirring constantly. Boil steadily without stirring until the syrup reaches a temperature of 230° on a candy thermometer, or until a bit dropped into ice water immediately forms a coarse thread. Then remove the pan from the heat and stir in the vanilla. Cover the syrup and keep it warm while you fry the *pastelitos*.

Divide the shortening equally between 2 deep-fryers or deep, heavy saucepans, using enough to make a depth of 3 inches in each pan. Simultaneously, heat one pan of fat to a temperature of 375° and the other to 175°. Drop as many *pastelitos* as the pan will comfortably hold into the 175° fat and fry for 3 to 4 minutes until the petals of dough begin to separate and open somewhat, basting with the fat once or twice. Do not let the *pastelitos* brown. Immediately transfer the *pastelitos* with a slotted spoon to the pan of 375° fat and fry on both sides for 2 minutes, or until golden brown. With tongs, remove the *pastelitos* from the fat and drain on paper towels. Then dip them in the warm syrup and place them on a serving plate. Fry and glaze the remaining *pastelitos* in precisely the same fashion. Serve at room temperature.

NOTE: The *pastelitos* may also be filled with a cooked meat or seafood filling and served as an hors d'oeuvre. Naturally, the syrup is then omitted.

1 To make *pastelitos*, roll the pastry into a 32-inch square *(left)*. Butter, flour and fold the dough in half. Then butter, flour and fold it 3 more times *(above)*. Roll it to 15 by 15 inches and cut into 36 squares *(right)*.

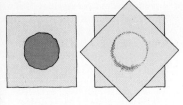

2 Center a spoonful of filling on each of 18 of the pastry squares. Pair these with the remaining 18 squares, set at an angle to make 8-pointed stars.

3 Lay a forefinger across one upper point of a star, its tip toward the filling. With your thumb and middle finger, pinch the two adjoining points of the bottom square around your forefinger. Repeat at each upper point. The *pastelito* will look like a flower.

Glossary

ANNATTO SEED (also known as *achiote* seed): Rusty-red dried seed of a tropical American tree. In crushed form it gives food a delicate flavor and a deep golden-orange color. Available in 1-ounce packs and jars at Latin American groceries or stores specializing in foods from India. Keeps indefinitely in a tightly covered jar. No substitute.

AVOCADOS: Pear-shaped bland, buttery fruit available the year round at fine groceries and fruit and vegetable stands. Especially plentiful from January to April. Avocados vary widely in color, texture of skin, and size. Skin may range from smooth light green to pebbled dark green or purple. Avocados may weigh from a few ounces to as much as 2 pounds. Their flavor has no relationship to their color and size. When ripe, this fruit yields to gentle pressure of the fingers. Hard avocados will ripen in a day or so. If a ripe avocado is not to be used at once, it may be refrigerated for a day or two. When the fruit is cut or peeled, sprinkle its exposed surfaces at once with fresh lemon or lime juice to prevent discoloring.

BANANA LEAVES, FRESH GREEN: Rarely available in the United States. Some Puerto Rican markets may carry them in December and January. Will keep indefinitely if stored in the freezer after wrapping in foil. Substitute parchment paper.

BEANS *(frijoles):* Most of the beans used in these recipes are dried and can be found easily in Latin American markets. The especially popular red kidney beans are also generally available in all U.S. groceries. Dried beans should be stored in a bag or can with a tight lid in a cool, dry place for no longer than two years. Below are descriptions that enable the cook to identify the various kinds of beans called for in the recipes in this book.

BLACK BEANS (also known as *frijoles negros*, turtle beans or black turtle soup beans): Small, flat, less than 1/2 inch long. Charcoal black with white spot.

CRANBERRY BEANS, FRESH (also known as shellouts): Sold in pods to be shelled and cooked during brief season, which varies with locality. Pods are mottled beige and red; shelled beans are flat and about 1/2 inch long. Available in some neighborhood Latin American and Hungarian markets.

CRANBERRY BEANS, DRIED: Similar to pinto beans *(listed below)* but plumper and deeper pink, mottled with reddish-brown, about 1/2 inch long.

PINK BEANS (also known as *rosadas):* Oval, pale pinkish-tan, about 1/2 inch long.

PINTO BEANS: Light pink, mottled with brown, about 1/2 inch long.

RED KIDNEY BEANS: Large, reddish-brown, of a definite kidney shape.

CASSAVA, BITTER: See *Manioc meal.*

CASSAVA, SWEET: See *Yuca.*

CHAYOTE (also known as *christophine, chuchu, xuxu):* A round or pear-shaped white to dark-green tropical squash. May be smooth or corrugated, 3 to 8 inches long, sometimes covered with soft spines. The firm, crisp flesh is more delicate in flavor than the familiar summer squash. Available in some Latin American markets the year round. Keeps two to four weeks in refrigerator.

CHILIES AND PEPPERS: Every podded pepper—sweet, pungent or hot—has a New World origin. The chili-pepper family, called *Capsicum,* includes Hungarian paprika as well as the fiery peppers of Indian curry, the pickled peppers of the Middle East and the common sweet bell pepper. There are a number of groups within the family—Cayenne and tabasco are examples—and within each group there are hundreds of varieties of different shapes and hotness. Growers and canners of chilies rate the pungency, or heat, of chili peppers on a scale of 1 to 120. A *jalapeño,* which to our palates is a relatively hot chili, measures 15 on this scale. The chilies and peppers listed below appear in the recipes in this book. They are described here by appearance, size, flavor and pungency. Remember that chilies lose their flavor quickly. Even dried chilies must be stored in a cool, dry place—preferably the refrigerator—in a tightly covered jar or tin.

ANCHO: A deep-mahogany, heart-shaped chili, about 3 inches long by 2 1/2 inches wide at its widest point. The *ancho* (meaning "broad" in Spanish) is a member of the Cayenne group. Full-flavored and mild. Available dried in Latin American markets.

CHIPOTLE: A dark brick-red chili about 2 inches long, plump, tapered and twisted. Very hot, with a pungent, distinct flavor. Available canned in Latin American markets.

GÜERO (also known as California green pepper): A pale plump yellowish-green mild chili, 3 to 4 inches long and about 2 1/2 inches in diameter. Slightly curved and tapered. Widely available in the fall in vegetable and supermarkets. Available canned in California where it is much used in Californian-Mexican cooking.

HONTAKA: A red, thin, somewhat wrinkled chili 1 to 2 inches long. Very pungent. Largely grown in Japan and exported for wide use in Latin American cooking. Sold dried in jars and cellophane packets in specialty and Latin American stores.

JALAPEÑO: A grass-green, smooth-skinned chili, about 2 inches long. Hot and juicy, rather stringy: The *jalapeño* is widely available canned, in Latin American markets and gourmet shops.

MALAGUETA PEPPER: A small green or red chili resembling the slender tapering tabasco pepper. Very hot. Used in Bahian cooking, it is unobtainable in the United States.

MULATO: A darker, larger and more pungent chili than the *ancho,* with which it is often combined in cooking. Sold dried in Latin American markets.

PASILLA: A thin, mahogany chili, about 7 inches long. The flavor is not so marked as the *ancho*'s but it is more pungent. Available dried in Latin American markets.

PEPPERS, GREEN OR RED, MILD (also known as bell peppers, sweet peppers or, in the Midwest, mango peppers): Although slightly pungent peppers do exist within this variety, only a fresh, mild form is usually found in markets. The kinds most commonly sold are plump and block-shaped, 4 to 5 inches long, tapering slightly toward the bottom. Dark green when immature, they will ripen to a brilliant red. Available fresh everywhere.

PEPPERS, GREEN OR RED, PIQUANT (usually Cayenne): Peppers ripen from green through orangey-yellow to red, and continue to ripen after they are picked. Color should not affect pungency, but flavor is sometimes more pronounced in the fully ripened ones. Some are tapered, twisted and wrinkled, some are smooth and shiny. Within the same strain some may be mild, others hot to very hot. Sizes vary anywhere from 3 to 8 inches. Available (usually in the fall) in Latin American and Italian markets and some other groceries, depending upon neighborhood and region.

PEPPERS, YELLOW, PIQUANT: Smooth and waxy, bright yellow, maturing to orange-red, about 5 inches long by 3/4 inches. These peppers are often found under the name "Hungarian yellow wax," and vary from mildly piquant to very pungent. Available fresh in groceries and supermarkets, usually in the fall.

PEQUÍN (also known as *tepín):* Tiny bright-red oval chilies about 1/2 inch long. Very hot. Available bottled or dried, in Latin American markets.

POBLANO: A dark-green chili, about the size of a bell pepper though more tapered and with a richer flavor. Usually mild, but occasionally slightly hot. Available fresh in the Southwest and canned in Latin American markets and gourmet shops elsewhere.

SERRANO: A tapered bright-green smooth pepper, 1 to 2 inches long. Mildly hot and very savory. Available in cans in Latin American markets.

TABASCO: Bright red, smooth-skinned and tapered, about 1 1/2 inches long. Hot. It is sold bottled whole, and is not to be confused with Tabasco sauce.

CHOCOLATE, MEXICAN: Solid bars of granular sweet chocolate, flavored with almonds and cinnamon. Available in some Latin American specialty stores in 15-ounce packages of two bars each. Keeps indefinitely in plastic wrap or tightly covered container. No substitute.

CHORIZO (Spanish sausage): Lightly smoked sausage of coarsely chopped pork, generally seasoned with garlic, sweet red pepper and hot paprika. Varies in piquancy. Will keep refrigerated for several months but should not be frozen. Available in 4-inch links at Latin American or Spanish groceries. Also available packed in lard in tins ranging in size from 5 ounces to 4 1/2 pounds. Occasionally found as *estilo Cantimpalos,* a 10-inch dried sausage. Substitute any smoked, spiced, uncooked French, Italian or Polish sausage.

CORIANDER, FRESH (also known as *cilantro, coriandro, culantro,* Chinese parsley): Aromatic herb sold by the bunch in Chinese and Latin American markets. Do not wash or remove roots before storing. Will keep about a week if refrigerated in covered jar or in plastic bag with roots wrapped in damp paper towel. If necessary, refresh before using by soaking for five minutes in cold water. No substitute.

CORIANDER SEED (also known as *cilantro, coriandro, culantro*): Round pale to yellowish-brown ridged seed of the herb coriander, slightly smaller than a peppercorn. Available in packets or jars in Latin American, Oriental and Middle Eastern groceries, or gourmet shops. To some it suggests the taste of lemon peel and sage, to others a mixture of caraway and cumin. Keeps indefinitely in a tightly covered jar.

CORN, DRIED: Coarsely cracked pearly-white corn, in ¼-inch bits. Sold by the pound in Latin American markets.

CORNHUSKS, DRIED: Sold in packages or by weight in most Latin American specialty food stores. Will keep indefinitely. Substitute parchment paper.

CUMIN (*comino*): Yellowish-brown seed of a plant of the parsley family, strongly aromatic and reminiscent of caraway. Available in small packets, whole or ground, in Latin American food stores and gourmet shops. Keeps indefinitely when tightly covered. No substitute.

DENDÊ OIL: A heavy, yellow-orange palm oil used in Bahian dishes. A cultivated taste. Rarely available outside Brazil. No substitute.

EPAZOTE (*pazote,* goosefoot): Strongly flavored, crumbled dried herb leaves used in Mexican tortilla dishes and beans. Packaged in California as "Jerusalem oak *pazote*" and sold in ⅛-ounce packets in some Latin American markets. Store tightly covered in a cool, dark place.

HEARTS OF PALM: Tender ivory-colored hearts or shoots of palm used as a vegetable or salad ingredient. Sold canned in most fancy grocery stores. Can sizes range

from 10 ounces to 1 pound 14 ounces. After opening, store the hearts in their own juice in a covered jar in the refrigerator. Keeps for about 10 days. No substitute.

HOMINY (hulled corn): Whole kernels of dried corn prepared by removing the hulls—by soaking in baking soda or lye—and then boiling. Available, prepared and canned, in some groceries and supermarkets.

MANIOC: See *Yuca.*

MANIOC MEAL (*farinha de mandioca*): Fine, grainy, flourlike meal prepared from the dried pulp of the bitter cassava or bitter manioc, a Brazilian root. Available by the pound in Latin American food stores. Keeps indefinitely when stored in tightly covered container. No substitute.

MASA HARINA: Corn flour. Instant varieties are available in Latin American markets in 5- to 50-pound packages. In general, domestic milled brands preferable. Store tightly covered in a dry place. Available in Latin American markets and some supermarkets.

MATÉ (*yerba maté,* Paraguay tea): Dried leaves of a South American holly used to make a stimulating caffein-rich tea. Derives its name from the gourd, or *maté,* in which it is usually brewed and served. Available in Latin American and health-food stores. Store tightly covered. No substitute.

NOPALITOS: The tender, green, fleshy, broad and flat paddles of the prickly-pear cactus. They are diced and packed in water (*nopalitos tiernos al natural*) or are sold as small spiced slices (*nopalitos en vinagre*). Latin American grocers and specialty stores sell them canned and bottled, in sizes ranging from 7¼ ounces to large tins of about 10 pounds. After opening, cover and store the contents in their own juice in the refrigerator. No substitute.

ORANGE FLOWER WATER: A flavoring agent made from distilled orange-blossom petals. Available at fancy apothecary shops and Middle Eastern grocers.

PALM, HEARTS OF: See *Hearts of palm.*

PANELA: Oblong loaves of hard dark-brown Colombian sugar, sold in 1-

pound-10-ounce boxes containing 6 loaves. Available in Latin American groceries. Store in a dry place in a tightly covered container. Substitute dark-brown sugar or *piloncillo.*

PILONCILLO: Cone-shaped loaves of hard dark-brown Mexican sugar, often 1 inch at the base and 1 inch high, sold by weight at Latin American groceries. Store in a dry place in a tightly covered container. Substitute dark-brown sugar or *panela.*

PINE NUTS (most familiarly known as *piñon* seeds, and as *pignon, pignolia* and Indian nuts): A white, cylindrical soft-textured nut, tender and not highly flavored, about ¼ inch long. They are used extensively in Italian and Middle Eastern cooking and are widely available, either in jars or by weight.

PLANTAINS (*plátanos*): Fruit belonging to the same family as bananas and similar in shape, but larger (9 to 12 inches long). Sometimes called cooking bananas, but coarser and not so sweet. Must be cooked before eating. Available in most Latin American fruit and vegetable markets in all degrees of ripeness from greenish yellow to yellow to brown. They may be cooked whatever their color; recipes will specify ripeness desired. They continue to ripen at room temperature, but when fully ripe may be wrapped in plastic and stored in the refrigerator for two or three days. After peeling, remove the fibrous strings before cooking. No substitute.

PUMPKIN SEEDS (*pepitas*): Small, plump, delicately flavored seeds, shelled, toasted in oil, and salted. Sold in glass jars by specialty grocers and gourmet food sections of supermarkets. Substitute squash seeds.

QUESO BLANCO (white cheese): A fresh, moist, unripened whey cheese made from partly skimmed cow's milk. Compressed and slightly rubbery; in appearance it is somewhat similar to fresh *mozzarella,* although the flavor is more reminiscent of a lightly salted fresh ricotta. Will keep in plastic wrap in the refrigerator for about two weeks. It is carried by Latin American markets and some specialty cheese stores. Substitute fresh *mozzarella* or Münster cheese.

QUINCE PASTE (*membrillo, dulce de*

membrillo, membrillate): Thick dull-pink concentrate of quince pulp cooked with sugar. Packed in 1- and 2-pound flat tins or various sizes of cellophane-wrapped bars. Available in Latin American groceries and in some shops specializing in fine imported European foods. After opening, keep covered or wrapped in plastic in a dry place. No substitute.

RICE FLOUR (*harina de arroz*): Rice milled into flour form. Available in 10-ounce cellophane packages in Latin American markets and in various sizes at Oriental and health-food stores. No substitute.

ROSE WATER: Distilled water flavored with rose extract. Available at fancy apothecary shops, but a heavier rose water, specifically sold for food flavoring, can be found in Middle Eastern grocery stores. No substitute.

SHRIMP, DRIED: Tiny shrimp with a sharp salty flavor, sold by weight or in 1-ounce cellophane packages in Chinese or Latin American specialty food shops. Store in refrigerator in plastic bag or covered jar. No substitute.

TOMATOES, MEXICAN GREEN, CANNED (*tomatitos verdes, pelados; tomatillos enteros*): This small green tomato with a distinctive flavor was the *miltomatl* of the Aztecs. It is sold canned in Latin American food stores, delicacy shops and gourmet food sections. No substitute.

TORTILLA FLOUR: See *Masa harina.*

TORTILLAS: If it is not convenient to make your own tortillas, they may be purchased freshly packaged in Latin American specialty shops, and occasionally in groceries and supermarkets. Tortillas are also sold in specialty and gourmet shops in cans containing 1½ to 2½ dozen.

YERBA MATÉ: See *Maté.*

YUCA (also known as *aipím,* sweet cassava or sweet manioc): Long, irregularly shaped root at least 2 inches in diameter, with rough brown barklike skin and hard white starchy interior. Available fresh year round in most Latin American and Puerto Rican groceries and vegetable markets. Sold whole or in pieces. Store refrigerated for 2 or 3 weeks. No substitute.

Recipe Index: English

NOTE: An R preceding a page refers to the Recipe Booklet. Size, weight and material are specified for pans in the recipes because they affect cooking results. A pan should be just large enough to hold its contents, comfortably. Heavy pans heat slowly and cook food at a constant rate. Aluminum and cast iron conduct heat well but may discolor foods containing egg yolks, wine, vinegar or lemon. Enamelware is a fairly poor conductor of heat. Many recipes therefore recommend stainless steel or enameled cast iron, which do not have these faults.

Recipe Index: Spanish and Portuguese

General Index

Numerals in italics indicate a photograph of the subject mentioned.

Credits and Acknowledgments

The sources for the illustrations in this book are shown below. Credits for the pictures from left to right are separated by commas, from top to bottom by dashes.

All photographs in this book are by Milton Greene except: 4—Walter Daran—Toby Hunt, Ted Hardin. 11—Clayton Price. 12, 13—Map by Nicholas Fasciano photograph by Robert S. Crandall overlays by George V. Kelvin type by Lothar Roth. 14—Bruno Barbey from Magnum. 15—Cornell Capa from Magnum. 16, 17—Paul Schutzer. 18, 19—Lisl Steiner from Keystone Press Agency—Dr. Georg Gerster from Rapho Guillumette. 22, 23—Douglas Faulkner. 25—Lee Boltin. 26—Constantine Manos from Magnum. 28—Lee Boltin. 29—Map by Gloria duBouchet. 30, 31—John Dominis—Constantine Manos from Magnum. 32, 33—Constantine Manos from Magnum. 38—Clayton Price. 40, 41—Constantine Manos from Magnum. 42—Charles Phillips. 47—Bottom rows Clayton Price. 48—Constantine Manos from Magnum. 52, 53—S. Byron Stone. 54—Constantine Manos from Magnum except top right Carter from Black Star. 55—Constantine Manos from Magnum. 58, 59—Richard Jeffery. 60—Map by Gloria duBouchet. 62, 63—Herbert Mason Jr. courtesy the Girard Foundation. 65, 108, 111, 113, 114—Constantine Manos from Magnum. 120—Paulo Muñiz. 147—Bernard Wolf. 151—Clayton Price. 156—Richard Jeffery. 165—Leonard McCombe. 168 through 171—Constantine Manos from Magnum. 182, 183—Sergio Larrain from Magnum. 191, 195—Clayton Price. 197—Drawings by Matt Greene—photographs by Clayton Price.

Special consultants for this book included: Mrs. Margarette de Andrade, Brazil; Mrs. Nelly de Oppes, Argentina; Mrs. Miguel Solano López, Paraguay; Mrs. Gossi Lares, Venezuela; Mrs. Barbarita Massa, Venezuela; Mrs. Edyth Ziffren, Chile; Miss Luz Llano-Gregory, Colombia; Miss Letitia Paez, Peru.

For further assistance in the preparation of this book the editors wish to thank the following: in Chile, Mrs. Paul Hegermann; in Mexico, Mr. and Mrs. José Ramón Albarrán y Pliego; Mariano Dueñas Astrónomos; Dick Debler, San Angel Inn; Hugo Farías; Rafael Delgado Lozano; Javier Frías; Guillermo Moreno, Consejo Nacional del Turismo; Fernando Rodríguez, Asociación Nacional de Charros; in Indiana, Dr. Charles B. Heiser; in Peru, Maria Pia T. de Alzamora; in New York City, Henrique Albu, H. Stern Jewelers; Arte de Colombia; Dr. Junius Bird, American Museum of Natural History; Gertrude Conner; Dr. Frederick Dockstader, Heye Foundation, Museum of the American Indian; Graziella Dubra, Uruguayan Delegation to the United Nations; Pablo Ford, Pablo's Restaurant; Howard S. Irwin, New York Botanical Garden; Jean's Silversmiths Inc.; Georg Jensen, Inc.; Ruth Jiménez, Carmen Miguel, LIFE EN ESPAÑOL; Fred Leighton Imports Ltd.; Peter Anderson, Chacho López, Ernest Silverman, Mexican National Tourist Council; Mexican Art Annex; Felix Maier, Fred Rufe, Restaurant Associates; Mr. and Mrs. Jesús Moneo, Casa Moneo; The Phoenix Pan American Shop; Piñata Party, Inc.; Corina de Rada, Bolivian Consulate; Violeta Ríos; RMH International; Scherr and McDermott, Products of the Alianza.

Sources consulted in the production of this book include: *The Art of Mexican Cooking* by Jan Aaron and Georgine Salom; *La Cocina en Bolivia* by Aida de Aguirre Achá; *Brazilian Cookery* by Margarette de Andrade; *Manual of Cultivated Plants Most Commonly Grown in the Continental United States and Canada* and *A Socialist Empire: The Incas of Peru* by Louis Baudin; *Comidas Criollas Peruanas* by Francisca Baylon; *El Gran Libro de Cocina* by Marta Beines; *The Food and Drink of Mexico* by George C. Booth; *The Art of Brazilian Cookery* by Dolores Botafoga; *These Are the Mexicans* by Herbert Cerwin; *El Libro de Tía María II* by María Chappelin; *Mexico* by Stuart Chase; *The Maya* by Michael D. Coe; *The Discovery and Conquest of Mexico, 1517-1521* by Bernal Díaz del Castillo; *La Cocina*, Andrés López Dominovich, ed.; *La Buena Mesa* by Olga Budge de Edwards; *Eating in Mexico* by Amando Farga; *The Masters and the Slaves* by Gilberto Freyre; *El Libro de Doña Petrona* by Petrona C. De Gandulfo; *El Plato Criollo* by Lola Llano de Gallardo; *Tropical Trees* by Dorothy and Bob Hargreaves; *A History of Latin America* by Hubert Herring; *South America, A to Z* by Robert S. Kane; *Recetas de las Rengifo* by María Paz Lagarrigue; *Folklore and Odysseys of Food and Medicinal Plants* by Ernst and Johanna Lehner; *El Asado Criollo* by E. Rodríguez Long and Jewel B. Groves; *Mexican Cookbook* and *Viajando por Las Cocinas de la Republica Mexicana* by Josefina Velasquez de León; *La Cocinera Criolla* by Marta; *The Ancient Civilizations of Peru* by J. Alden Mason; *Cocina Peruana* by Misia-Peta; *The Complete Book of Mexican Cooking* by Elisabeth Lambert Ortiz; *Meet Flora Mexicana* by M. Walter Pesman; *History of the Conquest of Mexico* and *History of the Conquest of Peru* by William H. Prescott; *Margarita Cocinando* by Margarita Mayor de Racedo; *Made in Mexico* by Patricia Fent Ross; *A Alegría de Cozinhar* by Helena B. Sangirardi; *Mi Cocina* by Luisa Wilson del Solar; *The Ethnobotany of Precolumbia Peru* by Margaret Tolle; *Three Worlds of Peru* and *A Treasury of Mexican Folkways* by Frances Toor; *The Romance of Coffee* by William H. Ukers; *Brown Gold* by Andrés Uribe; *Plants and Plant Science in Latin America*, Frans Verdorn, ed.; *Foods America Gave the World* by A. H. Verrill; *Epicuro Andino* by The Women's Auxiliary of Pfeiffer Memorial Hospital; *Coffee* by Frederick L. Wellman; *Elena's Famous Mexican and Spanish Recipes* and *Elena's Secrets of Mexican Cooking* by Elena Zelayeta.